In Praise of DIFFICULT WOMEN

In Praise of DIFFICULT WOMEN

LIFE LESSONS From 29 HEROINES Who DARED to BREAK the RULES

KAREN KARBO

ILLUSTRATIONS BY KIMBERLY GLYDER

NATIONAL GEOGRAPHIC

Washington, D.C.

Published by National Geographic Partners, LLC
1145 17th Street NW Washington, DC 20036

ISBN: 978-1-4262-1774-6

Since 1888, the National Geographic Society has funded more than 12,000 research, exploration, and preservation projects around the world. National Geographic Partners distributes a portion of the funds it receives from your purchase to National Geographic Society to support programs including the conservation of animals and their habitats.

Get closer to National Geographic explorers and photographers, and connect with our global community. Join us today at nationalgeographic.com/join.

For information about special discounts for bulk purchases, please contact National Geographic Books Special Sales: specialsales@natgeo.com

For rights or permissions inquiries, please contact National Geographic Books Subsidiary Rights: bookrights@natgeo.com

Interior design: Nicole Miller

Printed in the United States of America

18/QGF/1

This book is dedicated to Fiona and Stephanie,
and to daughters everywhere:
Be difficult.

"Whatever you choose, however many roads you travel, I hope that you choose not to be a lady. I hope you will find some way to break the rules and make a little trouble out there. And I also hope that you will choose to make some of that trouble on behalf of women."

—NORA EPHRON,
Wellesley Commencement Speech, 1996

Contents

FOREWORD

THE FIRST DIFFICULT WOMAN I KNEW was named Myrtle. Elderly and white-haired, single and childless, she lived next door to my family when I was five. *A spinster,* my father told me one day, his tone so disparaging it sparked my interest. *She thinks she can do whatever she wants to do,* he said. Even at five, I knew this to be in violation of a cardinal rule in the unwritten but widely known rule book of what it means to be female.

Intrigued, I studied Myrtle from afar, deeply curious about what a woman who thought she could do whatever she wanted to do might actually *do.* But my findings were a disappointment. Doing whatever she wanted to do, at least in this particular case, turned out to be nothing more than to play her piano in the early evenings—the melodic thunder of it spilling from her windows into our yard, where I did gymnastics with my sister while pretending not to be a spy. I don't recall a single conversation with Myrtle, and yet the fact of her existence stuck to me like a burr. Perhaps because even all those years ago, I knew that I, too, wanted to be the kind of woman who did what she wanted to do.

In my 20s, I named my truck after Myrtle. I'm not generally one to assign human qualities to automobiles, but this truck was different, and the name fit. A 1979 Chevy LUV pickup, Myrtle was more companion than vehicle, more confidante than mass of metal and machinery. In her I could go anywhere, and did. From New York to Alabama to Minnesota to Wyoming to Arizona to California to Oregon and points in between, that truck was my home away from home on countless weeks-long, low-budget road trips. I slept alone amid the vast darkness of national forests on a futon I'd laid out in the truck's long bed, cooking dinner solo in small-town parks on a camp stove propped on the tailgate. In Myrtle's rusted body—onto which I'd plastered bumper stickers that said things like Feminism Is the Radical Notion That Women Are People and Question Authority and Well-Behaved Women Seldom Make History—I had my first taste of what it felt like to do what the original Myrtle had done. I too had defied one of the cardinal rules in the unwritten but widely known rule book of what it means to be female: Into the wildest places, I'd ventured alone.

I thought of those two Myrtles and the two younger versions of myself as I read this book, which is chock-full of people who remind us, by the example of their lives, that rules are powerful only if we obey them. These 29 fascinating, moving, entertaining, and inspiring essays explore the many facets of what it means to be female and "difficult"—which is really another way of saying female and "brave enough to express the full range of one's humanity." Instead of carrying out the wishes of others, the accomplished women in these pages did what they wanted to do, the way they wanted to do it. Without apology, they decided to be ambitious and bold, adventurous and emotional, brainy and defiant, incorrigible and outlandish, determined and badass.

They said no in a world that expects women to say yes, and yes in a world that doesn't even bother to ask them the question.

Their stories matter because they teach us how to live, much in the same way that old, outdated-from-the-start rule book of what it means to be female tried to do. Each story offers us another version, another path, another way of seeing women and being one.

They're also a lot of fun to read. Each chapter felt to me like I finally had the goods on the mysterious woman who lived next door. We are led to vividly imagine the young Jane Goodall doing her first research while camping in the central African bush with her mother, as well as the unflinching pain that informed Frida Kahlo's most exquisite paintings. We contemplate Laverne Cox's undaunted courage as a trans woman and the nerve it took for Lena Dunham to flaunt what most perceive as imperfection. We delve into the essence of Elizabeth Warren's persistence and Billie Jean King's competitive drive and Eva Perón's fanaticism, among so much more.

And, through these perceptive and personal portraits, we get a portrait of Karen Karbo herself. I happen to know she's also a woman who threw out the rule book of what it means to be female. She replaced it with this book instead.

—Cheryl Strayed
Author of *Wild* and *Tiny Beautiful Things*

INTRODUCTION

THE BOOK YOU HOLD IN YOUR HANDS is about women who insisted on being difficult.

A difficult woman, as I define her, is a person who believes her needs, passions, and goals are at least as important as those of everyone around her. In many cases, she doesn't even believe they're more important—many women in this book were devoted, loving wives and mothers—but simply *as* important. A difficult woman is also a woman who doesn't believe the expectations of the culture in which she lives are more important than what she knows to be true about herself. She is a woman who accepts that sometimes the cost of being fully human is upsetting people.

A difficult woman isn't a bitch, although on occasion she might be. She isn't cruel or selfish or mean—although, again, on occasion she might be. Just like anyone (by which I mean men), she has bad days, she makes mistakes, she loses her temper. A difficult woman is a woman who insists on inhabiting the full range of her humanity.

Difficult women tend not to be ladies-in-waiting. Waiting for love, waiting for someone to notice their excellent job performance, waiting for the kids to go to bed, or off to school, waiting until they lose weight and fit into their skinny jeans. Instead, they are driven by their internal engines. They make *other* people wait. It's immaterial whether these others worry about her, grow impatient with her, find her frustrating, or call her names. Difficult women may not enjoy causing a stir (though most seem to), and sometimes their feelings get hurt, but the bumps along the way fail to deter them from their mission.

The 29 iconic women included in this book have inspired me over the years, and to this moment. Obviously, there are many more difficult women worthy of inclusion in these pages. But these were the ones who spoke to me.

My mother died when I was 17, my father quickly remarried, and I was more or less on my own. Throughout college, I ministered to my loneliness with biographies of great women. Into my life came Martha Gellhorn, Coco Chanel, Josephine Baker. They were women of a long-ago era, but they felt alive to me: singular, bold, different, difficult. Gloria Steinem, Jane Goodall, and Nora Ephron were in my personal pantheon of living legends I adored; now, I watch the uber-difficult Margaret Cho, Rachel Maddow, and Lena Dunham walking their talk, generating outrage (and tweets) all along the way.

As I read and wrote, I was a little delirious to discover the many ways in which women can be difficult.

We can be good-natured and competitive (Billie Jean King); sarcastic and vulnerable (Carrie Fisher); quiet, well behaved, and braver than most men (Amelia Earhart); completely unapologetic about taking everything that is our due (Shonda Rhimes); zany and so off-the-charts talented people don't know what to make of us (Kay Thompson); ambitious beyond measure (Hillary Clinton).

They come from every background and upbringing, my difficult women. Wealthy, but neglected (Vita Sackville-West); of modest means, but rich in love and attachment (Elizabeth Warren); and straight-up middle-class (Janis Joplin). Many of these women had stable early childhoods, but if their fathers left or died, the family descended into poverty (Helen Gurley Brown, Eva Perón, Amelia Earhart). Some were conventionally pretty (Elizabeth Taylor, Gloria Steinem), some were what the French call *jolie laide* (Diana Vreeland, Frida Kahlo).

But all of them have embraced their messy, interesting lives. All serve as an inspiration for more accommodating women, who like me long to be braver, bolder, more courageous, more outspoken, more willing to upset the status quo.

I love these women because they encourage me to own my true nature. They teach me that it's perfectly okay not to go along to get along. They show by example that we shouldn't shy away from stating our opinions. Their lives were and are imperfect. They suffered. They made mistakes. But they rarely betrayed their essential natures to keep the peace. They saw (and see) no margin in making sure no one around them is inconvenienced.

These difficult women give us permission to occupy space in our worlds, to say what we think, and to stand our ground. They give us permission to be ambitious, passionate, curmudgeonly, outspoken, persistent, sassy, and angry. They tell us, by their words and deeds, that it's all right to occupy our humanity.

I hope you will come to revere them—and be inspired by them—as I have.

CHAPTER 1

J. K. ROWLING

Feisty

GIVEN HER MONUMENTAL LITERARY SUCCESS, happy marriage to a loving Scottish doctor, three beautiful children, posh residences scattered around the UK, blond English-rose beauty, and ability to rock dangly earrings, there is no reason on Earth for J. K. Rowling to be difficult. And yet she is. Tetchy on Twitter, out and proud about her progressive politics, Jo (as she calls herself) isn't interested in remaining imprisoned by her role as creator of one of the most beloved fictional universes in literary history. Instead, she stays in the fray, enjoys stirring things up.

Jo has always been scrappy, so either old habits die hard or she sees no reason to stop now. Her own origin story has become as well known as Harry Potter's. She grew up in middle-class English villages—the first outside Bristol, the next farther west in the Forest of Dean.* Her father, Peter, was a Rolls Royce aircraft engine mechanic; her mother, Anne, a science technician in the chemistry department at Jo and her younger sister's high school. Anne was diagnosed with multiple sclerosis when Jo was 15, which put an abrupt end to the luxury of being a bookish, sheltered child. She became the girl with heavy eyeliner, binge-reading Tolkien while The Smiths pumped through her headphones.

In 1982, Jo applied to Oxford, didn't get in, and wound up studying French and classics at Exeter. In 1986, after graduation, she worked for Amnesty International. Four years later, while sitting on a delayed train

---

* If I had an indie rock band, I would totally name it Forest of Dean.

en route to London, she got the idea for a book about a boy wizard who takes a magical train to his magical boarding school. She started writing, but when her mother died, she lost her momentum.

It was 1991. Jo was 25 and suddenly lost. On a whim she moved to Porto, Portugal, where she met and married journalist Jorge Arantes. A daughter, Jessica, was born in 1993—but the marriage didn't last, and Jo soon found herself back in England with an infant, three chapters of her wizard book, and not much else. "I was jobless, a lone parent, and as poor as it is possible to be in modern Britain, without being homeless . . . By every usual standard, I was the biggest failure I knew," she confessed.

Hoping to make a new start, Jo moved to Scotland at the end of 1993. *Harry Potter and the Philosopher's Stone* was written in Edinburgh cafés while she lived hand to mouth and cared for her baby. After she was finished, the manuscript was rejected a dozen times. People apparently thought the boarding school trope had been played out, even if it was a wizard boarding school that featured a partially decapitated ghost named Nearly Headless Nick.

Then, an editor at Bloomsbury, aka the Smartest Man in Publishing, bought the manuscript for $2,250. Pretty much every superlative came to pass. The seven Harry Potter books became the best-selling literary series in history. The last four of the seven volumes hold records for the fastest sales. They've been published in 73 languages (including Latin and ancient Greek, just for kicks), and have sold 450 million copies, give or take.

The books begat the movies, which begat the theme park attractions. More than 600,000 pieces of Harry Potter fan fiction have been produced, and about a hundred more pieces have been posted online since I began writing this sentence. A two-part West End stage play, *Harry Potter and the Cursed Child,* opened in 2016. It takes place 19 years in the future after *Harry Potter and the Deathly Hallows,* the seventh book in the series. In the sequel, Harry has become an employee at the Ministry of Magic. I haven't seen the play, but I'm a bit disheartened to think that after his epic childhood and teen years, Harry grew up to become, essentially, a civil servant.

But wait, there's more. In 2001 Jo expanded her Potter oeuvre to include "textbooks" from Hogwarts—*Quidditch Through the Ages* and *Fantastic Beasts and Where to Find Them* (writing as the fictitious magizoologist Newt Scamander)—and in 2012 published her first adult novel, *The Casual Vacancy*. She also writes the Cormoran Strike crime series, under the pen name Robert Galbraith (described by the publisher as, "a former plainclothes Royal Military Police investigator who had left in 2003 to work in the civilian security industry"). All this has made Jo literally richer than the Queen of England, and people have become obsessed with her financial status, before and after the Potter books. In 2016, the *New York Times* offered an in-depth accounting, but the takeaway is:

Then, not a pot to piss in.

Now, billions or millions, depending on whether you're counting the vast sums she's given away to charity.

ROWLING FINISHED THE FINAL POTTER installment in 2007—and now that she's off the leash, she's known for being "thin-skinned." These days "thin-skinned" is the insult du jour—but long before politicians were calling each other thin-skinned and pundits who disagreed were calling each other thin-skinned, Jo was smacked with the label. In 2007, *Time* magazine described her as "a woman of high energy and a short fuse." In 2012, the *New Yorker* weighed in with, "She has a reputation for being likable, but shy and thin-skinned."

To be female and be thin-skinned means you react, sometimes strongly, to things you don't like, choosing to voice your opinions instead of swallowing them because they may cause problems. It's that straightforward: Rather than tolerating something, you speak up. Perhaps you're even a little bit *angry*. You don't pretend it's okay, or (as I sometimes do) bend over backward to see the other point of view, or try to magically convert rage to empathy. (I'm sure Hermione has a spell for that.)

In 2004, when Rowling's 19-month-old son, David (from second husband, Neil Murray, whom she married in 2001), was "papped" by a photographer with a telephoto lens while she was out walking him in his baby buggy, she sued everyone who could possibly be sued for invasion of privacy.* I think it's safe to say she never thought, The guy's just doing his job.

Rowling is also reputed to be "famously reclusive"—a descriptor that's vaguely disapproving. If there was ever a word that needed to be redefined for the digital age, it's recluse. Although it's true that Rowling doesn't throw neighborhood potlucks or get sloppy drunk doing karaoke at the local pub, the woman has almost 10 million Twitter followers, and has been known to tweet many times a day about rugby, Scottish politics, her favorite charities, and various Potter arcana (there are Jews at Hogwarts but not Wiccans, oddly enough).

Before I go any further, I should point out that I am no devotee of Twitter. I suspect you need to be either famous or an existential masochist to enjoy it. Nothing makes it clearer that you're a lone soul living out your uneventful days on an undistinguished planet orbiting a mediocre star in a far-flung arm of the Milky Way than blasting out a few wickedly insightful or funny tweets, only to have them met with . . . nothing.

Obviously, Rowling doesn't have that issue. The downside of her visibility and influence is that she's routinely held to task for refusing to behave like a proper children's book author (which seems to be a mix between a Sunday school teacher and full-time literacy advocate).

When Jo published *The Casual Vacancy,* a hefty adult novel about a local city council election in the small English town of Pagford, the parents of young fans apparently took umbrage with the clearly grown-up content (by which I mean that Rowling used the word "vagina"). Her tweet on the matter was a delicious snippet of the snark to come: "There's

---

* The landmark ruling strengthened privacy laws across the land, protecting the children of celebrities who wish to keep their kids out of the public eye.

no part of me that feels that I represented myself as your children's baby-sitter or their teacher."

She was just warming up. During the 2016 presidential election, she regularly weighed in about her disdain for Trump. After the third debate, she tweeted: "Well, there you have it. A highly intelligent, experienced woman just debated a giant orange Twitter egg. Your move, America. #debate." She went on to offend legions of Trump-supporting trolls who shot back that they were going to burn all their Potter books and DVDs and never read her work again.

Her takedown: "Well, the fumes from the DVDs might be toxic, and I've still got your money, so by all means borrow my lighter."

Of course, the more success a woman enjoys, the more complicated things become. Sometimes, there is no winning for women—for deep and deeply infuriating reasons that legions of feminists, sociologists, psychologists, and culture anthropologists have spent entire lifetimes attempting to sort out.

In 2016, *Slate* posted a piece called, "J. K. Rowling's Twitter Feed Is Slowly Ruining Everything I Love About J. K. Rowling." The tone is tongue-in-cheek, but the message is unmistakable: Stay in your lane, Jo. Don't ruin our image of you as the sweet, slightly eccentric author of the best books of our youth by being an adult woman with thoughts and feelings of her own. Please spend your life being an emissary for Harry Potter.

Over on *Gawker*, however, she was mocked for doing exactly that. A regular J. K. Rowling feature headlined "God, Get a Life!!!" pictured Jo either reading from a Potter book, or holding one up. As authors are wont to do.

Luckily for Jo, she doesn't mind being called thin-skinned. She owns it. She isn't thin-skinned about being called thin-skinned.

To be blasé about what others view as a shortcoming is pure difficult woman. Please join me in a thought exercise: That thing you hate about yourself? Accept it now. Make no excuses for it. Be inspired by Jo Rowling, and embrace your complexities! Your public, like hers, will simply have to deal with them.

CHAPTER 2

ELIZABETH TAYLOR

Notorious

DIFFICULT WOMEN SHARE many commonalities. But the one trait they all possess is complete indifference to what people think. There was no one for whom this was more true than Elizabeth Taylor.

During her seven decades in the spotlight as America's sexiest, most gossiped-about film actress, there was never any doubt that Hollywood's first modern movie star was doing exactly what she wanted to do, regardless of what people said about her. She rarely explained herself or interpreted her behavior to put other people at ease. She was both wondrous and terrifying: a hyperfeminine and hypersexual woman who couldn't be contained or controlled by public opinion. To be a woman like Elizabeth—who tells you to take your scarlet A and shove it—is to be difficult, dangerous, and powerful.

Her résumé is well known, though less so as time marches on. When I asked my 24-year-old daughter what she knew about Elizabeth Taylor, she said Liz had a lot of husbands and rocked the eyeliner in *Cleopatra*. True! But she also was a child actor whose breakout role in *National Velvet* (a film my horse-loving daughter adored and apparently forgot) occurred when she was 12. From that moment on, Elizabeth Taylor was a star, and would remain one of the brightest in the firmament for the next 67 years, until her death in 2011 at age 79.

Elizabeth made a handful of classic films, including *A Place in the Sun* (1951), *Giant* (1956), *BUtterfield 8* (1960), and *Who's Afraid of Virginia*

Woolf? (1966); the last two earned her a pair of best actress Oscars. But the real show was the way she conducted herself. She was a sexy woman who did nothing to hide her appetites; she lived her very public life with gusto and a complete lack of remorse during the buttoned-up 1950s.

In 1964, she married Richard Burton, with whom she costarred in *Cleopatra*. They would divorce, then remarry, then divorce once and for all in 1976. Every public quarrel, separation, and tearful reunion was front-page news.

During and after the Liz and Dick years, Elizabeth made some great and terrible movies (*Doctor Faustus,* anyone?*), spent two stints in rehab after becoming addicted to booze and prescription pain pills, got fat, got thin, married a few more times (Republican senator John Warner, construction worker and mullet-rocker Larry Fortensky), launched a series of fragrances that made her extremely rich, and founded what would be the first important organization to battle AIDS. And these are only a handful of the high points.

ELIZABETH ROSEMOND TAYLOR was born in London to American parents in 1932. The Taylors traveled in rarified circles: Elizabeth's father, Francis, was an art dealer with a posh gallery on Bond Street; her mother, Sara, had acted a bit on the stage. From the time she was a toddler, people remarked on Elizabeth's beauty: her black hair, her alabaster skin, and her stunning eyes that were in fact a lovely medium blue (and not violet, as everyone would one day have it**). Eye color aside, she was also blessed with a genetic mutation called distichiasis: double eyelashes. (I know: I feel for her too.) In 1943, Elizabeth costarred with Roddy McDowall in

---

* Renata Adler, in her blistering review in the *New York Times* wrote, "[Burton] seems happiest shouting in Latin, or in Ms. Taylor's ear."

** Go ahead and Google the color violet. You'll see.

Lassie Come Home. McDowall liked to tell the story of how the director ordered Elizabeth to wash off her mascara the first day on set. Except: She wasn't wearing any.

More evidence, as if we needed any, that life is unfair.

Elizabeth's eyes may have been beautiful, but they were also alarming. Studio heads at Universal, where she had a brief contract that was allowed to expire, said she didn't look like a child, but had "old eyes." In those days, the studios were all looking for the next Shirley Temple, with her sausage curls, jaunty pinafore, and chirpy songs about the Good Ship Lollipop. But that was not Elizabeth Taylor. There was something too knowing about her, something unsettling and a little wild.

The 11-year-old Elizabeth had been a huge fan of *National Velvet*, the 1935 novel by Enid Bagnold. Together, she and her mother lobbied Pandro S. Berman, the head of MGM, for the costarring role of Velvet Brown. Berman turned her down flat, saying that she was simply too short for the role, which required her at one point to pass herself off as a male jockey. In one of the first, great apocryphal stories meant to convey the sheer tenacity of Elizabeth Taylor, she went home, willed herself to grow three inches, then came back and landed the part.

Velvet Brown is a young English girl who wins a horse in a raffle and aspires to ride him in the Grand National Steeplechase. She's aided in her quest by a down-on-his-luck jockey (is there any other kind?), played by Mickey Rooney. Because girls weren't allowed to ride in the Grand National, she disguises herself as a boy and rides to triumph. Rooney is ostensibly the star, but Elizabeth steals the show. It's a treat to see her in a prepubescent moment: that blink of a cultural eye before she became a woman to be reckoned with.

That was the thing about Elizabeth Taylor: There were no coltish years during which she languished awkwardly on the cusp of womanhood. She was a kid, and then suddenly, she was a va-va-va-voom hottie. In 1949, she starred with 38-year-old Robert Taylor in *Conspirator,* complete with torrid-for-the-time love scenes. She was a mere 16 during the film's production.

These days, there are some women who take pride in being called "girls," shopping in the junior (or even children's) department, and banishing post-baby pooches as soon as is humanly possible. But Taylor reveled in her hourglass figure and looked to cash in on the spoils of adult womanhood as soon as she could.

As a child star, Elizabeth had been cloistered by her parents and managed by the studio; she had no real friends. "Without the usual crowd of peers most teens use to define themselves, I knew I would have to grow up even faster," she wrote in her 1987 memoir/self-help tome *Elizabeth Takes Off: On Weight Gain, Weight Loss, Self-Image, and Self-Esteem.* "I didn't have to be a genius to realize that I would have to find a place away from both my parents' house and the studio. After several failed attempts, I realized the only way I could escape was through marriage."

Which she did, to Conrad "Nicky" Hilton, in 1950. Even at the tender age of 18, marriage for Elizabeth wasn't marriage as we lesser mortals think of it. It was more like industrial-strength dating. For the rest of her life, she would breezily swing from one man to the next, like Tarzan from vine to vine. Mr. Right Now was always Mr. Right. "I've only slept with men I've been married to," she once said, "How many women can make that claim?" If that's true, she was more decorous than anyone gave her credit for.

There were the Major Husbands who rocked her world (Michael Wilding*, Mike Todd, Richard Burton, and Richard Burton). And then there were the Minor Husbands, companions who seemed only to keep her bed warm (Conrad Hilton, Eddie Fisher, John Warner, Larry Fortensky). She loved them until she didn't; then it was on to the next. Elizabeth was romantic, passionate, impetuous, but she had no aptitude for riding out the rough patches. Nor, in her entitled way, did she believe that she should.

The engagement to Nicky Hilton was multipurpose: an instance of boffo cross-promotional kismet. Studio publicists routinely stirred up gossip about romances between costars as a form of cheap marketing.

---

* Earned by virtue of being the husband of the longest marriage.

But rarely did something like this happen: In the spring of 1950 Elizabeth also happened to be costarring in *Father of the Bride* with Spencer Tracy as, you guessed it, a *bride*. MGM was thrilled to pick up the tab for Elizabeth's May wedding (including the dress). The church for the real wedding was decorated in the same way as the church in the movie wedding. The ceremony took place a month before the release of the film. The film was a hit, while the marriage was not; they were divorced after eight months. Elizabeth was still 18.

In 1951, she costarred in the classic *A Place in the Sun*. It was the height of the Hays Code era, when movies were censored within an inch of incomprehensibility. The Motion Picture Production Code, as it was also known, ruled Hollywood between 1930 and 1968—but it was particularly stringent during Elizabeth's early movies. Every page of every script was scrutinized to be sure that there was no nudity, profanity, shots of people in bed, or references to "sexual perversion," which included homosexuality, open or implicit criticisms of marriage, law enforcement, or religion. There was also a specially appointed BI, or Bust Inspector, to police the cleavage.

The film starred Montgomery Clift as George Eastman, the poor nephew of a rich uncle who manufacturers women's bathing suits. He meets vivacious, breathtaking socialite Angela Vickers (Elizabeth) at one of his uncle's parties. Assuming she's completely out of his league, he settles for innocent factory co-worker Alice Tripp, played to perfection by Shelley Winters. George and Angela meet again and fall in love, just as Alice learns she's "in trouble." George wants her to terminate the pregnancy; we know this because he makes a few phone calls from a sketchy pay phone and writes down the name of a doctor on a sad little crumpled piece of paper. Alice drags herself to the doctor, who apparently cannot help her (unless you consider his stern lecture about how she will make a healthy mother, "help"). Alice blackmails George into marrying her—but thinking better of it, he decides to drown her instead. In short order, he's apprehended and sent to the electric chair. The end.

The movie was provocative in its time because it dared to dramatize the plight of pregnancy out of wedlock. But it's also an unwitting cautionary tale for what happens to men who settle. Don't have unprotected sex with the first girl who says yes, sir. You're better than that! Have a little self-respect! With that handsome mug and full head of hair, you could land gorgeous, ditzy Angela Vickers.

A Place in the Sun won a slew of production Oscars, and Clift and Winters were both nominated. Elizabeth was not, and for good reason. *Variety* wrote: "[Taylor's] histrionics are of a quality so far beyond anything she has done previously, that Stevens' skilled hands on the reins must be credited with a minor miracle."

But it didn't matter. It would never matter. Whether she turned in an Oscar-worthy performance or something more typical of a community college theater department on the skids, Elizabeth Taylor on the screen—with that heart-shaped face and 19-inch waist—was a female force to be reckoned with.

Elizabeth Taylor would be called the Most Beautiful Woman in the World, but come on. Beauty is possibly the most subjective thing on Earth (after how people like their eggs). Grace Kelly, Elizabeth's peer, was easily as beautiful. But Elizabeth stirred up something in our wayward human hearts. In *The Accidental Feminist,* M. G. Lord writes about Elizabeth's genius for evoking primitive, nonverbal feelings: "Taylor spoke directly to our ancient aft-brain: our amygdala, the repository of love, hate, fear, and lust." Camille Paglia, in her usual overheated way, wrote, "[A]n electric, erotic charge vibrates the space between her face and the lens." Elizabeth was, in fact, the perfect screen siren for the Hays Code era—because she could evoke deep, dirty, confusing thoughts simply by standing there.

IN HER WOMANLY WAY Elizabeth was also a prodigy of procreation. In 1952, a year after she cast aside Hilton, she tied the knot with British actor Michael Wilding in a low-key wedding at the registry office. He was 40, she was a month shy of her 20th birthday. He was a friend-and-protector-style husband. A year later, their son Michael Jr. was born. Two years later, another son, Christopher, was born. An heir and a spare. Done and done.

Elizabeth had been making movies all along, as best she could. Her pregnancies stalled her career. Weddings were great publicity, but the pregnancies that followed? Not so much. A pregnancy wasn't romantic. It wasn't something the Hays Code could reframe, and the specter of a wasp-waisted lovely gaining 50 pounds, as Elizabeth did with both pregnancies, was too appalling for words. There was no provision for maternity leave in a studio contract. Actresses who dared to get pregnant were suspended without pay. When they returned, wasp-waisted again, they were often given the lousy roles that less troublesome, nonpregnant actresses had turned down. I'm simplifying the situation, but not much. After her sons were born, Elizabeth dutifully appeared in a handful of forgettable films because she needed to work. Wilding was a rank-and-file actor, respected in London, but unknown in L.A. Touchingly, they needed the money.

At the tender age of 23, Elizabeth told the press she'd had it with Hollywood and was thinking about retiring to devote herself to her family. Had this happened, perhaps another actress would have been left to lay the groundwork for modern celebrity culture, where the so-called private life is the entertainment, and whatever the celebrity produces—movies, plays, paintings, fragrances, or Instagram accounts—gives us an excuse to form a devoted and completely illogical attachment.

Producer Mike Todd, husband number three, arrived on the scene in 1956. Elizabeth's rebound marriage to Michael Wilding was in tatters. He was unhappy in Hollywood, both at the state of his career and in his role as Mr. Taylor. He soothed his despair with strippers, thus proving he was also ahead of his time.

Out went the old Mike, in came the new, even older Mike. He was 49; she was 24. Best known for producing *Around the World in 80 Days* and developing Todd-AO, a widescreen theater format that improved the moviegoing experience, older Mike was loud and showbizzy, and sounds perfectly awful. He was one of those guys who, at a large dinner party, gestures to his wife with a chicken leg and says, "I'm going to eat this, and you, too." Wink.

Todd's proposal to Elizabeth was a statement, not a question. He asked her to come to his office at MGM. "He told me he was going to marry me," she said. "He didn't *ask* me, he *told* me. He was irresistible."

Really, Liz?

Clearly she saw something in this arrangement—and indeed, Mike Todd laid the groundwork for her transition to Difficult Woman Extraordinaire. He was the wizard-husband who demonstrated to Elizabeth how to make her natural beauty, sense of entitlement, and lack of expectation in having a private life, work for her. Todd showed her how, without any serious effort on her part, she might keep people watching and wondering what was going to happen to her next, which would make her even more celebrated, allowing her to eventually ask a cool million for *Cleopatra*. But I'm getting ahead of myself.

Never one to miss a marketing opportunity, Todd announced their engagement on the day *Around the World in 80 Days* was released, then slid a 29.4-carat engagement ring on Elizabeth's finger. The thing was as big as a postage stamp, and inaugurated Elizabeth's lavish fit-for-a-queen jewelry collection.* Pretty much every week that followed, Todd would present her with some astonishing new piece. The ruby and diamond Cartier suite (necklace, bracelet, and earrings). The diamond tiara (she liked to wear it by the pool at their rented villa outside Monte Carlo). The $42,000 black pearl ring.

If there's a page we can all take from Elizabeth's book, it's believing we're worth the gems. To no one's knowledge was there ever a moment when Elizabeth said, "Honey! What am I going to do with a tiara?!

---

* As it happened, she was still married to Michael Wilding—silly detail! After their quickie divorce she married Todd on February 2, 1957. She was single for less than a week.

Take it back and let's take a trip/remodel the kitchen/give it away to charity." What Elizabeth Taylor never said in her longish life is, "Oh, you shouldn't have." And neither should we.

LAYERED BETWEEN ANNOUNCEMENTS of what precious bauble was nestled in the latest black velvet box were bulletins about Elizabeth's health. They were surefire attention magnets: sparkling and very expensive gestures of love interwoven with alarming hospital visits. The birth of a baby girl, Liza, in 1957, added more luster to the love story.

Like her dramatic love life and growing world-class jewelry collection, Elizabeth's health issues were larger than life. Although she endured a lot of genuine and prolonged agony, she was also raced to the hospital for the sort of twisted ankles and phlegmy coughs that the rest of us treat with Advil and a day off from work. The best we can tell, no one ever said take two aspirin and call me in the morning to Elizabeth Taylor.

She broke her foot while filming *Lassie Come Home,* required surgery to remove a piece of flint from her eye, and underwent the usual appendectomy and tonsillectomy. She was hospitalized for the flu. She was hospitalized for a pinched nerve.** Her births were all C-sections. After she met Mike Todd, she underwent an extensive, multiple-hour back surgery to repair a crushed disk she'd suffered from falling down some stairs. These are only the greatest hits of her medical chart, all racked up before she was 24 years old.

Indeed, it was her dodgy health that saved her life. In March 1958, Mike Todd was scheduled to be in New York to receive an award for something or other, and Elizabeth, laid low by the flu, couldn't join him. En route, his private plane, the *Lucky Liz,* crashed in New Mexico, killing all aboard.

Elizabeth was throttled with grief. Who wouldn't be? As all the gossip rags would remind the world, she and Todd had only had 417 days

---

** The poor lamb was diagnosed with sciatica at 23. I'm a jaded old crone staring down the barrel of 60 and even I don't have sciatica, knock wood.

together. She was in the middle of filming *Cat on a Hot Tin Roof,* and production was shut down while she adjusted to her new life as a widow with three young children. But you know, she wasn't alone for long, because that was not how Elizabeth Taylor rolled.

Enter Eddie Fisher, wildly famous crooner (and father, incidentally, of Carrie Fisher—see Chapter 29). Or I should say, Eddie Fisher and Debbie Reynolds. They were couple-friends with Elizabeth and Mike Todd. Elizabeth and Debbie knew each other from girlhood, when they'd both been under contract at MGM and went to school together on the lot. Eddie and Mike were also friends. When Elizabeth and Mike married, Debbie was her matron of honor and Eddie was the best man. They were those kind of friends.

When Mike Todd was killed, Eddie was also throttled with grief. Debbie was perhaps also upset, but she had two very small children to tend to, plus her career. Here is Carrie Fisher on what happened next:

"Well, naturally, my father flew to Elizabeth's side, gradually making his way slowly to her front. He first dried her eyes with his handkerchief, then he consoled her with flowers, and ultimately consoled her with his penis. Now this made marriage to my mother awkward, so he was gone within the week."

The one thing I don't understand is why Debbie didn't rush to her friend's side upon the death of her husband. Think of it. One of your best friends is The Most Beautiful Woman in the World, and when her husband dies unexpectedly, *your* husband rushes to her side?

Many years later, Elizabeth would offer a commonplace—though rare for her—analysis: The marriage between Debbie and Eddie was over; she was not the home-wrecking Jezebel the world had made her out to be. But at the time, the only explanation she offered appeared in Hedda Hopper's gossip column. "Mike's dead, and I'm alive. What do you expect me to do, sleep alone?"

You can imagine how well that went over. The woman who could probably quite literally have any man in the world (except the gay men she loved like brothers: Roddy McDowall, Montgomery Clift, and Rock Hudson) could only be happy with her best friend's husband, also the father of two small children.

It was indefensible, and Elizabeth offered nothing in her defense.

When we generally think of difficult women, we think of those who are opinionated, who shoot off their mouths, who won't take no for an answer. Who refuse to sit down and shut up. Who nevertheless persist. But Elizabeth said nothing. Why should she?

In a much slower time, when you had to be home to catch a phone call and wait for monthly magazines to get caught up on Hollywood gossip, Elizabeth's reputation had nevertheless rocketed from heartbroken young widow to whore of Babylon in a matter of weeks. Meanwhile, *Cat on a Hot Tin Roof* was released and made a mint. Perhaps in her grief Elizabeth didn't have it in her to gild her performance with her usual actress-y flourishes. Whatever the analysis, she was sensational, and earned an Oscar nomination for best actress.

In May 1959, a year and two months after Todd was killed, Elizabeth and Eddie were married in Vegas. The bride wore brown, and a lot of the beautiful jewelry given to her by Mike Todd. The next year she starred in *BUtterfield 8* as high-priced call girl Gloria Wandrous—wearing, I swear, the same slip she immortalized in *Cat on a Hot Tin Roof.* She was a white satin slip–wearing husband stealer, and moviegoers came out in droves. She allegedly hated the role—but the movie was another hit, and allowed her to cheekily demand that historic seven-figure fee to play *Cleopatra.*

Eddie Fisher's career didn't keep pace with Elizabeth's. His TV show was canceled, and he was dropped from his record company. The general feeling among the public was that however grief-stricken he might have been over the death of his friend, he was a bit of a cad for leaving his family—especially because it was to be the lesser consort of a queen.

ELIZABETH MET RICHARD BURTON on the set of *Cleopatra* in 1962. This time, they were both married. It's likely her reputation would never have survived another round of juicy, flagrant adultery; however, the year before she had nearly died. And there is nothing we like better than celebrities who escape death. Especially, apparently, shameless hussies of whom we disapprove.

The movie was originally filming in England, and Elizabeth came down with a bad case of pneumonia. She was rushed to a London hospital. She stopped breathing. A quick-thinking doctor performed a tracheotomy on the most beautiful neck in the world, thus saving her life. But the media jumped the gun and reported that Elizabeth Taylor had died. Joan Collins, another light-eyed brunette with an hourglass figure, was tapped to replace her.

But Elizabeth did not die, and this is how weird human beings are: By not being dead after her death was reported erroneously, it was as if she had been resurrected. She was not a queen after all, but a goddess. Suddenly, all was forgiven. She was no longer the whore of Babylon. She won the Oscar for best actress for *BUtterfield 8,* even though she'd been much better in *Cat on a Hot Tin Roof.* Elizabeth was no dummy. She knew it was a sympathy award, but accepted it graciously anyway. As one does.

By the time she was fully recovered, the *Cleopatra* production had moved to Rome. Elizabeth arrived with a full entourage, including her three children, five dogs, two cats, hairdresser, personal physician, and Eddie, who was hired by the production to make sure she made it to the set on time.* They stayed in a 14-room villa just off the Appian Way.

Richard Burton was a mere seven years older than Elizabeth, and thus her peer. He was known primarily as a Shakespearean actor, famous for his rich Welsh accent and portrayals of Hamlet and Henry V on the London stage. (Later he would go on to star in the mid-century hit films *Becket, The Spy Who Came in From the Cold,* and with Elizabeth, *Who's Afraid of Virginia Woolf?*) When he wasn't on the set, Burton was usually drunk and

---

* That sound you hear is romance leaking out of the marriage.

trying to get laid. He was married to a nice, tolerant woman named Sybil who, in the British way, turned a blind eye to his carrying-on, as long as he was discreet. Burton was known for routinely bedding his costar, and knocked boots with whoever caught his eye in the same way other people go to the gym. (Actually, if you go to the gym less than three times a week, Dick was having sex more often than you run on the treadmill.)

Given that Liz and Dick fell in love and carried on in the country that invented the word "paparazzi," it will come as no surprise that when they tried to sneak away for a tryst, the whole world knew about it.

Poor Eddie Fisher, as I've come to think of him. He begged Elizabeth to deny the rumors. She refused. Furious, he did that thing that, then as now, is seriously uncool, even if you are being cuckolded. He rang up Burton's nice, tolerant wife, Sybil, and ratted them out. Burton was furious, and his surprising reaction was to break it off with Elizabeth. This had never happened to her before. Her response was less surprising. She was rushed to the hospital. There were varying reports as to why: either food poisoning or sleeping pill overdose.

Then they got back together.

These days, no one blinks an eye when a scandalous celebrity love affair dominates the media. It's hardly even news. In the mid 1960s, it was an entirely different enchilada: The studio asked Elizabeth to "desist" canoo-dling with Burton, and attempted to sue her for violating the morals clause in her contract. Elizabeth harrumphed and said, "Nobody tells me who to love or not to love." The Vatican weighed in with a very proper "open letter" that included the frankly adorable and completely nonsen-sical argument: "Even considering the husband that was finished by a natural solution, there remain three husbands buried with no other motive than a greater love that killed the one before." Later, when Liz and Dick went to Puerto Vallarta to film *The Night of the Iguana*** and shacked up together at a local resort, a local convent that had kept a vow

---

** Dick's costar was Ava Gardner, and Liz was not about to let him toodle off to Mexico alone. She arrived on a private plane with 74 pieces of luggage.

of silence as long as anyone could remember spoke out against the mortal sinners in their midst.

In 1964, after divorcing their respective spouses, they were married. Poor Eddie Fisher never quite recovered. He remarried a few times, struggled with a serious meth habit, and eventually declared bankruptcy.

My mother was a huge fan of Liz and Dick. I was maybe in second grade when they entered my consciousness. Because my dad was a Richard who went by Dick, and my uncle was a Richard who went by Dick, I was confused much of the time and thought perhaps Liz was somehow related. My mother especially loved *Who's Afraid of Virginia Woolf?*, which she took me to see when my dad was out of town on business and the babysitter had failed to appear. I felt terrified by the whole spectacle. So much shouting. And so boring. I was alarmed by how old and angry Liz looked, when I knew her to be a young, suntanned beauty who was often photographed wearing a big fur hat (also for reasons I couldn't under-stand, because we lived in California and so did she).

After the movie, I remember driving down Whittier Boulevard in my mother's Galaxie 500 convertible. It must have been summer, because we put the top down. I asked her what the movie was about, and she said, "It's what happens when a woman doesn't have anything of her own." I said, "Liz doesn't have anything of her own?"

You should have heard my mother laugh.

I ALMOST FORGOT ABOUT all the mad drinking. Dick, as we know, was a big lush. Liz liked to knock back a few herself. Together they were sauced a lot of the time, which led to a lot of arguments and crockery hurling. Since, as we know, Liz was also seemingly in a perpetual state of recovery from some surgery or other (in 1964 she had knee surgery; in 1966 she broke her big toe), prescription painkillers were also a regular part of her daily regime. Their romance, which was the most glamorous thing going, was a scrumptious layer cake of public arguments, hospitalizations, and staggeringly expensive jewels that made Mike Todd's offerings look like they came from the Dollar Store. Dick gave Liz pieces that were so extravagant they had *names*. The 33.19-carat Krupp diamond. The 69-carat Burton-Cartier diamond. The 55.95-carat La Peregrina, arguably the world's most famous pearl. Found in the 16th century by an African slave, it passed through the hands of kings and queens until Burton purchased it at Sotheby's to give to Liz for Valentine's Day. For a brief time the pearl was lost—Liz discovered the dog chewing on it—before finding a stunning home in a Cartier-designed necklace, set with pearls, diamonds, and rubies.

Still, it was not enough to keep them together. They divorced in 1974, remarrying in 1975. By then they were like two old prizefighters holding each other up in the middle of the ring. This second marriage lasted less than a year. They divorced in 1976, the same year Liz married Republican Senator John Warner. She then proceeded to get fat, which only endeared her to us further. The Most Beautiful Woman in the World was no different from the rest of us.

THROUGHOUT HER LIFE Elizabeth maintained deep friendships with a handful of gay men. Some of her biographers have posited that it was because her father had had a long relationship with a set designer, and may have been at least bisexual. Others claimed it was because these were men Elizabeth couldn't have. I'd like to think that it's because your standard-issue heterosexual male was only capable of responding to her beauty. Once sex was off the table, men were able to see that she also had other admirable human qualities worth appreciating. Like boldly speaking up about AIDS when her friends, family, and business managers advised her to be quiet.

During the filming of *Giant,* Elizabeth and Rock Hudson had become fast friends. In the summer of 1985, he was dying of AIDS in a Paris hospital. The general public knew next to nothing about the disease whose name kept changing, but was known informally as "the gay plague." Hollywood had more than its share of sufferers, and nevertheless turned a blind eye. Elizabeth was furious, and because she was a difficult woman, did absolutely nothing to tamp down her rage.

She was now a middle-aged woman of 53, and looked it. Two years earlier, she had entered rehab at the Betty Ford Center. The year before, Burton had died of a cerebral hemorrhage. Her last great movie had been *Taming of the Shrew,* where she went toe-to-toe with Burton in 1967. She had been through some things.

Oh, how Hollywood's apathy and homophobia galled her.

In September 1985, she founded the American Foundation for AIDS Research (amfAR). Her newfound passion was a difficult sell. Even friends who were sympathetic were wary. Her closest friends and allies advised her to steer clear. For the first time in her life, people didn't return her calls, which only made her more determined. She starred in television spots and testified before Congress. She attended fundraisers, and embarrassed politicians into getting involved. She even wrote an open letter to then President Reagan to press for his involvement.

"I am writing from my heart to ask if you both would attend the dinner—and if you, Mr. President, would give the keynote speech. I am so pleased that you, Mr. President, have already spoken out on the issue of AIDS," she wrote. Actually, up until that moment he'd sidestepped the issue. But he, like so many men who came before him, could not say no to Elizabeth Taylor.

In the end, she would raise $100 million for AIDS research.

Recently, Suzanne Venker, author of *The Alpha Female's Guide to Men and Marriage,* which basically advises women to hop in the way-back machine and defer to their husbands, 1950s style, writes, "In essence, being feminine means being nice."

Fair enough, except "nice" was never a word associated with the most feminine star of the last century. Elizabeth was a hyper-girly goddess before whom men lined up for the chance to buy Oreo-size diamonds. But she was still complicated, selfish, demanding, passionate—and unafraid to speak up and wield her power. We tend to write off Elizabeth Taylor's charisma as a simple function of her beauty. But the secret to her timeless allure was her complicated, difficult nature.

CHAPTER 3

GLORIA STEINEM

Activist

ON OCTOBER 7, 2016, THE *NEW YORK TIMES* published a profile of Gloria Steinem and her love of New York. The story began: "Gloria Steinem started her career as a CIA operative, got her break as a Playboy Bunny, married Christian Bale's father, and now produces a show for the cable television channel Viceland . . ." At 82, the story continued, Steinem still kept a "rock star's schedule," organizing, lecturing, fundraising, stumping for political candidates, and promoting her new book, *My Life on the Road*. The piece was a little flip, but generally balanced and positive—and if I were Gloria, slogging from city to city on a book tour, my roller bag bumping along behind me, I would be fine with it. Yes, the lead was stupidly reductive, but nothing a little self-soothing at the minibar couldn't fix. As I polished off a tiny bottle of Dewar's, I would congratulate myself for letting go of my irritation. After all, what could it possibly matter?

But that's why Gloria Steinem is a difficult woman. Things *do* matter. Language matters. History matters. Truth matters. Within the week, she fired off a response to the *Times* piece with a letter to the editor, clarifying facts behind the racy lead. She was not a CIA operative, but had attended two Soviet-backed youth festivals in the 1960s, her travel financed by a foundation subsidized by the agency. She had never been a Playboy Bunny, but donned the outfit to go undercover for 10 days to write an exposé. And David Bale, her late husband, was not simply the father of a famous actor, but actually had an identity of his own, as an entrepreneur and animal rights activist.

The tone was classic Gloria Steinem: cool, calm, and witty. I was impressed that she'd taken the time—especially considering that the sentence in question was misleading, but the facts weren't technically incorrect. Known informally as the World's Most Famous Feminist, Gloria has been pushing the women's lib rock uphill for 55 years. She shows no signs of putting her feet up and getting caught up on her binge-watching.

GLORIA'S OWN CHILDHOOD would make for an excellent show on premium cable. She was born in Toledo, Ohio, on March 25, 1934, during the height of the Depression. Her gregarious father, Leo, was "a traveling antique salesman," which sounds like an actual profession. In truth he was a charming nomad, pathologically unable to stay in one place, who dragged his wife, Ruth, and two daughters around the country in a trailer, buying and selling antiques simply to get to the next place.

It was a blast for little Gloria. She writes in *My Life on the Road* about the joy of stopping along the way for Nehi grape soda at middle-of-nowhere gas stations and checking into a hotel when the family needed a shower. Sometimes, at home in Toledo, her dad would get such an intense hankering to be on the road that they would leave the dirty dinner dishes sitting on the counter and just *go*. This was pretty much hell on her anxious mother, who worried about the things responsible women are always left to worry about, such as where the next meal might be coming from. Ruth was mentally fragile, and had suffered a breakdown or two before Gloria was born.

When Gloria was 10, Ruth and Leo divorced; her older sister was already off at Smith College. Leo took off for California, leaving Gloria alone to look after her mother. Her relationship with Ruth was challenging and poignant. Over and over again, she saw the doctors dismiss her mother's obvious distress and mental illness—and long before she was a feminist, recognized an anti-woman bias when she saw it.

Gloria enrolled at Smith, where she graduated Phi Beta Kappa in 1956. After college, she moved to New York to become a journalist. Her first meaty assignment was a story for *Esquire* on the state of contraception. It was 1962, and the Pill was big news—even though it would take 10 more years until it was available to all women, regardless of marital status. The notorious Playboy Bunny story, written for a magazine called *Show,* came a year later. Gloria zeroed in on the way in which the Bunnies were exploited and sexually harassed in Hugh Hefner's New York Playboy Club. Her radical conclusion: Just because Bunnies served horny businessmen highballs and medium-rare steaks didn't mean they were good with being felt up.

In 1969, Gloria reported on an abortion speak-out for *New York* magazine. Let us recall that freedom to choose would not come along until 1973, and that the women gathered in the church basement in Greenwich Village who stood up and told their stories were basically criminals who were probably lucky to be alive. Gloria had had her own secret abortion when she was 22, performed in London by the doctor to whom she dedicated *My Life on the Road.* She traces the speak-out and the story she wrote about it to her active embrace of feminism.

In 1971, Gloria co-founded *Ms.* magazine with African-American activist Dorothy Pitman Hughes. For the next two decades, she was on a plane every few days, traveling to get the word out about why the lives of women were every bit as important as the lives of men.

In *The Feminine Mystique,* Betty Friedan addressed the ennui felt by educated middle-class white women pressed to surrender their ambitions and identities to the rigors of the suburban home and hearth. But Gloria's view was always global. She understood that race, class, and caste (she traveled for two years after college in India) tend to double and triple the degree of oppression to which women are subjected. She herself was dismissed as a "girl reporter" and had trouble renting an apartment because landlords believed that single women were too irresponsible to be financially reliable. (The feeling was that if by some miracle they *were* able to pay their rent every month on time, it was because they were prostitutes or some man's mistress.) Although that attitude was infuriating, Gloria was already well aware that it was nothing compared with the injustices women of color and women of the developing world suffered.

SOMETIMES YOU'RE A DAMNED-IF-YOU-DO, damned-if-you-don't sort of difficult woman. Gloria is an empathic, good-natured consensus builder, with a dry, self-deprecating wit. She is smart, and by all reports, kind. She *listens*. She allows people to crash at her cool Manhattan brownstone whenever they want. Really, what's not to like?

Oh, so much.

Beginning in the early 1970s, after launching *Ms.,* Gloria found herself to be the so-called face of feminism. *Esquire* dubbed her "the intellectual's pin-up."

She was (and still is) despised by conservatives (some of whom think that feminism is an evil capable of bringing down the nation). But many of her own feminist sisters were openly disgruntled with the media's interest in Gloria. New thinking, radical ideas, bold analysis, and a collective of raised consciences were supposed to float the feminist boat— and not a woman who so thoroughly rocked a miniskirt.*

A lot of the backlash went back to that damn 1963 *Show* story—and the accompanying picture of Gloria in full Bunny regalia (strapless satin

---

* It isn't fair, but what can you do? I will tell you one thing: Ugly crying about the injustice of it all doesn't help matters—nor does pitching a fit, however justified.

one-piece, weird little collar with tiny black bow tie, matching satin cuffs, and large, frankly ridiculous satin ears attached to a headband). The fallout from the Bunny story lasted decades. Whatever it was Gloria aimed to do—investigative journalism, political activism, magazine founding, and editing—she was dismissed for being too attractive. Complete insanity, because for women—like it or not, then as now, possibly forever and ever, amen—being considered attractive is always one of the highest cards in our respective decks.

The common wrongheaded thinking about feminism (still!) is that only plain women want equal rights because they aren't hot enough to attract a husband. In other words, they would play the patriarchal game if they could. You would think all the erudite people opining about second-wave feminism in the 1970s would have been smarter than that—or at least have been aware that life was complicated. (Clay Felker, founder of *New York* magazine and Gloria's one-time boss, once said that child care was the only real problem of women; if they just imported more nannies, everything would be fine.)

But what if a beautiful wife's husband died, divorced her, or turned out to be such an abusive jerk that she couldn't stay married any longer? What if, beauty notwithstanding, a woman was smart enough to want a credit card in her own name? (Not possible until 1974.) What if her boss pressed himself on her at work? (Sexual harassment not actionable until 1977.) Or she got pregnant? (*Roe* v. *Wade*, 1973.) That stuff happened, and happens every day. Why wouldn't women want laws to protect themselves?

When I was in grade school, a friend's mother was pregnant with twins and I remember being frightened by her size. She couldn't sit down or stand up without the help of two people. Her feet were so splayed, they'd broken the sides of her shoes. I told my mother I never wanted to get pregnant. When she asked why, I said, "because what if someone chases me? I won't be able to run!" She said, "That's what your husband's for." I looked at her and said, "That doesn't make any sense." I was eight years old. Even at that age, I knew women could only rely on men for so much.

In any case, Gloria's beauty wound up being good for the feminist cause. She wrote, "When a reporter raised the question of my looks as more important than anything I could possibly have to say . . . an older woman rose in the audience. 'Don't worry, honey,' she said to me comfortingly. 'It's important for some who could play the game—and win— to say: The game isn't worth shit.' "

Gloria became the face of feminism, and also, because this is how the world works, the voice. "A woman needs a man like a fish needs a bicycle," was famously attributed to her, but in fact was coined by Australian activist Irina Dunn. Gloria also never said, "If men could get pregnant, abortion would be a sacrament." That was coined by an Irish woman cab driver.

BEING PRETTY DIDN'T MAKE Gloria Steinem's love life any easier. Women who play by the rules are excused for changing their minds— that's just what we silly ladies do! Move the sofa over there. No, there. Let's go to that Indian place for dinner—no wait, I want Mexican. I love you, but I'm not in love with you, or actually, maybe I do love you.

If you're going to be difficult, people are much less forgiving. If you insist on planting your flag in the sand for your politics or other beliefs—even if it's just a belief in yourself—be prepared to be called out the moment you evolve, rethink something, change your mind, contradict yourself, or just behave in an inexplicably human way. It's as if by flouting expectations, we've also unwittingly agreed to be held to impossible standards.

In the early 1990s, Gloria and New York real estate developer Mort Zuckerman were an item. It was a difficult time: She was struggling with a book, had survived a bout of breast cancer, and would soon turn 60.

People were appalled by her choice of Zuckerman. He was a rich capitalist who was known to send a limo to pick up Gloria when she returned from one of her speaking engagements. This was viewed as flagrant hypocrisy on Gloria's part. It was as if, as a feminist, she was never allowed to be exhausted, depressed, or in need of cosseting by a beau with enough money to send a car to pick her up.

Rumors raced around Manhattan with such speed that it's a wonder the city didn't spontaneously combust. The completely inaccurate gist was: Mort Zuckerman said he would marry Gloria if she could give him a baby, and she was frantically, desperately dashing from one fertility specialist to the next. She *was* frantically, desperately dashing to specialists, but they were oncologists. The relationship didn't last, but the disapproval did. In 2000, she married younger man David Bale (he was 59, she was 66). More uproar: We thought Gloria Steinem hated marriage!

"I didn't change. Marriage changed," she said. "We spent 30 years in the United States changing the marriage laws. If I had married when I was supposed to get married, I would have lost my name, my legal residence, my credit rating, many of my civil rights. That's not true anymore. It's possible to make an equal marriage."

NOW IN HER 80S, Gloria is my role model for aging. On March 25, 2014, she celebrated her 80th birthday by riding an elephant in Botswana. After that she was on her way to India, then California. She still dyes her hair, but has passed on plastic surgery. She still has terrific bone structure. One thing she loves about being older is her lack of libido. "The brain cells that used to be obsessed are now free for all kinds of great things," she remarked. "I try to tell younger women that, but they don't believe me."

Some difficult women become more difficult with age, but Gloria doesn't even have to do anything. She is one of those women who rankle people merely by still being aboveground. You would think the collective cultural impulse would be to treat Gloria Steinem as a cool old person, a grand dame of a time gone by when tinted aviator glasses were not worn ironically. This, sadly, is not the case. Controversial old guys tend to get a pass (see adopted daughter–marrying Woody Allen)—but not so crusading, outspoken women.

For half our divided nation, Gloria is a beloved icon.* For the other half, her politics are problematic. In spring 2016, CEO Federica Marchionni, formerly of ultracool Dolce & Gabbana, was hired to bring a bit more style to the traditional American clothing company Lands' End. The company launched a series called Legends, "our ode to individuals who have made a difference in both their respective industries and the world at large. We honor them and thank them for paving the way for the many who follow."

Gloria Steinem was invited to be the inaugural Legend. She was photographed wearing a perfectly respectable blazer and scarf. Her interview with Marchionni was standard "You go, girl!" issue, covering such seemingly mainstream issues as equal rights and women in the workplace. Reproductive freedom was never mentioned. It didn't matter.

"What are you thinking to glorify a pro-abortion feminist when you are trying to sell clothing to families?!" wrote one unhappy customer on the company's Facebook page.

Without stopping to think that the damage had already been done, Lands' End pulled the profile and issued an apology. In so doing, they effectively alienated everyone: the people who will never forgive them for having thought to celebrate Gloria in the first place as well as a lot of left-leaning pro-choice women. "You have lost my business by succumbing to pressure from the far right," one woman wrote in an email. "I have

---

* And in case you think it's just graying baby boomers who love her, Emma Watson, aka Hermione, selected Gloria's *My Life on the Road* as her inaugural Twitter book club pick.

been a Lands' End customer for 40 years. Gloria Steinem is indeed someone to be honored."**

Federica Marchionni stepped down not long after.

At the time, Gloria wasn't available for comment as she was on the road. But she said, through an assistant, that her "stance on all issues remains the same."

I read this and laughed. Gloria Steinem is not going to change her tune at this late date to placate a clothing catalog. Or anyone else, for that matter. But appreciate the lightness of her words, the playfulness. If Gloria has taught us anything, it's that we can stand our ground, speak our truth, and fight the good fight—all without sacrificing our wit or cool hair.

** My email said: Stand your ground, Lands' End. Gloria Steinem is absolutely someone who made a difference, paved the way, etc. Just because not everyone agrees with everything she says doesn't change that!

CHAPTER 4

AMY POEHLER

Subversive

THERE ARE A HANDFUL OF contemporary comediennes I always mix up—but never Amy Poehler. Perhaps because she looks like a cross between Alice in Wonderland and a cute cartoon frog contemplating a felony. There's that arched eyebrow, that deadpan stare, that curled corner of the lip. She's very sweet-looking—but beware. Amy is one of those difficult women who fly under cover of adorable amiability, but when pressed, can throw some world-class shade faster than you can say "Live from New York, it's Saturday Night."

In *Yes Please,* her sort of a memoir, she tells a story about the time she was flying to Toronto with Tina Fey and Ana Gasteyer to shoot *Mean Girls.* They were in first class, and during the hour-long flight were chatting in a lively (loud) fashion as girlfriends often do. A White Businessman of a Certain Age in a fancy suit was seated nearby and mistook first class for a library. Fancy Suit was peeved at what he clearly viewed as disruptive visiting among the women. After they deplaned, he pushed past Amy and she did that thing where you say "Excuse me!" but what you really mean is You're the One Who Should Be Saying Excuse Me, Pal.

Fancy Suit said, "Excuse ME? Excuse you!" He then told Amy that because she and her friends had been yammering during the entire flight, they shouldn't have been allowed in first class.

Amy was enraged. She spun around and dropped a few F-bombs.

He turned on his heel, to get away from this madwoman, but she ran after him, shouting and cursing that he wasn't better than her, and that he could keep his entitled opinions to himself.

Brief digression for a sexism check: This nonsense wouldn't have happened to a man, so why is it happening to a woman? Is there any doubt that if Amy, Tina, and Ana had been three showbizzy guys talking sports, Fancy Suit would have wanted to join in on the Monday morning quarterbacking, stat swapping, and Super Bowl ad recounting? (I just decided our hypothetical guy makes commercials.)

This altercation took place in the early 2000s, before the iPhone-equipped masses became citizen journalists eager to record a celebrity losing her mind in an airport (the better to create memes, GIFs, and hashtags like #SNLStarChasesManInAirport). Still, Amy Poehler was a public figure: a young woman who appeared every weekend on *Saturday Night Live*. Tabloids were around, and surely someone could have snapped a picture of her looking unhinged.

Like many women (me), she could easily have complained under her breath but otherwise kept her objections to being patronized to herself.

Because so often, that's what we do. We stay silent, rather than cuss out someone and chase him down the moving walkway. Even difficult women who are stubborn, brave, outspoken, and won't take no for an answer tend to let this kind of thing go. Men, however, do not let this sort of thing go. That's why there are bar fights and the situation in the Middle East.

There are complex biological and sociological reasons why we ladies prefer to go along to get along (I'm guessing). But the one reliable woman-taming weapon that never loses its effectiveness is slinging the b-word. For some reason we think we will melt like the Wicked Witch of the West if someone calls us a bitch. The only time it's okay to be called a bitch is if you're about to get busy with a hot guy who growls "you're one sexy bitch."

Ugh. Even then. I totally take that back.

In 2008, Tina Fey hosted *SNL* and did a guest spot behind the "Week-end Update" desk, doing her best to take the sting out of the word and make it a rallying cry. It will come as no surprise that the bit was attached to Hillary Clinton.

"Some people say that Hillary is a bitch. I'm a bitch, so is this one [nodding at Amy]. Bitches get stuff done. Bitch is the new black."

Not that this did any good at all. The morning I wrote this, I was in line at Starbucks behind two girls who were maybe 19. One was tormented about whether she should tell her lousy boyfriend that it was uncool when he flirted with someone else while she was standing right there: "I don't want him to think I'm a bitch," she sighed. Amy would totally have told that girl to cuss him out and chase him down the street.

BORN IN NEWTON, MASSACHUSETTS, IN 1971, Amy Poehler was always a funny girl. After graduating from Boston College, she earned her comedy chops in Upright Citizens Brigade, the improv group she co-founded in Chicago in the 1990s. Improv is all about reading a situation, staying in the moment, and doing what feels right. "She was like a surreal anarchist punk comic . . . a total maverick," said Natasha Lyonne, a friend and fellow actor.

Amy appeared on *Saturday Night Live* a week after 9/11—not the best time for sketch comedy—and still managed to find a way to make people shoot beer out of their noses. She was rapidly promoted from featured player to full-time cast member, and was tapped for co-anchor of "Week-end Update"—first with *SNL* head writer and "comedy wife" Tina Fey, then with Seth Meyers. After the birth of her first son in 2008, she left *SNL* to star in *Parks and Recreation* as Leslie Knope, the nation's most upbeat, yet uncompromising, mid-level city bureaucrat. (Every feminist could take a lesson from Leslie: "You know my code. Hoes before bros. Uteruses before duderuses. Ovaries before brovaries!") No one was much surprised when Amy won a Golden Globe for her portrayal—the same year she co-hosted the awards with Tina Fey.

The woman is everywhere these days: producing, directing, writing, and starring in shows on all the TVs (network, cable, digital) as well as feature films. In 2008 she co-founded, with producer Meredith Walker, the online community Smart Girls at the Party, where the focus is on intelligence and imagination, rather than slavishly trying to fit in with a bunch of girls who, let's face it, are never worth it. Tagline: *Change the World by Being Yourself.* Pretty much the difficult woman credo.

That same year, Amy did something that should probably be in *Guinness World Records:* Most Epic Rap Song Performed by a Woman Hours Away from Giving Birth. It occurred on *SNL* in October 2008, when she was so pregnant that it's a true reproductive miracle that her water didn't break on air. Vice presidential candidate Sarah Palin guest-starred, taking a seat at the "Weekend Update" desk with co-anchors Amy and Seth Meyers. There was some back-and-forth between Palin (in full hot teacher mode with glossy updo and shiny teeth) and Meyers about a bit Palin chose not to participate in, as it wouldn't be good for the campaign. Amy graciously agreed to step in and dove into an epic rap. A pair of Eskimos appeared as her backup chorus.

Amy was so pregnant that her belly was no longer round, but more oblong and bargelike—something that happens at the very end when the baby, rather than floating sweetly in its amniotic bath, is wedged in there like a sumo wrestler stuck in economy. She looked pretty exhausted, but completely *owned* it—as if this wasn't simply one of a hundred bits she'd done over the years, but as if this performance would be the ticket out of her small town.

If there exists more convincing evidence that pregnant ladies aren't the delicate flowers our culture would have them be, I'd like to see it. All those comely pregnant celebrities on the cover of the glossy mags—boldly displaying their very round bellies and outie belly buttons, a Mona Lisa smile on their moistened lips—think they're showing the world what it's like to be a mom-to-be? Wrong. It's Amy Poehler, rapping *My name is Sarah Palin / you all know me / vice prezzy nominee / of the GOP.*

When asked by *People* whether it was bizarre to be sending up Palin, who was sitting right there, Amy said she felt no shame or embarrassment. "I was just trying not to give birth—that was my goal."

Amy's style of difficulty is inspiring because however winning or funny she may be, she takes herself and her life very seriously. Once, when she was in Cannes to promote a film, a reporter asked whether she ever dreamed she would one day be there. Clearly, this was her cue to confess that yes, she was thrilled and shocked and full of Hollywood guru-inspired gratitude with a twist of lemon. Instead, she gave him a look— I'm betting with an arched eyebrow—and said, "Sure I did."

It doesn't get any more difficult than that.

CHAPTER 5

RUTH BADER GINSBURG

Indefatigable

EIGHTY-FIVE-YEAR-OLD SUPREME COURT JUSTICE Ruth Bader Ginsburg does not do girl push-ups. During her twice-a-week workouts in the Supreme Court gym, she busts out two sets of 10 standard push-ups without stopping for a break. She leg presses 70 pounds. She easily nails one-arm side planks, one-legged squats, and a medicine ball toss. Since the death of her husband, Martin, in 2010, and best friend on the bench, Antonin Scalia, in 2016, Ruth jokes that the most important person in her life is her personal trainer, Bryant Johnson. Justice Ginsburg is not much of a wisecracker; I'd wager that she thought this probably sounded amusing, but she was actually serious.

Born in 1933 in Brooklyn, New York, Ruth Bader Ginsburg attended Harvard Law School, where she was one of nine women in a class of five hundred and the first female member of the *Harvard Law Review.* After transferring and graduating at the top of her class from Columbia Law School in 1959, she made a name for herself as a quiet yet stalwart courtroom advocate for gender equality. In 1972, she co-founded the American Civil Liberties Union women's rights project and became the first female tenured professor at Columbia Law School. Between 1973 and 1975, she argued six gender discrimination cases before the Supreme Court, and won five of them. In 1980 President Carter appointed her to the U.S. Court of Appeals for the District of Columbia Circuit, and in 1993 President Clinton appointed her to the Supreme Court. She was the second woman to serve, joining Sandra Day O'Connor.

If you were born after 1970, and have thus benefited from changes in the law Ruth Bader Ginsburg helped effect, you might be forgiven for viewing her ascent as a smooth escalator ride to the top—the obvious outcome for a woman who is clearly brilliant. (In the early 1960s, when Ruth went to Sweden to study civil procedure—something in which she holds a passionate interest—she learned Swedish.) But let's not forget that her Depression-era generation of women breathed sexism as if it were air. Most fell in line with societal norms, accepting the fallacy that female biology transcends individual intelligence, aptitude, ambition, or the understandable human desire to escape a lifetime of picking up the dirty socks of others. The kind of blatant, dispiriting discrimination Ruth experienced as she advanced in her career wasn't anything out of the ordinary. But whereas many women were thwarted, Ruth persevered. Misogyny was simply one more hill to climb. Ruth was difficult because she refused to be discouraged. She *really* persisted, one tiny foot in front of the other.

The daughter of Russian Jewish immigrants, Joan Ruth Bader was born during the worst year of the Great Depression. Her father, Nathan, was a furrier, when the last thing a person could afford was a fur coat. Her mother, Celia, denied a college education because of her gender, especially valued education for her daughter. She hoped that if Ruth studied hard, she might become a teacher. But Celia was stricken with cancer while Ruth was in high school, and died the day before her daughter graduated.

At Cornell, Ruth met Martin Ginsburg, whom she would marry a few days after she graduated in 1954. Together they went to Harvard Law, where the dean berated Ruth at a dinner party for taking a man's spot. Even though there were 491 men in her class of 500, she was made to feel guilty for displacing a presumably now-despondent male applicant whose life she'd made more difficult. During her second year at Harvard, Marty was diagnosed with testicular cancer. They also had a toddler, Jane. Ruth took care of her husband as he underwent surgery and chemotherapy, went to class for him, and typed up his papers from dictation, while also caring for their daughter. She managed, amid all this, to keep her own grades up and made the *Harvard Law Review*.

Marty recovered and graduated. He accepted a position at a firm in New York. Ruth dutifully transferred to Columbia Law School, graduating in 1959. She leaned in before it was a thing, had it all before women knew they could want it all. She made it work because her husband was a partner, and her views on motherhood—like pretty much everything else about RBG, as she's come to be known of late—were ahead of her time. "When I started law school, my daughter Jane was 14 months, and I attribute my success in law school largely to Jane. I went to class about 8:30 a.m., and I came home at 4:00 p.m.; that was children's hour. It was a total break in my day, and children's hour continued until Jane went to sleep. Then I was happy to go back to the books. So I felt each part of my life gave me respite from the other."

Despite being first in her class at Columbia Law, Ruth couldn't get a job. Think about it: First in her class, and not one offer. It was a discriminatory trifecta: Jewish, woman, mother. Gerald Gunther, a forward-thinking professor who believed in her, finally strong-armed Manhattan federal judge Edmund Palmieri into hiring her to clerk for him. "Gunther told the judge he'd never recommend another Columbia student to him unless he gave me a chance," Ruth said in a 2013 *New Yorker* interview.

But the challenges continued. In 1963, Ruth was the first woman to teach at Rutgers Law School, where the dean helpfully explained that because her husband made a good living, it was unnecessary to pay her what her male colleagues were making. When she became pregnant with her son, James, in 1964, she hid her condition.

If Ruth ever struggled with insomnia, tossing and turning while brooding over the heinous injustices she was being forced to endure, it never manifested itself in her approach to the law. She's a believer in baby steps. Goethe said about writing, "Do not hurry, do not rest"—a description that also describes Ruth Bader Ginsburg's jurisprudence. One day, her secretary was typing up a brief and suggested that Justice Ginsburg change the phrase sex discrimination to gender discrimination. The problem was the word "sex." Her secretary pointed out that like a dog distracted by a squirrel, the male justices were no doubt distracted from Ruth's argument by the constant repetition of the word. From then on Ruth used the term "gender discrimination," which stuck and is now used in court.

Ruth's radicalism flies under the flag of 1950s-era good manners; it's hard to believe a woman so genteel and soft-spoken is such a mighty litigator. Her mother-in-law once advised her that the key to a happy marriage was sometimes pretending to be a little deaf; Ruth has said the same applies to being a female Supreme Court justice. "When a thoughtless or unkind word is spoken, best to tune it out," she observed. "Reacting in anger or annoyance will not advance one's ability to persuade."

Dahlia Lithwick, in her *Slate* story tracing the rise of the Internet meme "Notorious RBG," wrote, "Ginsburg was so institution-minded and retiring in her first decade at the high court that it was often difficult to reconcile her presence with the monster Supreme Court litigator whose work . . . would reshape U.S. gender law forever. Yet, on and off the bench, Ginsburg always looked and sounded like the most dangerous weapon she could possibly be carrying would be a potato kugel." Proving, in case there was any doubt, that you don't need to possess the strapping badass countenance of Xena Warrior Princess to be a truly, deeply difficult woman.

Of everything Ruth Bader Ginsburg must have imagined when she was appointed to the Supreme Court, I'm confident that being a pop culture sensation was not on the list. Shana Knizhnik, a law student at New York University in 2013, was inspired by Ruth's recent dissenting opinions. In 2006, when Sandra Day O'Connor retired, Ruth didn't like being the only woman on the court.* She began to see that a lot of the work she had done for gender equality was starting to erode. Over the years, her dissenting opinions became positively scathing. She would read them to the court in her soft little voice. To some, I imagine this seemed out of character. Tiny, unassuming Justice Ginsburg! I don't think writing and delivering these historic opinions required the summoning of untapped reserves of strength and chutzpah. By this time Ruth had spent her entire life battling for her own right to excel. Without knowing it, she'd been in training for just this moment.

---

* She would be the lone woman for three years, until the appointment of Sonia Sotomayor in 2009.

Knizhnik followed Ruth's dissents, became inspired, and started a blog on Tumblr called Notorious R.B.G. (with apologies to the late rapper Biggie Smalls, also known as the Notorious B.I.G.) and subtitled *Justice Ruth Bader Ginsburg, in all her glory.* The blog went viral (with a name like that how could it not?), Knizhnik whipped up some cool T-shirts, and an Internet sensation was born. The tattoos, Halloween costumes, coloring books, greeting cards, mugs, and tarot cards were not far behind. In 2015, Knizhnik and MSNBC reporter Irin Carmon published a saucy biography, *Notorious RBG: The Life and Times of Ruth Bader Ginsburg.* It became a *New York Times* best seller.

The media also become interested in RBG's fashion choices. Ruth is known for sprucing up her somber black judge's robe with a collection of fancy jabots (lace collars). The website Bustle has respectfully suggested the justice might be termed an accessory hoarder. Her day-to-day jabot appears to be a white beaded collar from Cape Town, South Africa: very chic. She sports a black velvet-and-gold jeweled collar on the days she reads the dissenting opinion. It would not be out of place around the neck of Cleopatra, and looks as though it might conceal a tiny dagger. For majority opinions, she busts out a woven gold collar with dangly beads, given to her by her law clerks. The style is a little Harmless Grandma, but it's probably better, tactically, to come off as a tiny old lady with a crocheted doily around your neck when you're handing the losing justices their asses.

Now that she's captured our cultural imagination, we know things about Ruth Bader Ginsburg that we might not otherwise. She loves opera. She hates to cook (her late husband Marty was the chef in the house). In her 70s she developed a hankering for white-water rafting. She is also digging the attention and keeps a supply of Notorious R.B.G. T-shirts in stock. (She especially loves one that says "You can't spell truth without Ruth.") She's been blunt about her dislike of President Trump. During the election she called him "a faker"—a crazy outburst by her normally low-key standards. She later apologized, but barely. She is notorious, after all.

Ruth Bader Ginsburg—always determined, disciplined, and polite—has become in her great old age, difficult. And the world is loving it.

CHAPTER 6

JOSEPHINE BAKER

Gutsy

ON OCTOBER 2, 1925, moments after she appeared on stage at the Théâtre des Champs-Élysées, Josephine Baker became the red-hot toast of Paris. She made her entrance splayed across the back of her partner, Joe Alex. The number was called "Danse Sauvage," and their identical "savage" costumes included matching feather skirts accompanied by a collection of bracelets and necklaces made from shells and seedpods. Joe wore a feather headdress. Josephine already sported her trademark slick cap of black hair, a silver dollar–size spit curl plastered to her forehead. Also, for some reason, black flats (as people are known to wear in darkest Africa).

Josephine rolled off Joe's back and launched into a frenzied dance the likes of which no one had ever seen—even in sophisticated 1920s Paris. She shook body parts no one knew you could shake. She was a proto–hip-hop artist, popping and locking, isolating different joints, hips doing one thing, belly another, ribs yet another. Her arms flailed, and her head rotated on that long, elegant neck. All that bumping, grinding, and groove thang shaking that goes on during music videos, televised award programs, rock concerts, Super Bowl halftime shows, and fraternity mixers? It all can be traced back to Josephine Baker, the celebrated American-French singer-dancer who would go on to spy for France during World War II, agitate for civil rights in the States during the 1950s and '60s, and mesmerize audiences until four days before her death, at 68, in 1975.

In 1926, she followed up the "Danse Sauvage" at the renowned Folies Bergère cabaret with her most unforgettable act: *Un Vent de Folie,* also known as the banana skirt dance.* The performance made her the biggest African-American star in the world. "I wasn't really naked. I simply didn't have any clothes on," she explained. It was untrue, even metaphorically. Josephine was completely naked before her audiences, which was part of her stupendous charisma.

JOSEPHINE MCDONALD was born in 1906 in St. Louis, Missouri, into the sort of extreme poverty that turns children into adults before they've lost all their baby teeth. Her parents were song-and-dance people who performed at theaters in black St. Louis. Her father, Eddie, was a drummer. Her mother, Carrie, was admired for her quick steps and flair. They were poor but happy until the arrival of baby Josephine made them just poor. Eddie and his drum kit split before Josephine turned one. Carrie gave up dancing and started taking in laundry; she had three more children with another man, Arthur, who stayed home. Really stayed home. As in, never left his easy chair, even to go to work.

Josephine, her mother, stepfather, and three siblings all slept in the same bed. Her stepfather's feet smelled worse than the stinkiest French cheese Josephine would one day come to adore. She preferred to sleep on the floor beneath a blanket of newspaper. At the age of eight, her mother sent her to work as a maid for a white woman, where her sleeping conditions improved considerably—she slept with the dog in the basement. She grew attached to both the dog and a chicken named Tiny Tim, who lived in the yard; one day, her mistress ordered her to kill the chicken, which she dutifully did, after giving it a sweet kiss on the head.

---

* Beyoncé would pay homage to Josephine and her banana skirt several times, first in her "Déjà Vu" track, and again in "B'day."

By my subjective reckoning, girls grow into difficult women after experiencing extreme childhoods. If you're sheltered and well fed, and your loving parents believe you to be a complex, competent person who has a right to march through the world making an impact, you're likely to be difficult. Why shouldn't you be? Speak your truth, go for broke, give it everything you've got, be a person of consequence. But wretched, abject childhoods can also produce difficult women. Maybe because many culturally approved feminine traits—receptivity, submissiveness, not worrying our pretty heads about anything—are luxuries when we're talking day-to-day survival. That was surely the case with Josephine, whose hellacious American childhood would give Grimm's fairy tales a run for their money.

The larger world was also horrifying. When Josephine was 11, in 1917, race riots broke out in East St. Louis (located in Illinois, just across the river from the city of St. Louis). It was the usual thing: White people were afraid people of color were going to take all the jobs (rural blacks were moving to the city to snap up all the glamorous, sexy gigs at the Aluminum Ore Company and American Steel Company). This early experience planted a seed in Josephine's heart. She would flee American racism as a teenager, but would combat bigotry for the rest of her life.

At 13 or thereabouts, Josephine quit school. In 1919, she procured herself a job as a waitress at the Old Chauffeur's Club—and also a husband, Willie Wells. The women of Josephine's family had an uncanny ability to attach themselves to men who, once married to them, planted themselves in their easy chairs to be both supported and waited on. Josephine was also a magnet for slackers, and the union didn't last.

Soon after, Josephine fell in with a troupe of street performers, who would unwittingly provide her informal dance education. She schooled herself in the dances of the day—the Tack Annie, the Itch, the Mess Around, Trucking—cutting loose with abandon. She joined the Jones Family, a neighborhood crew who liked to pass the hat in front of the Booker T. Washington Theatre, a popular black vaudeville joint. One night the Dixie Steppers were headlining at the Booker T., and their opening act failed to show. The Jones Family was snagged to fill the breach. Teenage Josephine could dance, cross her eyes, and play the trombone at the same time. (Let's pause to imagine that.) She made the manager of the Dixie Steppers weep with laughter, and when the Dixie Steppers left St. Louis and headed to New York, Josephine went with them.

In 1921, she landed a role in *Shuffle Along*. In the pioneering revue—written, directed, and performed by African Americans—Josephine played the klutz at the end of the chorus line who cannot keep up. She falls over her own feet, makes a fool of herself—and then, at the end of the show, breaks into a dance so skillful and breathtaking that it puts the rest of the line to shame.

Josephine's great strength was her ability to optimize the one thing she knew she was good at: dancing without inhibition and making people laugh. It's instructive, I think, to imagine what our lives might be like if we were to invest 100 percent in even one thing at which we know we excel.

FOUR YEARS LATER, she was recruited for an all "African" revue in Paris at the Théâtre des Champs-Elysées. Her primary philosophy of living was *"pourquoi pas?"*—why not?—so off she went to France. Josephine would say later that her only real memory of her Paris debut was not the bright lights, the physical exhilaration of performing, or the thrill of applause. It was that after the show was over, "for the first time in my life, I was invited to sit at a table and eat with white people." The French adored her, and she them. They found her to be dazzling and sexy, her dark skin beautiful. That said, their love was complicated, and frankly, a little weird. To them, in what was a colossal and willful case of mistaken identity, Josephine was not a Missourian who escaped the grinding poverty and appalling racism of the United States, but a sexy, earthy, exotic African blossom from deep in the jungle.

It was pure fantasy, which bothered no one. Paris between the wars engaged in a mad romance with all things *primitif.* The *New Yorker* writer Janet Flanner was there the night of Josephine's debut in 1925 and summed it up this way: " . . . two specific elements had been established and were unforgettable—her magnificent dark body, a new model that to the French proved that black was beautiful, and the acute response of the white masculine public in the capital of hedonism of all Europe: Paris."

In 1926, the banana skirt dance sealed Josephine's celebrity. Wearing nothing more than a "skirt" of 16 rubber bananas, "she pushed forward her stomach, swung her hips, twisted her arms and legs and pushed up her bottom, as she clenched her fists and motioned her arms like a runner, her feet remained still as she shook the fruit backwards and forwards until it moved in angles of 180 degrees," wrote a contemporary observer.

Josephine's star shot into the Paris sky. Embraced by bourgeois night-lifers, artists, and intellectuals alike, Josephine was synonymous with the jazz age, art deco, freedom, joy, and everything modern. She subverted racial assumptions, proving that a black woman could be beautiful, sexy, cheeky, and au courant. Hemingway called her "the most sensational woman anyone ever saw." The country's most celebrated clothiers, Madame Vionnet and Paul Poiret, draped her in couture. Diamond bracelets adorned her wrists. A club owner thought it would be interesting to add a live cheetah to one of her acts; after the show closed, Josephine adopted her. From that moment on, Chiquita traveled in the backseat of Josephine's white Rolls Royce, sporting her own diamond collar.

"I was earning a great deal of money but I wanted to earn even more," she wrote in her autobiography. "It wasn't because of the money itself—which ran through my fingers like water—but because of the importance the world places on wealth. 'You can't change the world.' All right then. I would fight with the enemy's weapons."

That same year, Josephine met Pepito Abatino in a bar in Montmartre. A onetime Sicilian stonemason, now supporting himself as a gigolo,

Abatino also liked to pass himself off as royalty. Josephine didn't care about the ruse; she preferred a good story to the truth any day. They fell in love and di Abatino, as he called himself, would have become Josephine's third husband—had she not still been married to husband number two, Willie Baker, whom she'd never bothered to divorce.

Pepito, who had no real training as an agent or manager, nevertheless demonstrated his unwavering devotion to Josephine by spending every waking hour figuring out ways to promote her. Tirelessly, he worked to get her film contracts[*] and expand her sponsorship deals. (Pernod!) He struck a deal with a company interested in manufacturing the pomade Josephine used to paste down her hair. Called Bakerfix, it would increase her fortune by leaps and bounds.

By the mid-1930s Josephine Baker was the most successful black woman in Europe. Most of us would be perfectly happy with conquering the continent, but Josephine was more ambitious than she appeared. She wanted to be taken seriously in the United States—not as a black performer but as a *performer*. She wanted a standing ovation on Broadway.

At this point, Josephine had lived in France for 10 years. She spoke French, acted in French, and was richer than she could have ever possibly imagined. Still, in 1935, at the age of almost 30, she decided it was time to conquer her native land.

The childlike glee and abandon that made Josephine so popular with audiences made her difficult offstage. Like a child, she wanted what she wanted when she wanted it. External reality—and often the feelings of others—rarely factored into her calculations, such as they were. This would make her brave and dauntless when it came to risking her life for the French Resistance—but in everyday life, her demands could be exasperating. Fun at a party, hell at home—that was Josephine Baker in a nutshell.[**]

---

[*] *Zou-Zou* (1934) and *Princesse Tam-Tam* (1935), both written exclusively for Josephine, were popular in France, but largely sucked.

[**] Courtesy of author Elissa Schappell, from whose Twitter profile I pilfered this descriptor. *Merci bien,* Elissa!

She pestered Pepito about setting her up with something in the United States. He worked his no-account count magic and got her a role in the 1936 *Ziegfeld Follies*. The production was going to be the most lavish Follies yet. Vincente Minnelli had been contracted for the sets and costumes. George Balanchine was the ballet master, Ira Gershwin the lyricist. Could the classy vaudeville variety show inspired by the very Folies Bergère in which Josephine had become a star be more perfect for her return? You would think.

From the moment Josephine and Pepito arrived in New York and were told they had to use the service entrance at the swanky St. Moritz (welcome home) to the blistering reviews of her performance, the trip was a disaster.

Time magazine's review was par for the course: "Josephine Baker is a St. Louis wash woman's daughter who stepped out of a Negro burlesque show into a life of adulation and luxury in Paris during the booming 1920s. In sex appeal to jaded Europeans of the jazz-loving type, a Negro wench always has a head start. The particular tawny tint of tall and stringy Josephine Baker's bare skin stirred French pulses. But to Manhattan theatre-goers last week, she was just a slightly buck-toothed young Negro woman whose figure might be matched in any nightclub show, whose dancing & singing could be topped practically anywhere outside France."

Josephine expressed her heartbreak by blaming Pepito. He should have negotiated a better contract, or known that the theater wasn't right for her voice, something. Confident in Pepito's canine-like devotion, she indulged her callous, willful side. After the first horrific reviews surfaced in February 1936, she hooked up with some random Frenchman she met at a Harlem nightclub and abandoned Pepito to contemplate his crime in solitude, alone in their suite at the St. Moritz. When he gave up trying to win her back and, complaining of stomach pains, abruptly returned to France, she figured she'd just make it up to him back in Paris.

A word about Josephine's sex life: She was decades ahead of *Cosmopolitan* in believing sex was a good workout. It was fun, felt good, and was a nice alternative to doing the Charleston. She was an equal opportunity seductress, taking up with men or women as the mood struck her. Even though they weren't married, Pepito was old-fashioned, and expected at least a hat tip to fidelity on her part. Their preferred ongoing quarrel involved Pepito's "irrational" jealousy. He would discover she'd been out canoodling, which would send him into a red-faced, spittle-flying outburst, which would send her straight into the arms of some low-key, smiling lover, which fueled yet another red-faced, spittle-flying outburst, which sent her into the arms of yet another low-key, smiling lover, and so forth.

In New York, Josephine dutifully endured the rest of her contract. Then, a few weeks before the Follies closed, she received word that Pepito had died. The stomach pain he'd been experiencing wasn't caused by Josephine's wrath and cruelty, but by cancer.

Few things in life make you feel more like crap than being nasty to someone, only to have them kick the bucket before you can make amends. Between the disappointing, ego-bruising reception at home and the death of her greatest advocate, Josephine was shattered. But not for long. She was a positive sort and was, she reminded herself, only 30!

Back she went to Paris, where she took a role in another Folies Bergère nude revue—a little bit of a step backward, but no matter. Within the year she was being courted by Jean Lion, a French "industrialist" (code for "makes a lot of money doing something boring"). While in the States she'd finally finalized her divorce from Willie Baker, and in November 1937 Lion became her third husband. Jean was dashing, a sophisticate, and a risk taker, who basically married Josephine because he knew it would give his staid bourgeois family collective heart failure. But it wasn't her color the Lions found objectionable; it was her occupation. An exotic dancer, however celebrated, is fine for a mistress, but never a wife.

Jean courted Josephine in a way that made her swoon. Despite her firsthand experience of life's grim realities—or perhaps because of them—

she could be easily swept off her feet. She was a sucker for romance and the grand gesture. Jean flew her around in his plane. They rode horses in the Bois de Boulogne. They went *fox hunting,* for God's sake.

They seemed poised to become Jeansophine—but instead of the hottest couple in Paris, they became yet another living example of the proverb "marry in haste, repent at leisure." Turns out Jean and Josephine had wanted to *get* married, but not *be* married. He worked all day and she worked all night. Jean had no intention of changing either his bourgeois industrialist routine or his playboy ways. Presumably, he expected his new bride to change her schedule. As husbands of the early to mid-20th century had been known to do.

Josephine's biographers tell us that she yearned to be married and was eager to become a mother. But if Jean wasn't willing to give a little so that they could be under the same roof at the same time, then neither was she. Josephine's unwillingness to accommodate Jean's unwillingness to accommodate *her* makes her troublesome in a time-honored manner old as Eve. (When the lady of the house stands her ground, refusing to budge off her position, and thus causes domestic strife, boy howdy is she difficult!) After a mere 14 months Josephine had had enough. She was not a girl to let grass grow under her feet. Personally, I think it was one of her finest qualities. She filed for divorce and walked away with the one thing that meant more to her than anything: her French citizenship.

TWO YEARS LATER, in 1940, Josephine was dancing to standing-room-only audiences at the Folies Bergère, waiting for her divorce from Jean Lion to become final—when suddenly, and without hesitation, she heeded the call of Charles de Gaulle to resist German occupation and volunteered for duty. Remember when past-life regressions were all the rage? When people discovered they'd been Eleanor of Aquitaine in a past life, instead of an illiterate lice-ridden beggar? It's the same thing with the French Resistance. Nearly everyone claimed after the fact to have worked for it, when in fact the real number was closer to 2 percent of the population living in France that summer.

But Josephine Baker was the real deal. She had no interest in the complexities of politics, but she knew a racist when she saw one, and the Nazis became her sworn enemies. This, commingled with her devotion to France (which she loved with the same effortless affection she felt for her audiences), made her a formidable intelligence agent. She was happy to leverage her celebrity, even at the cost of ruining her life.

Often when I think of a difficult woman, I envision someone articulate, outspoken, and (that loaded word) "bossy." Josephine was none of those things. She was outwardly sweet, outwardly kind. But in always following her heart, she wound up behaving in ways that were both aggravating (the Folies-Pepito debacle) and breathtakingly courageous. What her heart commanded never gave her pause. She plunged ahead, even at personal risk to herself.

In the early 1940s, as the war engulfed Europe, Josephine crashed parties at consulates and embassies, batting her long lashes at Germans and Nazi sympathizers who mansplained to their heart's content. She would then excuse herself and go to the ladies' room, where she would jot down the intel on slips of paper she would then pin to her panties. "My notes would have been highly compromising," she wrote in her autobiography, "but who would dare search Josephine Baker to the skin? Besides, my encounters with customs officials were always extremely relaxed. When they asked *me* for papers, they generally meant autographs." She would then deliver her information to Jacques Abtey, her handler and the head of Paris counterintelligence.

Here is Josephine fleeing Paris in her fancy car as the Nazis march in, the backseat filled with as many Jewish refugees as she could squeeze and the trunk filled with champagne bottles bearing precious, hard-to-obtain gasoline. Here she is deciding at a moment's notice to tour Portugal, where she will smuggle strategic information about troop movement written in invisible ink on her sheet music; this will then make its way to Charles de Gaulle, who headed the Free French movement from his post in London. (He went on to become one of France's most beloved presidents—despite having said, "How can you govern a country which has 246 varieties of cheese?") Here she is traveling to Morocco, ostensibly to entertain the British, American, and French troops based in the French colonies, but actually to help establish a base for the Resistance. And here she is pulling strings to help none other than Jean Lion, her Jewish third ex-husband, get a visa to South America to escape the camps.

After the war ended, the newly liberated French government awarded Josephine a slew of medals. For her valor she received the Croix de Guerre, the Légion d'honneur, and the Médaille de la Résistance. Almost 20 years later, in 1963, she attended the March on Washington, where she was the only female speaker. It was the end of August, hot and muggy enough to melt your eyeballs, but she wore her woolen French Resistance uniform, complete with epaulettes and dark tie, with all of her impressive medals pinned in a row along her chest.

IN 1947, AT THE AGE OF 41, Josephine married French orchestra leader Jo Bouillon. This time, she finally seemed to have gotten it right. Like Pepito, he was devoted to her and supported her aspirations; like Jean Lion he hailed from an orderly French bourgeois family and helped to keep her grounded. At least for a while.

In 1936—the same year as her calamitous trip to the United States—Josephine had purchased her country house, Les Milandes, with the profits from Bakerfix. It was a decrepit, if romantic, château tucked away in France's rugged, remote Dordogne. After her marriage to Bouillon, she hatched a plan to refurbish it and create a tourist destination that would be a cross between Michael Jackson's Neverland Ranch and Downton Abbey. Josephine blew through money faster than she could shake her hips, and she was hoping Les Milandes would provide a nice revenue stream. She envisioned hotels, restaurants, stables, a miniature golf course, a farm with strolling peacocks, a big swimming pool in the shape of a J, and a wax museum depicting dramatic scenes from her life. To run the operation, Josephine installed families in the surrounding village—and because she was fundamentally kind and generous, provided them with decent housing and hot and cold running water.

As you might imagine, this kind of project costs a fortune. During the war Josephine had lived on her savings, performing for the troops for free; now she was broke. To fund Les Milandes, Inc. (as I think of it), she returned to the stage. So devoted was she to making this monumental vision come true that she was forced to go where the money was. Europe was still crawling from the wreckage of a world war, but nightclubs across the United States were flush. Her Ziegfeld Follies folly was a distant, prewar memory, and nightclub owners were happy to book her.

You probably won't be surprised to hear how this ended up. Even in the aftermath of a war that had engulfed the entire world, one of France's most esteemed citizens still could not get a room in a "white" hotel in her homeland. According to one account, she and Jo were turned away 36 times. This time, rather than hiding her pain and anger in a fling with a random Frenchman (although as distractions go, you could do worse) she just got plain old angry. And an unrepentant, angry woman is a difficult woman. If a city refused her request for a reservation, she would cancel her performance and tell the press why. She insisted on fully integrated shows, and would reserve a big table near the stage for local members of the NAACP; until they were all seated, she would not appear.

By this time, at the age of 45, Josephine was also completely over whatever lingering reputation she may have had as an exotic *primitif.* Her activism involved giving performances where she demonstrated that black people could be as sophisticated and worldly as anyone else. Dressed in Dior, Balmain, and Balenciaga (she made 13 costume changes over the course of the evening), she showed off her language acquisition chops by singing in French, Italian, Portuguese, even Yiddish. She told stories about the old days, chatted up the audience. She was lovely, but also fierce and uncompromising. Once, she overheard someone use the n-word in a restaurant and called the cops. As her biographer Phyllis Rose observed: "Like a comic-book superwoman, one moment Josephine was an innocuous celebrity eating a meal—and then (quick moral change in invisible phone booth of the mind)—an intrepid fighter for civil rights, leaping into the fray, clad in the uniform of the Free French Women's Auxiliary."

The New York branch of the NAACP deemed May 20, 1951, Josephine Baker Day, and *Life* magazine ran a feature story declaring that "La Baker is back." Six months later—perhaps further emboldened by these public affirmations—she accused Manhattan's celebrated Stork Club of racism when she was made to wait an hour for a steak. Accounts differed about whether this was a passive-aggressive display of bigotry or just really bad service (history has come down firmly on Josephine's side). But at this point, she had become such a staunch and respected foe of discrimination that the reputation of the club never recovered.

JOSEPHINE HAD ALWAYS EXPRESSED a desire to be a mother, but for one reason or another (timing, various female maladies), it never happened. In 1954, after seven years of marriage to Bouillon, Josephine decided that she wanted to create a family that would also make a political statement. They would all live at Les Milandes, where, for their visitors, they would demonstrate love and tolerance. "Jo and I plan to adopt four little children: red, yellow, white, and black. Four little children raised in the country, in my beautiful Dordogne," Bouillon wrote in his memoir. "They will serve as an example of true Democracy, and be living proof that if people are left in peace, nature takes care of the rest."

But Josephine and Jo did not adopt a tidy quartet of kids. They started a kid collection. In the same way some people get one tattoo, and then cannot help getting 10 or 12 more, Josephine started picking up kids there and then—pretty much whenever the spirit moved her.

The Baker-Bouillons' first four children were a pair of half-American, half-Asian babies adopted from a Japanese orphanage (their fathers were most likely GIs); a "white" Finnish toddler from Helsinki; and a "black" infant of indeterminate race. Four children that, alas, represented only three of the required colors. Josephine was a stickler for seeing her fantasy to completion, and she refused to call her family whole until she was able to adopt a "red" baby: an American Indian.

It escaped her (if she ever knew) that the skin color of Native Americans is actually a shade of brown. In any case, there weren't a lot (possibly any) Native American babies to be had in the orphanages of Western Europe after the war. This inability to easily fulfill her original mission inspired a new thought: Her tribe would have not only children of different races but also of different religions. Think of the possibilities!

They adopted Moïse (Jewish). They adopted Brahim (Muslim). She acquired a few more Catholics for spare parts, Jean-Claude and Marianne. I believe we're up to eight? Bouillon, who managed the money, started to lose his sense of humor. It was the usual thing: Josephine following her heart without a thought for how it might be affecting anyone else. She refused to consider the cost of raising all these children. A time-honored ongoing marital squabble ensued, where Jo called her impulsive and irresponsible, and she called him a petty bean counter. In 1961, he left. They had been married 14 years: a relationship of duration for the impulsive, difficult Josephine.

She spent most of the rest of the decade trying to save Les Milandes—the only home her kids had ever known—but was evicted in 1968. She had to be dragged bodily from the kitchen of her château, and sat on the porch barefoot, a patchwork blanket over her knees, a lunch lady bonnet on her head. She waited for photographers to record her injustice and humiliation for posterity. Here I am, she seemed to be saying, La Baker, trying to do good for the world—and this is how the world has treated me. She seemed to lack any responsibility for her current state of affairs.

But Josephine was nothing if not a survivor. That same year, she made yet another comeback, singing and dancing at the Olympia in Paris; five years later she played a sold-out show at Carnegie Hall. Four days before she died of a cerebral hemorrhage in 1975, she opened in *Joséphine à Bobino,* a revue that paid tribute to her 50 years on stage. The show was sold out; Mick Jagger, Sophia Loren, and Jackie Onassis were among the opening night crowd. Josephine, at 68, was still wicked and captivating: a drama queen with a heart of gold.

CHAPTER 7

RACHEL MADDOW

Brainy

I'M GOING TO APPROACH Rachel Maddow the way Rachel Maddow would approach Rachel Maddow: by taking my sweet time to build the story of how she's broken the rules of reporting, and continues to break them, daily. MSNBC's biggest star anchor, Rachel, is out and proud about being the smartest person in the (cable TV news) room. She refuses to dumb anything down—and if you cannot keep up, that's fine with her.

Almost 20 years into the new millennium, our political parties have devolved into warring factions that seem to be a spin-off of World Wrestling rather than a crucial component of a democratic government. Now it's the Red Team versus the Blue Team, and there's no discussion, just gamesmanship. It's as if we've slid into a parallel universe where invisible points are being totted up on an invisible scoreboard—the health and well-being of the republic utterly beside the point.

It wasn't always this way. I'm a lifelong Democrat raised by staunch Republicans. My dad was an old-school, nonreligious right-winger, tacking Libertarian. Our political debates, often unspooling during the all-important martini (or two) hour (or two) that preceded dinner, were textbook right versus left. My dad and I assumed a basic set of facts, gleaned from the news of the day. If one of us made a point that was irrefutable, the other conceded. We were united in our belief that facts were facts. Looking back, these debates seem so sweet and courtly. We were so old-fashioned!

The Blue Team's signature strategy is ad hominem attacks;* the Red Team's signature response is to label anything they disagree with as fake news. When the Blue Team proves to be true an event or accounting the Red Team spokesman has deemed "fake," the Red Team pivots, claiming their mistake is an "alternative fact."

This drives the Blue Team bonkers, which brings the Red Team deep and abiding joy. We Blue Teamers respect facts. We believe the world is complex, and politics and government tend to be really complex. We think there are way more than 50 shades of gray.

And this is why people adore Rachel Maddow. She is the patient, bemused explainer who puts our increasingly nutso nation in perspective. She is proudly brainy. She has no problem holding the floor, and is willing to get as detailed as necessary to explain the evermore Byzantine ins and outs of contemporary governing. She is the exact opposite of the woman who has been told (me, by my mother) not to be "a know-it-all." I have no doubt that when it comes to politics, Rachel probably does know everything worth knowing. And she's made it look as hip as it is necessary.

As host, since 2008, of *The Rachel Maddow Show* on MSNBC, Rachel is a tomboy nerd who has said of her political leanings, "I'm undoubtedly a liberal, which means that I'm in almost total agreement with the Eisenhower-era Republican party platform." Blue Teamers dig her dark cropped hair, black hipster glasses, black blazer, boyfriend jeans, and Converse sneakers. Her stylish butch mien sets her apart from the phalanx of overdone pageant queen–style newscasters.

It will come as no surprise that Rachel's academic credentials are impressive: In 1994, she graduated from Stanford with a degree in public policy, and in 2001 earned a doctorate in politics from Oxford, where she was the first openly gay person to be awarded a Rhodes Scholarship. Some on the Red Team disregard all this extreme book learning as yet another example

---

* I never really knew what ad hominem attacks were until the 2016 presidential campaign. Essentially, it means attacking the person, not the position, on an issue.

of elitism, therefore not to be trusted. Blue Teamers, however, believe this erudition makes her extra-trustworthy. Since the arrival of Rachel on the news scene, if the behavior of my friends and me is any indication, we've felt freer and more emboldened to argue our points at gatherings where we might otherwise distract ourselves with the Chardonnay.

Rachel Maddow doesn't report the news. Instead, she explains it, drawing connections that are often buried—either because they've been intentionally obfuscated by people in power or because they simply get lost in the increasingly complicated shuffle. She is the wonk's wonk, telling complex narratives (critics call them "convoluted and labored") in which she pulls in seemingly disparate facts to make a larger point that might not be obvious at first. Her show is the cable news embodiment of reading an article to the end, which no one seems to do much anymore.

For example: In early 2017 she began a broadcast with a short history of the United States' purchase of Alaska from Russia 150 years ago, followed by an introduction to the We the People petitioning system the Obama Administration created in 2011 (in which citizens could directly petition policy experts). She then made an easy joke about the nine million legalize-pot petitions before directing us to a very odd petition that popped up in 2014: the "Alaska Back to Russia" petition, which called for returning Alaska to Russia. The petition was bizarre, and not just because it was obviously translated from another language (we've all received those idiotic- sounding and obviously fake spam emails). It was also bizarre because it garnered a quick 39,000 signatures. "These can't all be from people who think this is hilarious," Rachel commented. It took her 10 minutes to get to the meat of the story (an hour in newscast time) about the role of bots in the Russian cyberattacks to influence the 2016 election.

No matter the implications of her nightly reports, Rachel is never angry. She never appears angry, nor does she ever report that something made her angry. As far as her viewers know, she has never been angry in her life. She explains the news with amiable astonishment: Can you even *believe* this? It's as if she's sharing some titillating gossip about the neighbors.

Somewhere in the world, there must exist a culture where female rage is appreciated: where the moment a woman raises her voice, the village gathers around, believing that if a woman is freaking the hell out, it's probably worth hearing what she has to say. That place is not American cable TV news—or anywhere in America, for that matter, except possibly spin class. Rachel has chosen to be of good cheer: the better to keep people watching. It's a con, in a way, because her devotion to telling the stories no one else has the patience or discipline to tell usually tips her hand.

Both teams blasted Rachel for a 2016 show that featured the issues raised by Donald Trump's refusal to disclose his tax returns. Financial reporter David Cay Johnston had received a portion of the returns through the mail, and asked Rachel whether she was interested. Was she ever.

At press time, the reasons for Trump's secrecy regarding his returns remain mysterious. Blue Teamers have been slavering for them, convinced the documents will reveal he's either not as wealthy as he's claimed—or that he's up to his eyeballs in investments from foreign banks that will prove, once and for all, his many financial conflicts of interest. Red Teamers don't know what the big deal is.

Ah, but I've now finally come around to what makes Rachel Maddow truly difficult: About 90 minutes before airtime, she tweeted that she'd obtained the president's tax returns. She didn't say what year, or how many pages. It was an epic tease. More than four million people tuned in that night. Tucker Carlson of Fox News normally dominates that time slot; she beat him out by 1.1 million viewers.

Rachel refused to treat the returns in her possession like breaking news. She told the story as if it were any other story. She carefully laid the ground-work, lingering on the nerdy details she always seems to find so interesting. She reminded us that every president since Nixon has released his tax returns as a matter of course, and speculated about what it may say about this president that he is adamant in his refusal to do so.*

---

* Before the show, the White House confirmed that the two pages of Trump's 2005 returns were authentic, but the president then tweeted that it was fake news.

Thanks to Twitter, the backlash erupted before the broadcast was even over. Journalists, both Blue and Red, berated her for the come-on tweet and commensurate lack of scandal (as if that's never happened on TV news). Others said she "flubbed" the story. My Facebook feed was a microcosm of the swift and rampant disapproval. My progressive friends who didn't call her a ratings whore said she should be shot for burying the lead. "Biggest Over-Hyped Live TV Epic Fail in History!" claimed one Red Team news site.

Actually, it wasn't. Actually, it was just Rachel Maddow doing her signature difficult woman Rachel Maddow thing. She talked about a topic of great interest in her customary, cool style. The degree to which people were clamoring to know had no bearing on her approach. She didn't flub the story; she just refused to adjust her style to accommodate the desire of viewers.

My father died in July 2000—before President Bush lost the popular vote to Al Gore, but won the electoral college, and before the Red Team versus Blue Team lunacy was in full swing. I can imagine he would enjoy Rachel Maddow, appreciating her charts, graphs, and statistics, but raise an eyebrow at what to me seem obvious connections, and what to him would seem like leaps in logic.

Rachel Maddow's audience has been growing steadily since 2016. Between March 2016 and March 2017 her ratings increased 107 percent—an unheard-of surge. As of this writing, her show is handily winning its time slot. When she was an under-the-radar girl nerd who was an acquired taste, no one cared about her approach; now that she's come up in the world, people seem to feel she owes them something. Ease, simplification, something. She's expected to give up her individuality and get with the program, to get straight to the point when, for Rachel, it's the *journey* to the point that intrigues her, the way her own mind works. For girls and women who are made to feel apologetic for being too brainy and too analytical, we have Rachel: difficult comfortable in her know-it-all skin.

CHAPTER 8

COCO CHANEL

Imperious

ONE CHILLY DAY in 1910 or thereabouts, Coco Chanel borrowed a pullover belonging to her lover, Arthur "Boy" Capel. She was perhaps 27 years old: tiny and dark-eyed, easily mistaken for a 12-year-old. Capel was a renowned British polo player, and Coco loved borrowing his clothes (something, I might add, none of her contemporaries would dream of doing). But hauling a pullover over her head had the unfortunate side effect of messing up her hair. To solve the problem, she cut the borrowed sweater straight up the middle with a pair of shears, belted it, and voilà! The cardigan was born.

Coco Chanel is the only fashion designer to appear on *Time* magazine's 100 Most Influential People of the 20th Century. It's not a stretch to say that almost every modern style can be traced in some way to her. Boxy jackets. The Little Black Dress. Pencil skirts, twin sets, trousers. That dress you love because it has pockets. Every dress that begs to be madly accessorized—along with the accessories themselves. (Coco gave us costume jewelry, believing it offered every woman the chance to jazz up everyday life.) The foundation of Coco's radical genius was that clothes should make a woman feel beautiful—and if she *felt* beautiful, she *was* beautiful. This seemingly simple philosophy dared to disrupt the primacy of the male gaze. Which made Coco *très difficile*.

A disclaimer concerning French women: They are born difficult and raised to be difficult. What's more, they're celebrated for it, which makes life easier for them in many ways. For example, they experience no cultural imperative to be "nice" in the way American women do; they feel little compunction to smile or be agreeable or do anything to suppress their eccentricities. They have no problem with saying *non, merci* (particularly to another slice of *tarte tatin*—because although they're not required to be nice, they are required to be thin). All those books about how to be more like French women? What they're really about is how to be difficult.

Coco Chanel was an extreme French woman: a super *française,* more imperious than most. She possessed an almost fanatical respect for her own time, refusing to make herself available to just anyone. She was a perfectionist, slaving away in her rue Cambon atelier for long hours on every garment (so as to make good on her theory that a dress should be as flawless on the inside as it is on the outside). And yet she made herself maddeningly unavailable to even her best clients: the better to shroud herself and her process in mystery. Perhaps the concept simply doesn't hold up in the digital age, where we've come to expect that every email and post be answered *tout de suite.* But I'm determined to think Coco had it right: Withhold a little. Be unavailable. Let people wonder.

GABRIELLE BONHEUR CHANEL was born in a poorhouse, in Saumur, Maine-et-Loire, France, on August 19, 1883. The city was ancient, boasting a château that dated to the tenth century, a military cavalry school, and a host of picturesque houses cut from the same pale stone (the excavation left tunnels in which the local wine was stored). Gabrielle's mother, Jeanne, was a laundry woman; her father, Albert, was a traveling street vendor. Apparently, the two had a standing arrangement, having five children together although Albert was rarely in town.

In 1895, Jeanne died of bronchitis at the age of 32. Albert, unable to cope with parenting, sent his three sons to farms, where they were given a place to live in exchange for labor. Gabrielle and her sister were sent to an orphanage, at the convent of Aubazine. There, she learned to sew.

Only girls who intended to join the order were allowed to stay at the convent after the age of 18. In 1901, Gabrielle drifted to the garrison city of Moulins. She worked as a seamstress and, like all modern girls, harbored vague aspirations of being a *"café-conc"* singer, that era's version of a rock star. She managed to land a gig at La Rotonde, singing between the appearances of the headliners. Even though Coco, as she came to be called,* was childlike, winsome, and innocent-looking, café concert singers inhabited the *demimonde,* along with prostitutes and courtesans. I'm sure this shady future was not what the nuns at Aubazine had in mind for little Gabrielle, but Coco, deep in her DNA, didn't care about rules, aside from the ones she made for herself. "I don't care what you think about me; I don't think about you at all," she once said. (Possibly it sounds less harsh in the original French, but I admire her certainty.) Imagine, for a moment, what it would be like to hold that view, to be a woman free of the shackles of judgment and expectation of others.

In 1903, at the age of 20, Coco caught the eye of Étienne Balsan, a onetime cavalry officer. Balsan, a horse breeder and heir to a textile fortune, spent most of his time raising horses at Royallieu, his château in northern France. When Coco was 23, he officially installed her there as his mistress. It was a little boring, frankly, and Coco spent most of her time at the stables, learning to ride. Balsan also had other, more traditionally appealing mistresses—think of the voluptuous, corseted beauties in a Renoir painting. Coco's flat-chested, boyish look was entirely different; she knew she would have to find a way to distinguish herself from those pink, bosomy ladies. She kept Balsan interested by showing off her excellent horsemanship and developing ambition: She wanted to be a milliner. (She became known as the offbeat mistress who could be found galloping off into the forest on a young stallion, and who had a talent for creating fetching chapeaus.)

Even with no money, no connections, no reputation, or anything to rely on but the benevolence of her paramour, Coco embodied what would later become her philosophy: "How many cares one loses when one decides not

---

* How did she get the name Coco? There are competing theories: Either it was short for *cocotte,* a kept woman, or referenced her signature song "Qui qu'a vu Coco." I cannot imagine Coco allowing herself to be slapped with a generic, dismissive nickname that could belong to anyone. Decide for yourself.

to be something, but to be some*one*." A female who is someone in her own right is a woman who has resisted being defined in relationship to others. You know those movies where there's a missing nuclear warhead and everyone in the Situation Room is panting with panic and fear? A woman who insists on being someone engenders the same sort of hysteria. Coco was always that kind of woman.

Although Coco loved Balsan, she wasn't "in love" with him. Also, she was tired of living the kept-woman life. Thus, after a few years, she fell in love with Balsan's good friend Boy Capel, owner of the aforementioned legendary pullover. Capel was of the British upper class, an intelligence officer and captain in the military, but also a self-made tycoon and polo player. It doesn't seem as if there were many tears shed or wineglasses smashed over this turn of events. In 1908 Coco left Balsan and Royallieu and moved into Capel's apartment in Paris. Like Balsan, Capel was captivated by Coco's ambition, and financed her first millinery boutiques. Two years later, she opened her first shops—one in Paris, at 31 rue Cambon, and the next at the haut-fancy watering hole of Deauville.*

Timing is everything, and part of Coco's genius lay in knowing it was time for women to dump the 20-pound platter hats and upholstered dresses of the Belle Époque. She is routinely credited with getting rid of the corset—but that was actually Paul Poiret, who was on the scene a good 10 years ahead of her. But Coco had the perfect historical moment on her side.

In the summer of 1914, Germany declared war on France. Men departed for the front lines. Women of means fled Paris for Deauville, where Coco's shop sold simple shirts and skirts in comfortable fabrics. The men were gone. There was no one to overdress for. Women were raising money for the war effort, or hopping on their bikes to ride to the hospital, where they would roll bandages. It was a new age, and Coco was leading the vanguard of fashion modernity. Just like that, the overelaborate trimmings, unnatural lines, and uncomfortable fabrics became a thing of the past.

---

* After she made her fortune, she paid Capel back in full.

Although she would go on to have many more suitors, Boy Capel was the love of Coco's life. (Give him a quick Google and you'll see why.) He taught her to read and to think. He believed in her talent and vision. They lived together discreetly—and for the most part, happily—in Paris for nine years. But in 1918 Capel jilted her to marry the Honorable Diana Wyndham, a British noblewoman considered to be more worthy of his social stature. Although Mademoiselle Chanel, now 35, had opened more successful boutiques in both Biarritz and Paris, was wealthy in her own right, and was on her way to becoming famous, she was still an orphan from the lower classes. And that simply would not do.

This didn't mean Coco and Capel couldn't keep seeing each other on the side. (You know, in the French way.) But in December 1919, on his way to visit Coco before spending Christmas with his family, Capel was killed in a car crash. Coco was devastated, and something inside her hardened. Like a man (or a difficult woman) she turned to her work for solace.

THE 1920S WERE COCO'S DECADE. Every society woman wore Chanel, and wealthy clients from London to New York found their way to her *maison de couture* for a fitting. Watching her work, her friend, the writer Colette, observed: "If every human face bears a resemblance to some animal, then Mademoiselle Chanel is a small black bull. That tuft of curly black hair falls over her brow all the way to the eyelids and dances with every maneuver of her head."

Before Chanel, couturiers were viewed as skilled service people, necessary to one's stylish existence but no more esteemed than shoe salesmen. Through her friendship with the renowned art patron Misia Sert, Coco changed that perception for good. Chanel's modern aesthetic was a perfect match for the avant-garde, and Misia made a point of introducing her friend to the cutting-edge artists of the day. Coco went on to create costumes for the 1920 production of Diaghilev's radical Ballet Russes and Jean Cocteau's play *Orphée;*

she befriended Stravinsky and Picasso. In Hollywood, she spent a brief sojourn designing costumes for Samuel Goldwyn—which she despised, because she really hated being told what to do.

I've no doubt I'm romanticizing aspects of Coco's difficult character. She could be stubborn, opportunistic, and combative, and not in a kicky, spirited way. Frankly, I don't care. Men with those qualities become celebrated leaders, innovators, and TED talk–givers. They are no nicer than Chanel was.

In the early 1920s Coco, working with master perfumer Ernest Beaux, concocted Chanel No. 5. To finance the production of what would become the world's most popular fragrance, she licensed the rights to Pierre and Paul Wertheimer, joint CEOs of the esteemed perfume house Bourjois. The Wertheimers provided full financing in exchange for 70 percent of the profits. The gentleman who brokered the deal received 20 percent, and Coco retained a mere 10 percent.

Though *Parfums Chanel* would make her rich—much richer than she would have been had she stuck solely with couture—Coco felt she was being exploited. In fact, she *was* being exploited. But as a woman, she was expected to set aside her concerns and be grateful for male patronage. For her, this was not an option. So instead, Coco spent pretty much the rest of her life suing and countersuing the Wertheimers, referring at one point to Pierre as "the bandit who screwed me."

It was an epic, contentious battle of wills and attorneys. During World War II, when Jews were forbidden to own businesses, Coco even tried to wrest control away from her partners. (She was outmaneuvered; with keen foresight the Wertheimers had temporarily transferred ownership into the hands of a trustworthy French businessman, Felix Amiot.)

But the most interesting part of the story is that this endless, Coco-generated fiasco didn't cause the Wertheimers to dislike her. This raises a key question: If we're to be difficult, do we really have to give up being liked? If we're argumentative and keep advocating for our own interests long after people wish we would just go away, will we wind up dying friendless?

If the relationship between Coco and the Wertheimers is any indication, the answer is no. Pierre Wertheimer became one of Coco's oldest friends (in addition to sharing the ongoing dispute over *Parfums Chanel,* they also bonded over a love of thoroughbred horse racing). In the 1960s he became the primary owner of the House of Chanel, and supported her in her old age. (Pierre's kindness paid off for his grandsons; Gerard and Alain currently own the Chanel luxury brand, and are said to be worth a breathtaking $19 billion.)

BY 1927, COCO HAD TRULY BECOME one of the most famous women in the world, beholden to no one. There was nothing she "needed" to do, other than what she chose to do. And *tout le monde* hung on her every fashion directive. When everyone else was wearing real pearls, Coco designed costume jewelry and decreed it be worn with sportswear. Then, at the height of America's Great Depression, when everyone was draped in costume jewelry, she debuted a fine jewelry collection, featuring diamonds set in platinum—because it amused her.

Coco never truly got over the death of Boy Capel. But life goes on and she was hardly ready to forego love completely. In 1923, she was introduced to Hugh Grosvenor, the second Duke of Westminster and, not incidentally, the richest man in the world. It seemed to be a good match, consisting of a lot of hunting, riding, fishing, and other outdoorsy things royals seem to live for, which Coco had enjoyed as a young woman at Royallieu with Étienne Balsan. Bendor, as the duke was known, showered Coco with jewels, gave her a parcel of land in the South of France on which she built her renowned villa, La Pausa, and introduced her to Winston Churchill, who found her to be a suitable mate for his friend. Still, when Bendor asked her to marry him, she said, "There have been several duchesses of Westminster, but there is only one Chanel."

Ten or so years later, before the relationship with the duke ended for good, Coco took up with fashionable political illustrator Paul Iribe. Sophisticated and witty, he shared Coco's modern sensibility. (Bendor, for all his wealth and influence, was definitely a man of the previous century—the kind of old-fashioned rich person who employed a man to press his morning newspaper.)

Coco was now in her late 40s, and as beautiful as ever. But she was aware of time passing. Children were not going to be part of her life—but would she remain unmarried as well? The gossip among the friends who came to stay at La Pausa was that an engagement announcement was imminent. Then, one day in late September 1935, Coco and Iribe were playing tennis. As she looked on, he staggered on the other side of the net, before dropping dead.

The loss of Iribe mirrored the loss of Capel so many years before. Coco would have found the idea of being retraumatized to be utter nonsense. But it's likely that her lover's death rekindled her grief. To make matters worse, her designs weren't as fashionable as they once were. She was in danger of being eclipsed by her rival, the spirited, playful Italian designer Elsa Schiaparelli, who popularized sportswear, the zipper, and "shocking" pink. In 1937, Schiap had collaborated with Salvador Dali on her "lobster" dress, lamb-cutlet hat, and a dress with pockets that looked like a chest of drawers: crazy, cheeky, and completely against Coco's more disciplined aesthetic. Her simple suits were starting to look drab by comparison. I imagine she was a bit depressed.

In 1939, at the beginning of World War II, Coco began an affair with Baron Hans Günther von Dincklage. His mother was English, but von Dincklage, an attaché at the German Embassy, was working for the Nazis. Coco was 56 when he moved into the apartment she kept at the Ritz. Von Dincklage was 43: a much younger, handsome man who made her feel desirable. At this stage, she had decided to close her shops, fire her employees, and hole up in her apartment to wait out the war.

After France was liberated, the government took a dim view of collaborators, especially women who had literally slept with the enemy. Bands of roving self-appointed *tondeurs* (head shavers) chased down female Nazi collaborators, shaved their heads, then marched them through the street, often tarred and naked. Coco escaped such treatment—most likely due to her friend Churchill's influence—but she was exiled to Switzerland in 1945. There she lived a quiet life.

In the late 1940s, part of France's recovery after the war included embracing the luxe designs of Christian Dior. Yards and yards of fabric—no more rationing!—were required to make his enormous dresses with their boned bodices, cinched waists, and padded hips.

"Oh *mon dieu*," I imagine Coco thinking. "Do I have to come back and teach everyone, again, that women must be comfortable in their clothes? That a woman must be able to stride along a city street in her skirt? That elegance is refusal? That luxury is simple, the opposite of complication?"

Back she came to Paris. She was more than 70 years old. In 1954, she put out a few collections, underwritten by her old frenemy Pierre Wertheimer. Parisians didn't love her new designs, which they felt looked a lot like the old designs. But by the early 1960s Americans, including Jackie Kennedy, discovered her easy suits, with their straight skirts and cardigan jackets. Coco was back on top. She returned to her workaholic ways, returned to creating fabulous pieces for fabulous women who could afford her prices.

On January 10, 1971, she was busy finishing the fittings for her spring line when, after a day's work she decided to go to sleep early. She lay down on her bed in her apartment at the Ritz and died.

IN 2009 I PUBLISHED *The Gospel According to Coco Chanel*, a celebration of Coco's life, style, and philosophy. During the Q&A after every reading, someone would always make the observation that Coco Chanel didn't seem very nice.

I would say, what does that have to do with anything? Or, she was nice to the people she cared about. Sometimes I would say, Chanel was a complicated, stubborn, ambitious visionary who transformed the way we dress, view ourselves in clothes, and walk through the world. You need her to be nice on top of everything else? What's wrong with you?

Then I would laugh, to diffuse the sting. Coco would never have done that, of course. She adored being thought difficult. And so should we.

CHAPTER 9

MARTHA GELLHORN

Brave

I WAS A COLLEGE STUDENT with a backpack, a Eurail Pass, and a head full of dreams about being a writer in Paris when I discovered the brilliant 20th-century war correspondent Martha Gellhorn. I picked up a copy of her celebrated memoir, *Travels With Myself and Another,* at Shakespeare and Company late one summer afternoon. It was obvious to me even then they'd stocked the book because Gellhorn had been the third wife of Ernest Hemingway, the most famous habitué of the bookstore. Martha would have hated that. "I was a writer before I met him and have been a writer for forty-five years since," she once groused to a reporter from the *Chicago Tribune.* "Why should I be a footnote to someone else's life?"

The question was rhetorical, but the literal answer is because that's where the wives, sisters, and daughters of men worthy of commanding the narrative have always resided. But Martha insisted on being the protagonist of her own story, responsible for her own accomplishments, disasters, and triumphs. This made her difficult: independent, disconcertingly intrepid (no damsel in distress, she), and whatever is the opposite of self-sacrificing. I read *Travels With Myself* in my tiny room off the Boulevard Raspail (the kind with a bathroom at the end of the hall with a light on a timer, forcing you to pee quickly). From the first sentence I was hooked: "I was seized by the idea of this book while sitting on a rotten little beach at the western tip of Crete, flanked by a waterlogged shower and a rusted potty." It was news to me that you could be this

snotty about the world in a travel memoir. Martha never referred to Hemingway by name; she referred to him as UC, or "unwilling companion." UC called her Gellhorn.

Martha's career spanned six decades. The author of five novels, 14 novellas, and two collections of short stories as well as the memoir, she was also a formidable journalist, having reported on every major war in the 20th century. *The Face of War,* her 1959 collection of wartime journalism, is a modern classic hailed by the *New York Times* as "a brilliant anti-war book that is as fresh as if written for this morning." In the late 1930s Martha wrote dozens of dispatches for *Collier's* magazine. In a squib on popular contributors, it was noted that she was "blond, tall, dashing—she comes pretty close to living up to Hollywood's idea of what a big-league woman reporter should be." In the campy 2012 HBO film *Hemingway & Gellhorn,* Nicole Kidman portrayed her as a force of nature with a gleam in her eye, wearing a snazzy pair of palazzo pants.

Martha was born in St. Louis, Missouri, in 1908. Her father, George, was a doctor; her mother, Edna, was an enthusiastic supporter of social causes. Little Martha cut her teeth on protests, rallies, and demonstrations for justice. She was made aware at a young age of just how unfair life could be, and it instilled in her a deep, lifelong hatred of politicians and power brokers. From the time she was a girl, Martha Gellhorn would never go along to get along.

Martha attended snooty Bryn Mawr (she was a year behind Katharine Hepburn) but dropped out in 1927 to work as a crime reporter. She knew she wanted to be a writer, and didn't see any reason why she shouldn't just get on with it. One presumes her parents were either on board with this or indifferent; there is no evidence of any awkward Gellhorn family meetings where Martha was encouraged to stay in school or face a future in retail. In 1930 she sallied forth to Paris, worked odd jobs, and had a proper French love affair. She then returned to St. Louis to write a novel, *What Mad Pursuit,* about a reporter who goes to Paris and has a proper French love affair.

The Great Depression hit its stride in 1932, when unemployment reached 25 percent. The stock market may have crashed in 1929, but it took a few years for the country to really fall apart: for unemployed fathers to start drinking, stealing, and beating their wives. For children to begin suffering in earnest, not only from malnutrition, but also from the diseases malnutrition wrought.

In 1933, the newly elected President Franklin Roosevelt created the Federal Emergency Relief Administration (FERA). He dispatched a troupe of 16 journalists that included Martha to collect data and file classified reports on how, exactly, the country was suffering (the better to assist FERA in administering its relief).

I want to pause for a moment to reflect on the common sense of this project, the thoughtfulness. Roosevelt wanted to act as quickly and efficiently as possible—and so he dispatched a bunch of professionals to gather facts and report back, allowing him to offer relief where relief was needed most. That today this would be considered a radical approach probably has Martha spinning in her grave.

At 25, she was the youngest journalist in the pack.

Martha's first assignment was the mill towns of New England and the Carolinas. She had an aptitude for the work and cared almost nothing about discomfort. She packed the completely inappropriate clothes hanging in her closet: a brown Schiaparelli suit with a Chinese collar and dainty French shoes (recall, please, that she was just back from Paris). She would talk to anyone willing to talk to her, obsessed with bearing witness. At night in her hotel room, she would type up her reports: precise, detail-driven accounts of the lives of regular people who suffered the folly of the wealthy and powerful.

She would live in a state of barely suppressed anger for the rest of her life. The most difficult women are the angry ones. The ones who refuse to "let it go," think happy thoughts, or eat their feelings. For reasons I will never understand, men are given a free pass when it comes to anger. But women are expected to figure out a way of disposing of theirs, as though it were a dirty diaper.

Martha spent most of her professional life infuriated about the stupendous injustices of the world, but she channeled that rage into her writing. And we would do well to follow her lead. Don't waste time trying to change your anger into something that makes you likable; you will only wind up disliking yourself. Write your rage, paint it, film it, dance it, lyricize it, poeticize it. You don't have to be good, just honest.

THREE OR SO YEARS LATER, in 1936, Martha met Hemingway at one of his favorite bars: Sloppy Joe's in the Florida Keys. He bought her a drink and revealed that he was off to cover the Spanish Civil War for a newspaper syndicate, the North American Newspaper Alliance.

Fresh from having published *The Trouble I've Seen,* a collection of four novellas based on her work for FERA, Martha thought that was a fine idea. She snagged an assignment from *Collier's* and, with a knapsack on her back and 50 bucks in her pocket, off she went. She ran into Hem at the Hotel Florida in Madrid. They proceeded to report from the front lines, drink a lot, carouse a lot, and fall in love.

Nothing appeals to me more than the idea of heading out into the world with a knapsack and 50 bucks. Have I ever done anything as remotely badass? Two summers ago I went to the South of France for a month with only a carry-on and a debit card.*

The simple fact is that Martha was free: tormented by her obsessions, but not weighed down by the soul-sucking monotony generally thought to be the province of women. She was the rare female who would rather duck mortar fire than sigh and submit to a lifetime full of Saturdays ironing sheets (which was something women spent an astounding amount of time doing in her day). Even when it came to packing her knapsack and taking off to one of the spots she wrote about in *Travels With Myself and Another*—

---

* So, no.

Cuba, Haiti, St. Thomas, and Kenya—I don't think she spent a second pondering whether she should have sprung for a new bathing suit or fretted over the degree of SPF in her sunscreen.

The dead glamour of Martha's approach to living has bewitched me for my entire adult life. Once, when she went to cover something or other going on in the Caribbean, she packed only two white linen dresses and a copy of Proust. This is so cool, and so exactly how I'd like to live, except for reality: I look terrible in white, have a love-hate relationship with linen, and would be woman overboard in about 12 minutes if Proust was all I had to read.

Martha was free, in part, because she was drawn to the world of men in action. She was addicted to going and doing. Women stay home and tend the home fires; men go, and men do. That was Martha's idea of a good time. She adored drinking, smoking, and talking shop. She was brave in the way a man was brave. She wasn't afraid of getting shot, blown up, or crushed amid the rubble. This is possibly a little mental, but she would rather be afraid than bored. Which did not make her a happy housewife and homemaker. Or a good one, either.

Three more years later, in 1939, Hemingway divorced his second wife, Pauline, to marry Martha. She was 32 years old; he was 40. He bought a ramshackle house in Cuba, Finca Vigía, 10 miles east of Havana. They were happy for a while, but Martha kept being seduced by the wider world. Long after the marriage was over, in 1959, she confessed in a letter to her friend Leonard Bernstein, "I have never been more bored in my life than during the long, long months when we lived alone in Cuba. I thought I would die of boredom. But it was very good for me. I wrote more with him than ever before or since in my life, and read more. There were no distractions; I lived beside him and entirely and completely alone, as never before or since."

Hemingway wanted Martha to stay home and take care of him, little woman style. And really, who can blame him? Hadley and Pauline, his first two wives, had devoted themselves to his comfort and to supporting his writing. Martha wasn't like that. She didn't do well in captivity.

It pains me that my favorite Martha Gellhorn story is one that involves Hemingway. (The poor woman can't get a break from even her most devoted readers.)

The beginning of the end came in the spring of 1944; the two of them were at home at La Finca. The United States had entered World War II, and the only thing Martha wanted was to be on the front lines covering it. Hemingway wanted her to stay home and be a deferential wife. They fought. He accused her of being selfish, a "pretentious bitch." She called him a drunk and a pathetic liar.*

Getting to the front in Europe would not be a simple matter. Journalists needed to be accredited by a news agency to gain access. At the beginning of the war, the U.S. military forbade women from embedding with troops. The multipurpose excuse for this was trotted out with regularity: no bathroom facilities. Permission denied.

This obstacle was no big deal for Martha. She was the queen of work-arounds, and knew she could figure out a way to get where she needed to be. She rang up *Collier's* to confirm her credentials, but her editor hemmed and hawed. She was confused, until Hemingway announced he had called the magazine, *her* magazine, played the celebrity card, and snatched her accreditation out from under her nose. Every magazine could send only one reporter, so Martha was out of luck.

Hem took off for New York, where he grabbed a seaplane bound for London. Martha, undeterred (and probably so spitting mad she was determined to make him pay), coaxed a friend into calling in a favor and getting her a berth on a Norwegian freighter transporting explosives. The crossing took 20 days. She was the only passenger. The captain and crew spoke no English, and for reasons that were unclear, drinking and smoking were not allowed on board. Martha passed the time reading D. H. Lawrence, stewing over her marriage, and writing letters to friends. "He [Hemingway] is a good man, which is vitally important," she observed.

---

* Not inaccurate.

"He is however bad for me, sadly enough—or maybe wrong for me is the word; and I am wrong for him."

Hemingway was already in London, and the moveable feast was in full swing. Any day the Allies would launch an invasion on a stretch of beach in Normandy, France. About 600 journalists and photographers had descended on London, waiting for the moment when they would be summoned to take their spot with the deploying troops.

Meanwhile, coming home one night from a party, Hemingway had been in a car wreck and smacked his head on the windshield. The deep gash on his forehead required 57 stitches and a few days of observation in the hospital. Martha, hearing the news, rushed to his bedside, only to find him drunk and carousing with some other journalists—including Mary Welsh, a sweet-faced midwestern blonde married to one of the reporters for *Time,* who would go on to become Hemingway's fourth wife. Martha was infuriated by her husband's ridiculousness, and also, I imagine, annoyed that like most famous men he was never held accountable for his high jinks.

With no accreditation, Martha had no way to get to France. On June 6, 1944, minutes after hearing the announcement of the D-Day invasion on the radio, she headed to South Devon, on the coast of England, to see if she could find a way across the channel.

Listen, how is it that men still haven't learned they underestimate women at their own peril? Martha spied a hospital ship, a big red cross painted on the bow. She approached the guard checking papers at the bottom of the gangplank, and said, "My magazine is writing a story about nurses." He waved her on, didn't even ask to see documentation. Can you imagine what the soldier thought? Oh, a silly woman writing about *nurses.*

Martha stowed away in a bathroom. When the ship arrived on Omaha Beach, thousands of troops were already wading through the tide toward shore. It was the biggest seaborne invasion in history, taking place in broad daylight. Planes roared overhead. Giant minesweepers worked the beach, detonating mines. The troops making landfall were easy targets for Germans in their sandy foxholes. Before the end of the day, 9,000 Allied troops would be wounded or dead. Martha disguised herself as a stretcher bearer, though actually, there was no need for a disguise. In the chaos, any able hands were welcome hands. The beach was a hellscape of smoke, eardrum-busting noise, and the smells of gunpowder and burned flesh.

Martha was the first woman on the beach at Normandy. When the hospital ship returned to London, its 400-plus bunks groaning with wounded, she immediately was arrested for entering France illegally. They didn't know what to do with her, so they sent her to a nurses' training school. She easily escaped. She wrote a long piece about the landing, focusing as she always did on the human stories. Hemingway, for his part, never left the transport ship, and never made it to shore. This didn't stop him from writing a braggy first-person account about his role in calming nervous young soldiers. Even though *Collier's* had awarded her accreditation to her more-famous husband, they were happy to run her scoop. The magazine ran both pieces in the same issue. Of course, Hemingway was on the cover.

In 1945, nine years after they'd first hooked up, Hemingway and Martha divorced. She was the only wife who'd ever done the leaving, and Hemingway was furious. It's possible that Hemingway loved her like no other—which of course meant that when it went bad, he hated her like no other. He indulged in some public name-calling, insisting she was "the product of a beautician" and "a career bulldozer." She was very private, and also silent on the matter of the marriage. She hated being thought of as an appendage to Hemingway, and the less said the better.

Martha went on to cover conflicts in Israel, Vietnam, El Salvador, and Nicaragua, and would never live in the United States again. She made homes in France, Italy, Mexico, and Kenya, before settling in England. Men—there were a few. Also, another husband. She didn't care much about romance, and even less about marriage, which she found to be excruciatingly dull. She once referred to herself as "the worst bed partner in five continents."

She wasn't completely without familial instincts, however; after the war she adopted a toddler, Sandro, from Italy. She re-christened him George Alexander, but she continued to call him Sandy, raising him as a single mom. Motherhood was exhausting and perplexing for Martha—a nice way of saying she pretty much sucked at it. For in the end, Martha was a loner. "Difficulty" is always in the eye of the beholder. Usually, it's just a woman being her complicated self.

Even into her 80s, Martha was cantankerous—and still, always eager to get herself to some far-flung front line. "If you have no part of the world, no matter how diseased the world is, you are dead," she once wrote in her diary. She was a woman determined to bear witness to every god-awful thing the world has to offer. This included her own complex nature. Martha Gellhorn was complicated and imperfect. But refused to pretend she was anything else.

CHAPTER 10

SHONDA RHIMES

Unstoppable

AT THE BEGINNING of her 2016 TED talk, TV show runner extraordinaire Shonda Rhimes had this to say about the current state of her workload:

"Three shows in production at a time, sometimes four. The budget for one episode of network television can be anywhere from three to six million dollars. Let's just say five. A new episode made every nine days, times four shows—so every nine days, that's 20 million dollars' worth of television. Four television programs, 70 hours of TV, three shows in production at a time, sometimes four, 16 episodes going on at all times. That's 350 million dollars a season. My television shows are back to back to back on Thursday night. Around the world, my shows air in 256 territories in 67 languages for an audience of 30 million people."

Just reading those stats makes me tremble with anxiety. In Shonda's TED talk, she refers to herself matter-of-factly as a titan, as she should. When she says she owns Thursday nights on ABC, that's not hyperbole: The woman created *Grey's Anatomy, Scandal, How to Get Away with Murder,* and executive produces *The Catch*. Her shows seem to run forever. My personal favorite, *Grey's Anatomy,* has been around so long that in an early season, one episode pivoted around that newfangled phone thing, texting.[*]

Shonda Rhimes sits at the pinnacle of TV-land achievement. And yet she sees no reason to rest on her laurels, or refrain from gobbling up the time slots, the production money, the producing credits, the Emmys, and

---

[*] It premiered on March 27, 2005.

probably one day soon, Oscars. Her disinclination to take it easy, go off and eat pray love, distract herself with a disastrous affair, or launch a life-style website trafficking in fancy yoga mats makes her difficult. Her ambition is a perpetual-motion machine, by which I mean she's as enterprising as any man. Like the famous female characters she breathes life into, she keeps smacking open life's piñata and grabbing all the candy she can get her hands on. She seems perfectly nice about it. But the woman is unstoppable, and an unstoppable woman—especially one who already owns an entire night of network TV—is a difficult one.

Shonda Rhimes's work ethic derives, I imagine, from having grown up watching her mom earn a Ph.D. while raising six kids. Born in Chicago in 1970, she was the baby of the family, shy and introverted, and found solace in books. Her storytelling genius revealed itself early. She liked to hide out in the kitchen pantry, where she constructed elaborate scenarios using canned fruit and vegetables as players and props. That her mom allowed this, only asking her to pass a can of peas or corn when the need arose during dinner preparation, tells you a lot about the sheer excellence of her parenting.

Shonda is a difficult woman, good girl division. She works hard, achieves a lot, and mows down the competition (pretty much everyone in her path). She has compared herself to Tracy Flick, the hyper-driven anti-heroine of the 1999 film *Election*. She is a cheerful, self-professed workaholic and type-A perfectionist who's happy in the overworking zone. Shonda graduated with honors from a Catholic high school and attended Dartmouth (more honors), then the University of Southern California School of Cinematic Arts (more honors), where she earned her MFA in 1995. Despite all the honors, once she got out of film school it was the usual thing: dull jobs that allowed her to write at night. Aspiring screenwriters can spend a decade trying to sell a script, but a mere three years later, in 1998, she caught a break and sold a script to New Line Cinema. In 1999 she was hired to co-write HBO's Halle Berry vehicle *Introducing Dorothy Dandridge*. In 2001 she wrote another script, *Crossroads*, for Britney Spears's film debut (panned by the critics, $60 million at the box office). On 9/11 she was holed up in Vermont working on another film script—and in a matter of days, she reexamined her life, her priorities, and what couldn't wait. The top of the list: becoming a mother.

Perhaps surprising for a perfectionistic titan of achievement, snagging the perfect husband—or any husband for that matter—was not on the list. In fact, although she likes having boyfriends, "I do not want a husband in my house," she told Oprah. "I have never wanted to get married. I never played bride. I was never interested."

She did always long to be a mother, however. Less than a year later she adopted Harper. (She would go on to adopt two other daughters with equally cool literary names: Emerson and Beckett.) While home with the baby, she flipped on the TV and discovered a world she wanted in on. She wrote and filmed a pilot for an ABC show about female war correspondents (I would totally watch that), but it wasn't a go. Her next pilot script was *Grey's Anatomy*, after which came *Private Practice* in 2007, and *Scandal* in 2012, as well as the shows she executive produces under the ShondaLand banner: *The Catch, Off the Map, How to Get Away with Murder,* and *Still Star-Crossed.* In 2017, at the age of 47, Shonda Rhimes is queen of network TV's most successful empire, the most powerful show runner in Hollywood. Not "the most powerful black female show runner," which is how she's sometimes described in the more boneheaded press releases. No. Most. Powerful. Show runner.

When she was creating *Grey's Anatomy*, Shonda Rhimes did something that in retrospect doesn't seem revolutionary, or even that creative: She cast African Americans, Asians, and Latinas as brilliant doctors, then wrote them as fully dimensional human beings with fully dimensional lives.

Have you ever been to a hospital? Have you taken a good look at the health care providers there? They do not look like the cast of *How I Met Your Mother.** There are men and women. There are Asians, African Americans, Latinos. It's a profession that attracts all races, colors, genders, and sexual preferences. It seems as if the advances of the civil rights movement and the women's rights movement should have made the diversity on

---

* Possibly the whitest cast of all time. Also: *Friends, Dawson's Creek, Buffy the Vampire Slayer.*

Grey's Anatomy routine—and yet Shonda was hailed as a visionary. Network TV became more genuinely diverse. When *Scandal* premiered in 2012, it was the first show to star an African-American woman in 38 years.* Both shows enjoy consistently high ratings, and on Thursday nights Twitter is generally afire as fans of the shows share their thoughts in real time.

I'm all for hailing Shonda Rhimes for pretty much everything.** She is bold and unapologetically enterprising, and she creates difficult women characters who make no bones about wanting what they want and doing what they need to do to get it. They are brilliant, determined, and complex. They are a lot like Shonda herself. Her genius further rests in making us *prefer* difficult women over their easier, more accommodating counterparts. In someone else's hands Cristina Yang, the selfish, headstrong cardiac surgeon-genius of Seattle Grace Mercy West Hospital played by Sandra Oh, or Olivia Pope, the whip-smart, uncompromising crisis manager and political "fixer" played by Kerry Washington, might be unlikable: the cardinal sin of both imaginary women and real women. But Shonda has managed to make them role models. Cristina Yang was written out of *Grey's Anatomy* after season 10 (she left Seattle Grace to move to Zurich to commandeer a cutting-edge cardiac center). But I still summon up her wisdom, which is, of course, Shonda's wisdom: The men in our lives "may be dreamy but are not the sun. You are."

IN 2015, SHONDA PUBLISHED a self-empowerment manifesto/memoir called *Year of Yes: How to Dance It Out, Stand in the Sun and Be Your Own Person*. It took me a bit to get my head around the premise: Didn't Shonda, storytelling genius and unstoppable show runner, get where she was, in part, by saying yes to all those deal memos and series orders, to pitching yet another blockbuster show, to becoming a single mom of three, and all

---

* In 1974 Teresa Graves starred in *Get Christie Love!*

** We are both alumnae of USC film school, a proud and insular clan.

that that entails? But it turns out that saying yes to work stuff is easy when you're a workaholic. Pretty much everything else sent her into a social anxiety–fueled tailspin.

Like public speaking. (To deliver that TED talk was *huge*.)

Like refusing to answer emails after 7 p.m.*** (To be unavailable to everyone in the digital age takes a depressing amount of courage and discipline.)

Like losing 150 pounds. (I'm tucking this impressive accomplishment in here, without fanfare, because Shonda despises the obsession with her transformation. "After I lost weight, I discovered that people found me valuable. Worthy of conversation. A person one could look at. A person one could compliment. A person one could admire. A person. You heard me. I discovered that NOW people saw me as a PERSON," she wrote in her newsletter, *Shondaland*. Take that, weight-obsessed world.)

Like saying yes to rethinking motherhood. "I find it offensive to motherhood to call being a mother a job. Being a mother isn't a job. It's who someone is. It's who I am." She's also against the celebration of the mom as martyr, and goes on a fine rant about how perverse it is to celebrate mothers for their ability to suffer, to make themselves small and without needs for the sake of their family. She wants to start a line of Mother's Day greeting cards that say stuff like "Happy Mother's Day to the mom who taught me to be strong, to be powerful, to be independent, to be competitive, to be fiercely myself and fight for what I want."

Shonda is difficult because she's all about owning her tremendous competence and badassery. Her achievements are huge, and there's no reason on Earth she should pretend otherwise. Let's take a page from her book, instead of falling over ourselves to write off our great job, our promotion, our special award as good luck or the universe smiling down on us or anything else other than our own intelligence, dedication, discipline, and talent. Let's be like Shonda and strut a little.

*** Email her and you will read this signature line—"Please note: I will not engage in work emails after 7 p.m. or on weekends. IF I AM YOUR BOSS, MAY I SUGGEST: PUT DOWN YOUR PHONE."

CHAPTER 11

EVA PERÓN

Fanatical

MOST OF US KNOW EVA PERÓN from the 1978 rock opera *Evita,* during which Patti LuPone, her hair slicked back in Evita's trademark honey blond chignon, belted out "Don't Cry for Me Argentina." Or, in my case, from the commercial that played every morning during the *Today* show for what seemed like months. I was a college student, and would watch it while I ate my Frosted Flakes before heading off to class. I still remember the spot, pretty much shot for shot. While LuPone beseeched her beloved nation to love her back, sexy, bearded Mandy Patinkin as Che Guevara (that beret!) sat backward in a chair, watching the first lady with a smoldering look that ignited in me a brief interest in finding myself a nice revolutionary to date. And also inspired a lifelong fascination in the glamorous, difficult Evita.

Between 1946 and her death in 1952, Evita—a onetime radio star and B-list actress—was the most powerful woman in the Americas. Fanatically devoted to her husband, President Juan Perón, Evita was instrumental in gaining the vote for women and creating an astonishing network of modern social services, while also sanctioning extortion, bribery, and corruption. To her followers, she was a saint sent by God. To her detractors, she was a cheap tart from the provinces. Before she died of cancer at 33, the bought-and-sold Congress bestowed upon her the accolade "Spiritual Mother of All Argentines." She was, in the end, a complicated woman: opinionated, compassionate, vengeful, high-handed. In other words, difficult.

EVITA WAS BORN IN 1919 in Los Toldos, a poor village 150 miles west of Buenos Aires. She was the fifth illegitimate child of Juana Ibarguren, mistress of Juan Duarte, a ranch manager and big man around town. Juan Duarte had a nice car and a title, justice of the peace. He was so well liked that everyone looked the other way when it came to Blanca, Elisa, Juan, Erminda, and Eva María, the children he'd sired with Juana.

That Juan had a proper wife and three other children in another village shocked no one, nor did anyone disapprove. He came and went as he pleased, tossed some money in Juana's direction now and then, and in all ways behaved like a typical Argentinian man of his time. Nevertheless, people chose to condemn Juana for behaving as if she were a proper wife. She was an excellent seamstress, and she and her children were clean and had nice clothes. She wore perfume, which was viewed as pretentious. The true scandal was that a simple, unmarried seamstress dared to exhibit self-respect. (She, too, was a difficult woman.)

Juana Ibarguren got her comeuppance soon enough. When Eva was only a year old, Juan Duarte returned to his former village and his first wife for good, effectively abandoning Juana and their children and plunging them all into poverty. But then he was killed in a car accident. Once Juan was gone, Juana was reduced to accepting handouts from people in the village—some of whom were men. They gave her the occasional chicken, some vegetables, milk, and bread to feed her children. Immediately she was deemed a common whore. Her daughters were considered damaged goods by proxy, even though they were still little girls.

Be prepared: The phrase "common whore" pops up a lot in Evita's story. In her short life, any time she branched out, made a decision, got a break, leaned in, moved on, soldiered forth, or spoke out, someone somewhere explained it away as the result of sexual favors. It's the go-to insult in a culture so macho that any time a woman does anything aside from the laundry, she's a common whore. Even the great Argentine writer Jorge

Luis Borges, who you would think had a more developed vocabulary, would refer to the first lady by this moniker. It's of note that there's no obverse, no uncommon whore. But if there were anyone worthy of being called an exceptional whore, it would be Evita.

In 1930, Juana left Los Toldos for the provincial city of Junín, where she hoped to attract more clothing clients, and where her older children were able to get work. Eva was sent to school, where her teachers would remember her large, dark eyes and porcelain skin, but not much else. She apparently loved to recite poetry, and would do so at the local record shop in a sort of open mic arrangement. Mostly, she loved American movies, which reached the cinemas of Junín a good five years after they were released in the States. No matter. Eva was hypnotized by the clothes, jewels, lipstick, nail polish, and glamour. She now had a goal: to be a movie star!

Legend has it that in 1934, at 15, Eva dropped out of school and became the mistress of a local tango singer, Agustín Magaldi, and made her way to Buenos Aires on his arm to pursue her dream. There's also a screwball comedy version, wherein she attempted to seduce him; when the married Magaldi turned her down, she sneaked into his train compartment as he traveled back to Buenos Aires. Neither of these stories is true, as it turns out, for there is no record of Magaldi visiting or performing in Junín the year Eva left.

From this point on in Evita's life, there would be at least three versions of everything that happened to her: the version put forth by Evita's supporters; the version put forth by Evita's detractors; and the version valiantly put forth by legitimate historians who have no political skin in the game. Given the dearth of official records in early 20th-century Argentina, Eva's refusal to acknowledge or elaborate on her personal history after she married Juan Perón, the robust suppression of the press during his presidency, and the tonnage of mawkish hagiography that does exist, the valiant historians are at a clear disadvantage. Still, we do the best we can.

It is highly likely that Eva made her way to Buenos Aires the way most teenagers without a driver's license do: by pestering her mother in the usual relentless teenage fashion. At some point, Juana probably shouted

"FINE! ALL RIGHT!" and together they traveled to the capital to investigate what sort of work might be available. Juana helped settle Eva in a small *pensione,* then returned to Junín. In March 1935, Eva landed her first theatrical role, in the play *Mrs. Perez* at the Comedias Theater.

BUENOS AIRES WAS THE MANHATTAN of Argentina, seasoned with extra macho sauce. Settled by Spain in the 14th century, further colonized by Britain in the 19th, and heavily influenced by France, the city felt European—that is, if you replaced the dainty shops with football stadiums and boxing rings.

The world of the theater in the mid-1930s was a microcosm of Buenos Aires society. The stars were usually related to the producer and well compensated, and their living and travel costs were picked up by the theater company. The other players practically starved. They weren't paid for rehearsals and had to foot the bill for their own costumes and lodging. In any case, actresses were presumed to be—all together now—common whores, and were expected to find a sugar daddy to help them along the way.

Did Eva have one? Maybe? Probably? She certainly accepted the help of men with whom she would fall in and out of love and lust. When she married Juan Perón at the age of 26, she was no longer a virgin, so make of that what you will.

At the beginning of her career, she barely scraped by. After *Mrs. Perez,* she landed a tiny part on a sci-fi radio show and emceed a tango contest. She also appeared in the traveling company of *The Fatal Kiss,* a cautionary tale about the ravages of syphilis, produced by the Prophylactic League of Argentina.

Evita may not have been educated, or even particularly intelligent. But she was sensitive to the unspoken, unwritten rules about the way the world actually worked. Somewhere around 1937, she figured out that it would be good to have her name appear in *Sintonía,* a popular movie rag. She began showing up at the magazine office claiming she had an appointment with the editor. He refused to see her, and didn't know why she was wasting her time and hoping to waste his. She came the next morning with the same story. She was cheerful, but persistent, determined to succeed, and the receptionist gave in and let her sit there. Sometimes, Eva would paint her nails. One day, a gossip columnist wondered aloud in his column what business the pretty young actress Eva Duarte (she always used her father's name) had with the powerful editor-in-chief, thus linking her name with his—which had been her intention all along.

Eva cozied up to a radio scriptwriter, who cast her in his next soap opera. *Sintonía* reported the news, calling her a "dynamic" actress. Most of what was written in movie magazines was completely bogus, but in this case dynamic might be an accurate euphemism for Eva's acting style, which verged on the hysterical.

The radio market in Argentina was second to the United States in programming and listeners. Soap operas were the most popular, appealing as they did to the Argentine love of melodrama and tragedy. Writers hacked out a "chapter" in the morning, and the actors performed it in the afternoon. By 1943, at the age of 24, Eva had become a radio star with her own production company, assembled with the help of her brother, Juan, who worked in the soap manufacturing business and had secured Radical Soap as a guaranteed sponsor of her programs. She now made 6,000 pesos a month—more than any other radio soap opera actress—and moved into a chic apartment in Barrio Norte. Among her peers she was not especially well liked, but people found her to be reliable, and she was very good at the overemoting required of the genre. Little did the world know that pretty, dynamic Eva Duarte's aptitude for the stagy and overwrought would change the course of world history.

THE ARGENTINE POLITICAL SYSTEM is modeled on that of the United States, with executive, legislative, and judicial branches. The country also holds elections, which have a tendency to be fraudulent, and is subject to occasional military coups.

Evita couldn't have cared less about politics, and when there was a coup on June 4, 1943, what annoyed her most were the restrictions now placed on soap opera production. A guy from the military with no experience in radio or entertainment was placed in charge of regulating her shows, and seemed to pick his rules out of a hat. There were to be no more bugle calls or whistles, or people speaking in foreign languages. Scripts now had to be submitted for approval to the new Inspector for Posts and Telecommunications.

Eva's new show, *Heroines of History,* managed to make it past the censors. The gossip, of course, was that she was a common whore having an affair with the officer in charge of assigning airtime. Was she? Maybe? Probably? Or was the show just upstanding and dull enough to appeal to a military guy stuck reading bad scripts all day?

Meanwhile, in January 1944, an earthquake caused a few books to tumble from shelves in Buenos Aires but left the city of San Juan, in the Andean west, in rubble. Col. Juan Domingo Perón, then the secretary of labor, hatched an idea for a fundraiser: a gala with plays, comedy acts, tango, the works.

I hate to waste ink on Evita's future husband, Juan, but as she would go on to become the world's most fanatical Perónist, I have no choice.

Juan Perón was also the illegitimate son of a ranch manager—but perhaps because his parents eventually married, it didn't bother him much. At the age of nine, he was sent away to boarding school, then military college. Perón was rugged, handsome, and macho. He fenced and played polo. He could easily have been mistaken for a Hollywood character actor of the time—the one who was routinely cast as a world-weary detective with a drinking problem.

He was career military. In 1939, a year after the death of his first wife (of cervical cancer; more on this later), he was sent to Europe to train with

Italy's alpine warfare division and to study fascism on behalf of the Argentine military. He found himself captivated by the Nazi gift for pomp and ceremony. When he returned to Buenos Aires, he wasn't shy about proclaiming his admiration for Hitler and Mussolini. He was fairly convinced the democracies of France and Britain were not long for this world, and why shouldn't Argentina, neutral in World War I, throw its lot behind the winners this time around?

Not that anyone cared what Juan Perón thought at this moment in time. When he returned in 1941, he was sent to a far province where he served as an army ski instructor. After the 1943 coup (the one that gave Evita such headaches about her radio scripts), he was appointed secretary of labor. It sounds like an important job, but he may as well have been the minister of silly walks.

No one in government gave much of a thought to workers in Argentina in 1943. They were all just . . . there . . . operating the trains and buses, cleaning the streets, making things in factories. They had no rights, because no one in the oligarchy, which historically ruled the nation before the military started butting in, thought they required them. Charity was the name of the game. Poor people, like workers, were dependent on what the rich felt like tossing their way.

Around the time of the earthquake, the press took a shine to the 48-year-old Perón. Unlike the rest of the sourpusses in the ruling junta, or military government, he was chatty and personable. He tended to mirror the attitudes of whomever he was speaking to, and depending on his audience, he came off as either a social justice warrior or a Nazi sympathizer.

AT THE EARTHQUAKE FUNDRAISING GALA, Evita and Perón were introduced, and left together at the end of the evening. After that they were a couple. She left her nice apartment in Barrio Norte and moved in with him. She continued doing her radio plays, sometimes as many as three a day. She still had dark hair, although she wore it swirled atop her head in a pompadour, in keeping with the style of the time. In late 1944, Eva was cast in a starring role in *La Cabalgata del Circo,* a historical melodrama about a theater troupe. She was required to go blond for the role, and once she did, she never went back.

Film stock was hard to come by in Argentina; it came from Mexico or the United States. Through her connections with Perón, Evita was able to get her hands on enough to make a film. She presented the stock to the studio, with herself attached as a star. *The Prodigal (La Pródiga)* was an odd choice. Evita played an aging beauty from the aristocracy whose generosity toward the less fortunate would be her downfall. There was no shooting schedule; instead, they'd expose a few rolls whenever Eva had some free time.

Meanwhile, back at the secretary of labor's office, Perón—singlehand-edly and in an impressively short amount of time—improved the life of the working class. A strong supporter of unions, he increased their clout and legal rights by instituting a minimum wage, paid medical care, paid time off, retirement pay, and a 40-hour workweek. He created work tribunals to deal with labor disputes; the old way involved the police throwing disgruntled workers in jail until they decided they weren't that unhappy after all.

I'm sure you're reading this and thinking, Juan Perón—what's not to like? But pay close attention: In another maneuver, which would become a hallmark of his special brand of authoritarianism, he "closed" the existing unions, scrubbing the leadership of its sharpest thinkers and possible future dissenters. Then, he reestablished *another* union under his own leadership, populated with devoted supporters and sycophants. Never-theless, the lives of millions of workers improved drastically, and they became lifelong Perónists. The discarded unionists and conservatives were furious, and everyone else was confused. Which was business as usual, for the most part, in Argentine politics.

Evita was fiercely devoted to Juan Perón. Despite their 24-year age difference, they were in many ways a perfect match. She was passionate; he was reserved (for an Argentine). She was ruled by her heart; he was ruled by a Machiavellian need, not uncommon in autocrats, to quash any and all dissent. They conducted their love affair in a shockingly modern fashion. Perón would sometimes hold meetings at his apartment. Here would come well-educated lawyers, stodgy generals, erudite politicians; Eva the sassy radio star would serve coffee, then sit down and join the conversation. The men were horrified. A wife would never be allowed to take part, yet here was Perón's *mistress?* Why wasn't he doing the acceptable thing—passing Evita off as his daughter, then hiding her in a back room?

Once again, points for Juan Perón. He didn't care enough to lie, and there was something else. He saw something fierce in Eva, and thought it would be prudent to educate her. She became his mentee, his pupil, or, as he once called her, "a second I." (This is also problematic, but it's better than being cast in an incestuous relationship against your will and locked in a back room.)

Evita, for her part, was an eager student. Perón taught her everything she knew. She attended union meetings, swearing-in ceremonies, and political rallies. Once, before a cabinet meeting, Perón appeared with a record player and forced the members to listen to a revolutionary poem recited with soap operatic flourish by Eva. Around this time, all the common whore accusations began to take root. Prostitutes weren't just beneath contempt from a moral perspective; they were also thought to be capable of putting men under magical spells. Clearly, this is what was happening to Juan Perón.

AFTER A SLAPDASH FAILED COUP on October 9, 1945 (from what I can tell, an Argentine specialty), Perón was forced to resign his post at the Department of Labor. He was then tossed into military prison on

Martín García Island.* Evita was immediately fired from her current radio series, a sci-fi show in which she was playing an astronaut. Suddenly, she found herself with no man, no job, no round-the-clock police protection. Rich ladies made a point of coming to spit on her doorstep.

For the next few days chaos ensued. There was no cabinet. The meat plant workers went on strike, and so did the sugar workers. The tram drivers walked out. The newspapers announced the end of Perón and his "Nazi-fascism." (Oh, they had no idea.)

This is the moment in time when the alternative facts concerning Evita really get rolling. There are two prevailing legends: Determined to save her man, stories say she either disguised herself and went from union leader to union leader, soliciting support—or, she was pulled into back alleys and physically beaten by members of the opposition, her bruised and battered face then serving as a disguise. Either way, both theories posit that she heroically orchestrated the workers of the nation to rise up and demand her beloved's release.

What she actually did was file a writ of habeas corpus for Juan's release, a standard and surprisingly dispassionate procedure, given the circumstances. The federal judge who heard and denied her claim was named Juan Atilio Bramuglia. He would rue the day he crossed her, but that comes later. Afterward, she went home and sat in her apartment.

Still, the workers *did* rise up, clamoring for Perón to declare his presidency and lead them. On October 17—a week after the coup—they simply didn't go to work. Instead they headed toward the center of the city. Many of them had never been there before. Now they flowed to the Plaza de Mayo, ground zero for Argentine protests since the foundation of Buenos Aires in 1580. They took over the buses. They climbed on top and hung on the back. They chanted *Viva Perón! Viva Perón!* The police joined the marchers. They sympathized with Perón

---

* There were many complex political reasons, aside from the Evita business. People were getting sick of the pro-fascist military in general. Argentina, long proud of its neutrality, was pressured—largely by the United States—into supporting the Allies. Every time they won a battle or beat back the Axis, the oligarchy and politically savvy upper-middle-class citizens celebrated it as a symbolic victory against their own Nazi-positive regime.

because he was a military man. Before the day was over, Perón would be released. The *descamisados,* or shirtless ones, as the workers came to be called, were thunderstruck to realize they had substantial political clout after all.

It was on this day, October 17, 1945, that Evita claimed to have been "born." The next day, in a small civil ceremony in Junín, she and Juan were married.

Almost overnight, her past vanished.** She had never talked about her childhood, so ashamed was she of her illegitimacy and poverty. Now, it was as if she'd never been a radio star, never appeared in a movie. All prints of her films were confiscated and destroyed, except a copy of *La Pródiga,* which she and Juan would watch from time to time. She was now the nation's most ardent Perónist, and that was all that mattered.

At the end of the year, Perón announced his presidential candidacy. He ran with no party and no funds. The descamisados and various radicals supported him, while progressives, conservatives, socialists, communists—all of whom were well funded and well organized—opposed him. It mattered not. On his arm he had Evita: young, blond, beautiful, glamorous. People ate it up, and on February 24, 1946, Perón won 52 percent of the vote in the first legitimate election since 1928. He immediately got busy appointing all his friends to important positions. He appointed his dentist, Ricardo Guardo, to a cabinet position. Evita's brother, Juan, the soap salesman, was appointed private presidential secretary.

Evita was the perfect modern first lady. She wasn't interested in the traditional wifely duties. She wasn't into hosting parties, and she never cooked. Cabinet members sometimes showed up at the presidential residence unannounced, and when they did, she would offer to open some cans and pass out the forks.

She was, however, interested in her wardrobe. She only knew how to

** Except, you know, all the common whore stuff.

dress like a cheesy radio star, and she understood that would not do. She enlisted the educated, well-bred Liliane Guardo, wife of the dentist/cabinet member, to assist in a makeover. At her first official state banquet she wore a subdued (for her) gray silk sheath dress, one shoulder completely bare. Everyone was appropriately scandalized.

IN JUNE 1947, EVITA WAS SENT on a grand tour of Europe. The reason for the trip was vague. Some typical morsel of nonsense was floated in the press about a rainbow of peace stretching between the continents. Perón had originally been invited by brutal Spanish dictator Francisco Franco—but Argentina had only recently been invited to join the UN (not a fan of Franco), and his visit would be too tricky politically to pull off. But Evita could go on her husband's behalf. Once her trip was announced, the usual travel logic took over: She was going to be over there anyway, so why not visit some other countries?

Evita had never been on an airplane. She had been out of the country only once before. Her brother, Juan, and friend Liliane Guardo accompanied her, as well as someone whose sole job was to keep an eye on her jewels. Also some speechwriters, diplomats, and photographers.

Three million supporters were there to welcome her in Madrid. Spain spent a fortune feting her: banquets, pageants, parades, presents, and long speeches, all in her honor. In France she received the Légion d'honneur, and had private viewings at the Paris fashion houses. (After this trip, Christian Dior would make most of her clothes.) At the Vatican, she was accorded 20 minutes with the pope—the same amount of time allocated to European queens. Some wag referred to her as "the South American Eleanor Roosevelt."

Still, every night, she asked Liliane to sleep in her room. She was lonely and homesick—and as much as she felt all this was her due, she also felt out of her depth, and thus a little frightened. No one would know this.

Her public speaking skills were improving rapidly. Her soap opera train-ing was perfect for the short, passionate, over-the-top declarations she would soon become famous for. She was also expert at seeming to answer questions without actually answering them, a foundational requirement for a politician.

IN 1947, WOMEN GAINED the right to vote. Evita is routinely credited with leading the charge—but as with everything else, it's hard to know what actually happened. What we do know is that after Perón appointed her head of the Perón Feminist Party, women quickly came into their own politically. Universities reported enrolling twice the number of female students as the previous year. In the next elections, in 1951, seven female senators were elected. Argentina now boasted the most female legislators in the world.

Evita's genuine passion was giving—but in that confusing way where it was really as much about her as it was about the person on the receiving end. The world would come to wonder what lay at the heart of Evita's spectacular obsession. Did she remember, clearly, what it was like to be poor? Did she feel indebted to the workers for supporting her husband? Or did she simply dig the adulation?

At first, she and Juan would do the Christmas thing, where they were chauffeured around to the poorest slums to distribute panettone and cider. Soon, she went alone and passed out food boxes during the off-holiday season and during frequent strikes.

People began to show up at her office with specific requests. Mostly women came. They were very poor. They were dirty, and—how to put this—they smelled. Eva's minions never failed to comment upon the odor of poverty in her office. The women asked her for shoes for their children. A new sewing machine because the one they relied on to make a few pesos here and there was stolen. Medicine to stop a husband's raging toothache. Evita kept a stack of new 50-peso notes beneath her desk blotter. Her hands were perfectly tended, her nails polished with red Helena Rubinstein polish each morning by a maid. She would pinch a note from beneath the blotter and press it into the hand of the supplicant, also making a note of their specific need. She would then stand up and hug and kiss them. Day by day, the lines grew longer. Evita worked longer hours—the hardest-working Santa Claus in recorded history.

JUAN PERÓN WAS NEVER your standard-issue dictator. He was elected freely and wound up dragging Argentina kicking and screaming into the modern age, and—at least at first—his supporters didn't mind being ruled in a paternalistic fashion. Plus, he had a beautiful, charismatic young wife and champion whose passion was giving over-the-top speeches singing his praises. It was quite a dog and pony show. He depended on the workers, but he was just not that into them. Evita was his heartfelt link. Once, she and Juan stepped from their limousine on the way to an event. Out of nowhere a *descaminado* in a filthy poncho swooped up and tried to embrace Perón. The president reflexively swatted him away, but Evita tottered after the man in her high heels. She bestowed a kiss upon his head, to make it up to him.

In the June 26, 1948, issue of the *New Yorker,* Philip Hamburger wrote, "They live happily in the presidential mansion. She now has fine furs and satins, and lots of big, sparkling diamonds, rubies, and emeralds. It's a dream come true. But Eva never forgets the Poor. She and the President, who love not only each other but the People, slave night and day doing good works and destroying the Enemies of the People. And so it goes, week after week after week. Wow!"

Evita and Juan viewed themselves as loving but strict parents who punished back talk—or really, any disagreement at all. The national labor union leadership comprised enthusiastic supporters who were nevertheless still capable of independent thought. When these men dared to disagree with or criticize Juan or Evita, they were fired and replaced with slavering toadies whose only qualification for the job was Labrador retriever–like loyalty. Both the driver of a biscuit truck and Perón's doorman were promoted within the ranks.

Perón found an arcane article in the Argentine Constitution that allowed him to impeach four Supreme Court justices. He replaced them with avid supporters, including one of Evita's brothers-in-law. Vast, complex plots to assassinate Juan and Eva would be hatched in-house and reported on state-run radio, giving Perón carte blanche to toss a select list of enemies in jail. There they would sit, awaiting a trial that would never occur.

Any newspaper that published anything aside from the most glowing editorials about Juan and Eva was soon visited by inspectors who would find reason to shut them down (lack of "proper" ventilation, inadequate washrooms). The Socialist newspaper published critical editorials and was shuttered because, allegedly, its printing presses violated local noise ordinances.

By 1948, the government was in charge of dispensing the printing ink. By 1950, most of the newspapers, publishing houses, radio stations, and news agencies were owned by a single entity chaired by the governor of Buenos Aires: a staunch Perónist.

Eva was given a newspaper, the nearly defunct *Democracia*. She was a hands-off publisher, but her staff knew without asking that each edition should feature the full texts of her husband's speeches, and plenty of flattering pictures of Evita in her red-carpet finery.* The only thing she absolutely insisted upon was that *Democracia* never mention Juan Atilio Bramuglia. Remember him? The federal judge who crossed her on the

---

* This was also a smart business move, because pictures of Evita sold papers; on the nights she wore a new dress to some gala, the housewives of Buenos Aires would buy out the run.

matter of Juan's imprisonment? If Bramuglia did something newsworthy, it was ignored. No pictures of him were printed. If he showed up in a group shot at some rally, meeting, or gala, his face was blacked out, without explanation.

THE EVA PERÓN FOUNDATION grew organically from Eva's charitable office hours. By the spring of 1948, hundreds of people would arrive every day at dawn to stand in line to see Evita. The supplicants would weep with gratitude. If they could write, they wrote thank-you notes.* Some would reappear at her office with goods from their factories: sugar, pasta, bread, shoes. These would be repackaged by Evita's growing staff, and redistributed.

Official photographers were now on hand for Eva's office hours. She arrived in her finery and the klieg lights *whoomped* on as though she were attending a Hollywood premiere. She got into the kissing and hugging in a way that made her seem Christlike. She was especially eager to dote upon those who were suffering from leprosy and various forms of venereal disease. Once, she kissed a man with a face ravaged from late-stage syphilis; when a maid stepped forward to wipe her face with a bit of alcohol, Evita took the jar and hurled it against the wall. The Catholics longed to have her beatified.

Even the oligarchy (sidelined politically, but still very rich), who otherwise considered Eva vulgar and cheap, got into the swing of donating goods and services to the foundation. They also had no choice, of course. Once Eva ordered a pharmaceutical company to cough up some much-needed vaccines for the poor. When the anti-Perónist CEO refused, the factory's electricity was shut off; after a week or so—with refrigerated medicines going bad in the Argentine heat—there was a pop inspection. The company was shut down and the CEO forced to flee to Uruguay.

---

* Which is more than you can say for the average American high school student upon receiving a birthday card from grandma containing a twenty.

By 1949, pretty much the entire Argentine economy circulated through Evita's foundation. She was 30 years old. But just when the whole deal began to seem like an outgrowth of her megalomania, she would do something smart and constructive—for example, opening new nursing schools and public hospitals.

Good medical care was available only to people who could pay for it, and Eva's foundation built 12 excellent public hospitals for the poor. Each facility was large and clean, with marble floors, sweeping staircases, and the latest medical equipment imported from Europe and the United States. She could have used her money more wisely—built twice as many hospitals with fewer bells and whistles—but she wanted to make a statement: Everyone deserves good health care. Naturally, she didn't want a single soul to forget who their benefactors were. Paintings of Jesus and Juan Perón hung on the walls, and her initials, EP, were carved into every bed frame.

IRONICALLY, you know who had really lousy health care? Eva Perón.

In 1950, during a ceremony celebrating the taxi drivers' union, she fainted. The press reported she'd undergone an emergency appendectomy. The doctor who performed the surgery diagnosed some other lady parts trouble, but Eva refused to hear of it and sent him away. No one could make her listen. She continued her workaholic ways, sleeping two or three hours a night, eating little. She lost weight and continued to suffer abdominal pains. More doctors were called, but none of them could bring themselves to give her anything close to bad news. Eventually, she underwent a hysterectomy** (although she was told it was just a "necessary surgery"). No one ever told her she had cancer.

Accounts differ as to whether Eva died of uterine or cervical cancer.

** So completely was she kept in the dark about her situation that her surgery was performed by an oncologic surgeon flown in from Memorial Sloan Kettering. She never met him. He was spirited in and out, while she was still under anesthesia.

Same goes for Perón's first wife, Aurelia. The discrepancy isn't clear. In any case, the current thinking is that both women died of cervical cancer, caused by an aggressive strain of HPV carried by Juan.

Perón, it seems, was a common whore.

BY 1951, IT WAS CLEAR that Evita—now 32—was failing. She continued appearing in public, and continued giving increasingly crazy and paranoid speeches. Argentines tend not to have the fear of death that we Anglos do. Or, rather, the fear of watching someone die.

On August 22, Evita stood before her countrymen and -women and gave a rambling speech on her usual topic, the greatness of her husband. She exhorted people to embrace fanaticism, to crush their enemies, to be soldiers for Perón. Another presidential election had been scheduled for June 4 of the coming year—10 months away. Evita's followers had been pressing for a Perón-Perón ticket. La Señora, Our Lady of Hope, would be vice president, a heartbeat away from the presidency!* The crowd roared that she should accept the nomination anyway, but she dithered and vague-talked. She weighed less than 90 pounds and, as someone recalled, was "as green as spinach." Her hundreds of thousands of supporters saw with their own eyes that she was not long for this world. A few days later, she declined the nomination.

Evita was bedridden when it came time for her to cast her vote for Perón. A ballot box was brought to her bedside, and when the election officials emerged from the residence, women who'd been praying outside rushed to kiss the box that held her vote.

He won, handily. She insisted on participating in the inaugural parade, and a special wire and plaster contraption was made to hold her up in

---

* Perón's third wife, Isabel, would be elected vice president. After his death, she served as president from July 1, 1974, to March 24, 1976. She was the first female president in the world. This should feel like good news, but she presided over a particularly horrific era of Argentine history.

the convertible in which she and Juan stood and waved. Even though she had no idea what was wrong with her, and didn't want to know, she knew false hope when she heard it. In the end, a sort of truth prevailed, and she sent away the devoted minions who offered her flattery.

After she died, on July 26, 1952, not a single flower could be found in the entire city of Buenos Aires. They were all piled in great towering stacks outside the ministry where Evita had dispensed her favors.

AFTER SHE WAS GONE, the spell Eva had cast was broken. The economy hit the skids. There had been a pair of bad harvests. The European countries that had been decimated by World War II were starting to regain their footing. Perón lost his focus. He tried to continue the daily giving on behalf of the foundation but couldn't summon any interest. On special occasions, he took to broadcasting her speeches instead of giving his own. Formerly so dashing and matinee idol–like, he got fat. He started riding a scooter around town in a Windbreaker. Once he was seen for who he truly was—a corrupt old autocrat like the rest of them—it was only a matter of time (three years, to be exact) before he found himself in exile.

MY PERSONAL THEORY ABOUT the rise of the cult of Evita is that macho Argentina was simply starved for the feminine. Evita brought glamour, generosity, beauty, and a spirit of *vive la différence* to public life. In many ways Juan Perón was her Trojan horse. By standing up day after day and proclaiming her devotion to her husband, she could get away with saying and doing pretty much anything she wanted. And in a country where women were viewed as chattel, her mere insistence on being seen, heard, and respected made her extraordinarily difficult. People couldn't look away—nor could they resist her exotic, female charm.

CHAPTER 12

HELEN GURLEY BROWN

Relentless

HELEN GURLEY WAS A 36-year-old copywriter at L.A. advertising firm Foote, Cone & Belding when she traded in her rickety Chevy for a car that would change her life. Frugal by design and necessity, she'd intended to spring for a slightly newer, yet still used, Thunderbird. Instead, she glimpsed a gray Mercedes 190 SL—a truly elegant ride. On a whim, she plopped down $5,000 in cash ($42,505.63 in 2017 dollars) and drove the car off the lot. She was equal parts horrified to have spent so much money and gratified because she felt she deserved it—a radical notion for a woman in 1958.

A few months later, when Helen met her future spouse, twice-divorced film producer David Brown, the sight of her sliding into that gray Mercedes would confirm his belief that she was different from the silly starlets, models, and gold diggers he'd been dating. He found Helen's ability to save, then *spend* on a fine car, to be intoxicating.

They married in 1959—and that's when Helen Gurley Brown, at the ripe old age of 37, began her singular career as writer, magazine editor, and lifelong advocate for single girls. David Brown had a background in publishing, and with his encouragement Helen wrote the groundbreaking best seller *Sex and the Single Girl.* Her message that women could (and should!) enjoy the same things in life as men—sexual freedom, love, and money—is unremarkable now.* But in 1962 it was revolutionary. Three years later, at the age of

---

* That somehow every generation has to refight the battle to defend the notion that women deserve the same things as men is another essay for another time.

42—with not a single day of magazine experience—Helen became the editor-in-chief of *Cosmopolitan,* a job she would hold for the next 32 years.

Since her first issue in July 1965, *Cosmo* has been almost exactly the same, publishing dizzily upbeat articles on sex, love, work, men, and money for independent working women. For many years it was one of the most profitable magazines in America, and even after Helen was forced to retire in 1997, her successors were clever enough to retain her seemingly magical formula.

I have always admired Helen's ambition, tenacity, vision, and stubborn adherence to a philosophy of women's liberation that began to sound a little daft as the decades rolled by. She was the first (and pretty much only) voice advocating for the so-called single working girl in the postwar dark ages of the late 1950s and early '60s—a time when every female over the age of 21 who wasn't married or engaged to be married, and who couldn't afford to enroll in college to pursue a so-called MRS degree, was looked upon as pitiful.

But Helen Gurley embraced her pink-collar, working-girl life, logging an impressive 17 secretarial and two copyediting jobs. She supported herself, made a home for herself, and had a lot of steamy affairs (highlights included brief canoodles with crooner Rudy Vallée, prizefighter Jack Dempsey, the CEO of Revlon, a French painter, and a Swiss skier). A high school–educated, self-made woman who'd been born without beauty—then as now the coin of the realm—she nevertheless built a full life. By all rights she should have been happy to settle for any man who would have her. Instead, she messed around and settled down only when she was ready—and in so doing, inspired women of modest means to embrace their freedom and love their lives just as they were.

But just when I begin to feel all *you go girl!* about Helen, reveling in her self-made womanhood, I recall my first experience reading *Cosmopolitan.* I was babysitting three boys in the neighborhood sometime in the early 1970s. I was in junior high, wearing (as I did that entire summer) a pair of brown cord cutoffs that had faded to a soft tobacco color and an oversize baby blue T-shirt from Oak St. Surf Shop in Laguna Beach.

I came upon the issue in a pile of magazines atop the toilet tank in the master bath. There was a cleavage-y lady on the cover with quotes marching down the page on either side of her. The only memorable offering was something about the "unexpected" joys of taking a Chinese lover. I could barely coax Billy Mohr into holding my hand after band practice, much less benefit from a story about "taking" a lover of any ethnicity. Inside, I eagerly turned to the fashion horoscope. As a Pisces, I was advised to wear diaphanous caftans in shades of aqua, and strappy, jeweled sandals to make the men in my life go mad with desire.

I burst out laughing. Pretty much the same response when I flip through an issue of *Cosmo* today.

HELEN GURLEY was born in tiny Green Forest, Arkansas, in 1922. As an adult she would claim to come from poor hillbilly stock, but her father, Ira, was an attorney who served in the Arkansas state legislature. He was one of those dashing extroverts who made life seem more exciting the moment he walked into the room. Not so her mother, Cleo Gurley, who was quiet and "nice" and came from a good family. She was average in all ways, and therefore grateful to have landed a suitable husband. In truth, she felt more passion for her job—Cleo considered teaching her calling—which Ira insisted she quit, as all good wives did in those days. Cleo went on to have a difficult experience giving birth to both Helen and her older sister, Mary. When Helen was an adult, she remembered her mother saying that even though she loved her daughters, having babies wasn't all it was cracked up to be.

The family had moved to Little Rock by the time the Great Depression hit in 1929. Ira managed to hold on to most of the family savings, as well as his good job at the State Game and Fish Commission. They were safely moored in the middle class until Helen was 10, when her father was killed in a freak elevator accident. Rumors swirled that he had been so intent on catching a ride up with a pretty woman that he didn't see the closing doors and was caught between the shaft wall and the moving car.

Ira had been a well-loved man about town. The newspapers ran front-page stories reporting his shocking death and honoring his achievements. Helen was confused by the commingling of grief and giddiness she experienced during her family's 15 minutes in the spotlight. She felt, for a moment, celebrated—just like the movie stars she read about in *Silver Screen.*

The Gurleys' fortune would change, but not overnight. There had been a bit of savings, and Cleo had received some compensation for her loss from the state of Arkansas. Never an enthusiastic mother, her solution for raising her now-fatherless daughters involved allowing them unlimited sweets, movie magazines, and tickets to the weekly double feature. Even as a young teenager, Helen was captivated by money, fame, glitz, and glamour. Cleo was an excellent seamstress, and after hearing her daughter rave about the clothes in *It Happened One Night,* she whipped up a copy of Claudette Colbert's swanky satin wedding dress.

In 1937, when Helen was 15 and Mary was 19, Cleo moved the family to Los Angeles. The month after they settled in, Mary came down with what was thought to be the common flu. She attributed her stiff neck, arms, and legs to the cheap mattress on the twin bed in the room she shared with Helen. At the time, polio was one of the most feared infectious diseases in the nation, causing permanent paralysis and sometimes death—and Mary had contracted polio.* Although Helen and her sister shared a small bedroom and a toothbrush glass in the bathroom, the disease passed Helen by. For the rest of her life, Mary would be in a wheelchair, and Helen would feel equal parts relief and guilt that she had not been stricken as well.

HELEN WOULD GO ON to coin the term "mouseburger" to describe the kind of woman she believed herself to be: dull, plain, and lacking in native

---

* Polio is spread via infected fecal matter entering the mouth, which is appallingly more common than you might realize. Remember to wash your hands before you eat, gentle readers.

feminine charm. I suppose it was her spunky spin on "mousy"—a perfectly good word that unlike "mouseburger" does not conjure up a meat patty made of mice, served on a sesame seed bun.

Aside from being a little plain and thin as a stick insect, Helen was not mousy, but a dynamo. In high school she was an "apple polisher": ambitious, driven, determinedly cheerful, a proto-Tracy Flick. She was the kind of overachieving girl who had nicknames (Guppy and Good Time). She was the class valedictorian, and if anyone was custom-built for a successful college experience, it was her. But the tuition was simply too expensive. After a semester at Texas State College for Women, she returned home to L.A., where she enrolled in the much less expensive Woodbury Business College. She was 18, and paid for her own tuition with her first job, at KHJ radio station.

In the late 1940s and early 1950s, few things were more poignant than a woman forced to work for a living. A few years earlier, during World War II, it was a different story. The government—desperate for humans with two arms, two legs, a working heart, and a brain—had impressed upon women that it was their patriotic duty to work. Rosie the Riveter, with her saucy red polka-dot bandanna and arched eyebrow, was created to inspire women to join the armed forces and step into the industrial jobs vacated by men who'd enlisted.

Suddenly, women were needed. They were busy, they were contributing, and they dug it. Then the war ended, and those who were married were released from duty first—presumably so they could race home to wash the curtains, vacuum the carpet, and make a quick pot roast in preparation for their returning husbands. Single women working stateside were fired to open up jobs for returning soldiers; if they were lucky, they would step away from their workstation and straight into the arms of a future fiancé, who would put a ring on it, quick.

After the war, if you were over the age of 22 and you weren't married or engaged to be married, you were considered an old maid. You were probably living at home and working in one of the lady-approved jobs—teacher, nurse, secretary—while looking forward to a life of caring for aged parents and being a beloved auntie. Maybe you were still a virgin, saving your virtue for the husband who would give your life meaning, but who'd failed to materialize as yet.

Helen Gurley said fuck that.

Literally, she probably said that, for she was known for her salty language.

SOMETIMES A WOMAN IS considered difficult simply by pointing out the obvious; sometimes it's for drawing attention to something people suspect but wish to ignore. Helen's practical nature, rooted in her ability to both recognize a good opportunity and trust her gut, allowed her to see the potential in situations others might have remained blind to, and act on them.

At KHJ, she observed that the office environment offered the chance for a young woman with no attachments to hang out with a lot of men, most of whom were bored with their jobs or bored with their wives and open to having a fling. The working world was raining men.

Duty and sacrifice were of no interest to Helen Gurley. Having watched her mother suffer a mediocre marriage, sacrificing her career so she could do the correct wifely thing, she was not about to fall down that rabbit hole. But wishful thinking was also anathema. She was well aware that the most powerful weapon in a woman's arsenal was her looks. Helen never struck me as particularly homely, but she did suffer from a ferocious case of acne and was self-conscious about her lack of "bosoms." But by the standards of the time, she felt she couldn't measure up, and would never be one of those women (see Elizabeth Taylor) who could capture the attention of men simply by entering a room.

Instead, she repurposed the Serenity Prayer, accepting the things she couldn't change and changing the things she could. She figured that if she wasn't pretty, rich, or well educated, she could always work 10 times as hard as everyone else, and also be really good at sex. She came to learn from her life as a single girl that when it came to men, as long as you were naked and smiling, they were happy. In the era of No Sex Before Marriage, this attitude was societal high treason.

"From nine to five is actually a marvelous time to sink into a man," she would write in *Sex and the Single Girl*. "Even though hordes of your male co-workers are married, plenty of unattached or 'detached' men from the outside should be calling on your firm, thus giving you access to them—salesmen, consultants, suppliers, clients, friends of executives, even naughty chaps from the Internal Revenue Service who are auditing the corporate books."

The only women among the disc jockeys, sound engineers, and managers at KHJ were secretaries and receptionists. Every so often, the guys would launch into an impromptu game called scuttle, whereby they would chase one of the girls around the office, pin her down, and pull off her panties. Helen considered this good, clean workplace fun, on a par with going out for a smoke or a stroll around the block. Scuttle, or the promise of impending scuttle, could make a dull job exciting!

Decades later, in the 1970s, Helen would still defend scuttle as something to help while away the time at work. No matter that her cheery endorsement of flagrant harassment horrified prominent feminists. No matter that most workplaces were blatantly sexist, harboring environments where men felt entitled to grope the women who made their coffee and typed up their letters. Places where a game like scuttle . . . wait, hold on a second. Before I go any further we need to stop and imagine being chased around an office in 1950-whatever. Did the guys have to yank off a garter belt and girdle before getting to the panties? Because bare legs in a pair of kicky heels for work wasn't a thing then. Were the men treated to a full OB-GYN view of things once the panties came off? Helen, Helen, Helen: How could you have thought this sort of thing livened up an otherwise-ho-hum workday?

DURING HER 20S AND EARLY 30S, Helen hopped from secretarial job to secretarial job. Once she was fired for sleeping off a hangover under her desk, and once she was fired for not sleeping with her boss. (Just because she was pro-office canoodling doesn't mean she wasn't discriminating.)

In 1951, at the age of 29, Helen entered *Glamour* magazine's annual "Ten Girls with Taste" contest, honoring young women of modest means who still managed to live with style. The contestants enthused, on a lengthy questionnaire, about their work wardrobes, cooking secrets, and personal credos. Helen made the finals but wasn't chosen. Two years later she tried again, taking poetic license with her application. She invented a new, more fetching wardrobe, feigned more interest in cooking for friends than she actually possessed, and fabricated an interest in being a copywriter. (A hunch told her that a girl with ambition would be more appealing to the judges.) This time, she triumphed. The grand prize was a trip to Hawaii; the grander prize was a personal phone call from a junior editor at *Glamour* to Helen's boss at Foot, Cone & Belding, where she worked as a secretary, suggesting it was time she was promoted. In 1952, at the age of 30, Helen became one of the agency's first female copywriters.

As we know from *Mad Men,* ad agency sexism is a species all its own. Women were generally thought to be too high-strung and emotional to write ad copy (find an occupation coveted by men and you will find a far-fetched reason why women cannot cut it). When women *were* allowed into the ranks, they were immediately saddled with all the products targeted at the ladies. Helen wound up working on campaigns for diet plans, bathing suits, and Max Factor eye makeup. Even though she was relegated to the lady-product ghetto, she became, over the course of the next half dozen years, the best paid female copywriter in L.A.

Helen enjoyed her freewheeling romantic life into her 30s. Some of her beaux were married, some weren't. But in the end she was like anyone else: She would get involved with the man du jour, become attached, and when the romance ran its course—as it inevitably would—she would be broken-hearted. She decided that maybe a spot of therapy was in order. Who knew there were so many kooky methodologies to choose from in 1957? She tried hypnosis, so-called touch therapy, and psychodrama. Nude group therapy was a thing: Patients took turns standing naked in the middle of the group, cataloging what they liked or didn't like about their bodies. Helen disparaged her too-wide hips, her too-small breasts. The point was to demonstrate that body shame was universal—though the most famous outcome would be Helen's insistence on using only big-breasted models on the cover of *Cosmo*.

In 1958, when Helen was 36 years old, a friend threw a dinner party and seated her beside David Brown, then·head of the story department at 20th Century Fox. After the party, David walked Helen to her car—the stylish gray Mercedes.

HELEN AND DAVID WERE MARRIED at Beverly Hills City Hall on September 25, 1959. She wore a long-sleeved fitted-waist dress and a strand of pearls, bought off the rack. (Hell if she was going to spend a fortune on a wedding dress.) David, known for being a gentleman with a literary bent, wore a dark suit. He had started out as a magazine journalist and editor before moving to L.A. Eventually he would partner with Richard Zanuck at 20th Century Fox to produce *The Sting, Jaws,* and other classics.

Helen was not interested in quitting her job to sit around being a wife—or God forbid, a mother. She remembered how miserable her own mother had been and, anticipating what pregnancy might wreak on her svelte figure, took childbirth off the table. Still, there were traditional components to the Browns' union. She fussed over him in typically wifely ways. It was a point of pride for her that no matter how busy she was, she would cook his dinner every night. She obsessed about his weight, in addition to her own, and made him weigh himself every morning.

But mostly, they were also a team: a pair of indefatigable workaholics. Helen loved to work. Her capacity for it was staggering. Over the years, what had originally been a matter of putting food on her table and a roof over her own head had given her life meaning. This runs counter to what so many of us are taught, and what we teach our children—to first *find* your passion, then go for it. In Helen's case, poverty and necessity had come first.

SEX AND THE SINGLE GIRL was David's idea. Then as now, "write what you know" was the cornerstone for aspiring authors, and David thought his wife's take on the open secret of workplace affairs might be intriguing. Helen loved the idea, and felt she had plenty to say about it. She knew it was a man's world: vastly unfair to women and particularly unfair to single working girls. Still, she didn't let inequity stop her; she was an eager proponent of gaming the system. The best chance a woman had for getting what she wanted, she asserted, was to figure out how to manipulate men and the world they claimed. Presumably, the two and a half million people who would buy *Sex and the Single Girl* when it came out in 1962 understood this as well.

The book is both ridiculous and empowering. Yearn for tips on some intensely creepy flirting? "Look into his eyes as though tomorrow's daily double winner were there. Never let your eyes leave his. Concentrate on his left eye . . . then on his right . . . now deep into both." Want to know how to decorate a man-pleasing apartment? (Did you even think there was such a thing until you read that sentence just now?) Aim to make yourself appear fascinating with "gobs" of pictures, travel posters, a TV set, books, and a hi-fi stereo. Your "sexy kitchen" should be equipped with a spice rack with at least 30 spices. This conveys that you love to cook—and nothing is sexier. (Even though you shouldn't cook too much; one of the main reasons for taking a lover is his willingness to pay for stuff, dinners at fancy restaurants included.)

Still, the money chapter reads, with a few exceptions, as if it were written last week, and under the tutelage of trendy Marie Kondo: Don't buy stuff you don't need. Only buy things you find beautiful, or that make you feel beautiful. Learn how finances work, learn how to manage your money, and take advantage of the fact that as a single working girl no one expects you to live beyond your means.

Published by Bernard Geis & Company, the book's original title, *Sex for the Single Girl*, sounded alarmingly prescriptive. So "for" was swapped with "and," and Helen was on the map. *Sex and the Single Girl* was the "it" book of 1962, selling an astonishing two million copies in three weeks. When people weren't worrying about the Cuban missile crisis, they were wondering how they'd missed the memo that it was a lot more fun being single than married. The reviews were mixed, verging on terrible. It was "tasteless" *(Los Angeles Times)*, "libel against womanhood" *(San Francisco Chronicle* letter to the editor), "racy and sassy . . . but full of hard-core common sense" *(Houston Chronicle)*.

Helen made no bones about the fact the book was for girls who had nothing, came from nowhere, and had to get by on their wits. When someone accused her of writing the book for money, she said, why of course she did. "I love money!" she laughed. She didn't read the bad reviews and seemed impervious to criticism.

Off she went on a book tour, becoming one of the first authors to do so. Thirteen weeks later, after visiting 28 cities and appearing on every television and radio show that would have her (even late-night call-in shows where incensed listeners who hadn't bothered to read the book phoned in to suggest she be burned at the stake), she had the country in the palm of her hand. She smiled, flirted, and shilled her way through appearances on the *Today* show, the *Tonight Show, Merv Griffin*. Her inner workaholic was fulfilled: Success begat success. The movie rights to the book were sold to Warner Brothers. Thirty-five countries snapped up the foreign rights. David was thrilled that she'd not simply found her niche, but created one that she alone occupied: an expert on how girls (they were always girls) could—and should—live it up before marriage. "I think marriage is insurance for the *worst* years of your life," she wrote in the book. "During your best years, you don't need a husband. You do need a man, of course—every step of the way—and they are often cheaper emotionally and a lot more fun by the dozen."

That Helen was no longer single, but loved, supported, advised, and promoted by a powerful, influential husband avoided irony by underscoring her book's main thesis: You don't have to be pretty to land a great husband; you simply need to use your single-working-girl years to "work like wharf rats" to develop your strong points and become independent, interesting, and sexy. And most of all, to have fun.

The book's sequel, *Sex and the Office,* appeared in 1965. Helen's editor, Bernard Geis, wanted a repeat of *Sex and the Single Girl.* He quashed Helen's more radical and progressive views. Out went the chapters on how to find the most effective contraception, what to do about date rape, lesbianism (it's bound to happen, she insisted, with all those young, sex-positive girls in the steno pool!), and how to get an abortion. The book did well by regular publishing standards, but wasn't the massive best seller they'd hoped for.

Part of the problem was the zeitgeist. The world was changing. There was a new, serious conversation beginning to brew about the status of women. In 1963, Betty Friedan had published *The Feminine Mystique,* in which she described how most of her fellow Smith College graduates dutifully got married after graduation, moved to the suburbs, had a few kids, and were now bored out of their minds (as Helen Gurley Brown, without her fancy college degree, might have predicted). Friedan's book precipitated the second wave of feminism. It received serious attention in all the correct, serious places. Even though Helen had blazed the trail, insisting that women and men deserved the same things, *Sex and the Single Girl* bore the cultural stigma of being too perky and full of advice (including a homemade solution for bleaching the hair on your arms).

The times may have been a-changin' but Helen still received so much fan mail that her postman in Pacific Palisades refused to deliver it. (She had to go to the substation and fetch it herself.) She had always been an avid letter writer, and tried to answer each one. She prided herself on being able to type 80 words a minute on her Royal 440 typewriter. David thought that if she had her own magazine, she could in a matter of speaking answer all the letters at once. To that end, Helen and David created a prototype for

Femme at their Southern California kitchen table. When they went to New York to pitch it, they discovered a better solution: to take over the ailing *Cosmopolitan,* a once-great literary magazine that had grown anemic in recent years.

Founded in 1886, *Cosmo* had an illustrious history. Some of the editors who blew through on their way to greatness: Ulysses S. Grant, Jr., and William Randolph Hearst. It published Ernest Hemingway, John Steinbeck, and Edna Ferber. Moreover, David had been the managing editor of the magazine in the late 1940s, and he also knew people who knew people. In a matter of days, it was decided that Helen would take over as editor in chief, folding all of their ideas for *Femme* into a new, improved *Cosmopolitan* to be targeted at Helen's readership: single working girls of modest means and education, hoping to make their mark in the world.

Helen was 43 when she took over as editor-in-chief. Her magazine experience was limited to reading them. She might as well have been entering an operating theater to perform an appendectomy. Every person on her staff had more experience than she did, including her own secretary. She had no idea how to manage people, oversee editorial budgets, and translate her vision into magazine-ese.

Later, when telling the story about the first few months at the magazine, she would admit how scared she was, and how she would call David and beg him to come collect her in their town car for a cruise around Manhattan. Cuddled together in the backseat, she would pour out her woes and they would brainstorm new stories. By the end of the ride he would have buoyed her up enough to face the rest of the day. No steel magnolia ever loved this damsel-in-distress business more than Helen. "Women are all female impersonators, to some degree," the celebrated author and activist Susan Brownmiller once said. And Helen was a master: an iron-willed she-wolf in silky sheep's clothing.

To whatever degree she felt truly terrified or insecure, Helen never abandoned the central organizing principles of her life: to trust her gut and work harder than everyone else. Her gut said, If I care deeply about men, sex, love, money, and looking hot at all times, other women will too. Her premise was simple and answered the hoary old Freudian question: What do women want?

What men want, silly.

The July 1965 issue of *Cosmo* was her first. The blond cover model wore a plunging red-and-white gingham top that displayed her "bosoms" to full advantage. David wrote the come-on headline.

In the dark contraceptive ages of the 1940s and '50s, a woman had to either prove she was married or pretend to be to be fitted for a diaphragm by her doctor. In 1960 the Food and Drug Administration approved the first oral contraceptive, but the Pill wasn't available to married women in all states until 1965; unmarried women didn't have access until 1972. Despite the fact *Cosmo* was geared to single girls (who presumably wouldn't be able to snag a prescription unless they lied), Helen ran a story about the Pill in her first issue. Hearst axed "The Pill That Makes Women More Responsive to Men" as being too risqué. The problem was solved by deleting the last two words. The story became "The New Pill that Makes Women More Responsive." What does that even mean? The would-be readership was in a sexy frame of mind, and took a wild (and accurate) guess. The issue flew off the stands.

As did the one after that, and the one after that. Under Helen's editorship, *Cosmopolitan* became the most successful newsstand magazine in the nation.

A few editors quit during her first few months at the helm. Those who stuck it out found Helen to be straightforward, fair, and exacting. She was against all forms of negativity, and also complex sentences. She was not afraid of italics, and she never met an exclamation point she didn't like! During editorial meetings, she either stood in front of her desk or kicked off her shoes and curled up on the couch. Her managerial style was essentially to flirt with everyone, because that was something at which she was expert—and it seemed to work. With nothing but faith in herself and what women wanted—which was, in essence, what *she* wanted—Helen upped the *Cosmo* circulation from 800,000 to three million.

BUT THEN CAME the 1970s and Gloria Steinem (see Chapter 3). Yes, there were other feminists of equal influence and importance—Betty Friedan, co-founder and president of the National Organization for Women; U.S. Representative "Battling" Bella Abzug; and Kate Millett, author of the seminal 1970 *Sexual Politics,* which was adapted from her doctoral dissertation at Columbia—but it was pretty freelance journalist Gloria, with her perfect features and aviator glasses, who captured the public's imagination.

Betty, Bella, Gloria, and Kate locked arms, and behind them marched a tribe of smart, college-educated women who thought Helen was the enemy. They despaired of Helen's determined belief in promoting female artifice; capped teeth, pancake makeup, push-up bras, wigs, and false eyelashes* made them want to pull out their unstyled hair. Helen further drove them mad by insisting that women enjoyed makeup, fashion, and looking sexy— and that women could be traditionally feminine and powerful, making her a *Sex and the City* feminist while Candace Bushnell was still awaiting her 14-year molars. But pro-nookie, pro-have your own apartment, pro-have your own money, pro-birth control, pro-choice Helen Gurley Brown was locked out of the feminist clubhouse.

One morning in 1970, a gang of feminists, led by Kate Millett, barged into the offices of *Cosmopolitan* and staged a sit-in. Fresh from a successful 11-hour occupancy at *Ladies' Home Journal,* where they pressed editor John Mack Carter to turn over an entire issue to the cause (they wound up settling for eight pages), they set their sights on Helen. They backed her up against the radiator, arguing that her magazine was sexist and woman hating and that she would do well to consider more feminist content.

"We're already a feminist book," said Helen. But to appease them, she agreed to consider any and all articles they wished to publish in her magazine,

---

* Which sorority girls now don with their yoga pants and Uggs to grab a post-hangover grande latte on Saturday mornings.

with the requirement that she would have editorial control. They agreed. As these things usually go, only a few articles were written and submitted, and Helen went back to work.

To further display her good faith in the movement, Helen agreed to go to a consciousness-raising session. Sometime before the end of 1970 she presented herself at a gathering but couldn't help being wry: "Twelve of us—I almost said girls, but they say I must stop that and refer to us as women—sat about and related our hang-ups. Frankly, I was only into my eighth hang-up when I had to relinquish the floor to the next hang up-ee." One could call her the Tenacious HGB.

But as the years passed, Helen was increasingly on the wrong side of history, and her famous instincts began to fail her. She refused to have anything to do with motherhood, claiming that nothing could be more oppressive or less sexy. Plus, it ruined your figure.

She also displayed her ignorance about HIV and AIDs. In the January 1988 issue of *Cosmo,* she ran a minimizing, inaccurate article called "Reassuring News about AIDS: A Doctor Tells You Why You May Not Be at Risk." Even after U.S. Surgeon General C. Everett Koop wrote an alarmed letter, she refused to print a retraction or update, for fear of seeming antisex.

IN 1997, AT THE AGE OF 75, Helen was asked to step down from the flagship magazine but stayed on as the editor of *Cosmo*'s 65 international editions. Her new office had pink silk wallpaper and leopard-print furnishings. For the next 15 years, she would get up in the morning, pack a lunch of tuna salad in a recycled yogurt container, slip into her pink Pucci miniskirt, black fishnets, and Manolo Blahniks, and head to the office, as she had done for more than 50 years. She refused to be philosophical about old age. As long as she was upright, she would wear perfume, bangles, and high heels and bat her false eyelashes at the doorman. People disparaged her for refusing to granny-fy herself, but why shouldn't she be the kind of woman she wanted to be for the whole of her life? This is how it should be. We should forget the calendar. We should stop tallying the number of high school reunions we've attended, and shrug it off that all the songs we once made out to are now golden oldies. We should all do whatever it is that makes us feel good about ourselves, and about who we are in the world, until we're bored by it. Helen was never bored by feeling frisky, feminine, and a little outrageous, and good on her.

Helen died in August 2012 at the age of 90,* but her spirit lives on in the pages of *Cosmopolitan*. Go to your local grocery store—not Whole Foods, or anywhere too concerned with the organic side of things—and there at the checkout stand behold the current issue. On the cover there will be a young woman with copious cleavage, framed by a series of come-ons that promise a better body, better sex, and a better way to make/save/spend your money. And on the cover of the issue I'm looking at this very minute, "The New Shows to Binge Watch." That seems a little outside *Cosmo*'s usual purview, until you get to #stayinbed.

Helen was at the swinging single-girl party first, and stayed there until last call. She remained defiant until the end, impervious to criticism, relentless in her defense of her own belief in what girls really wanted. "If you're not a sex object, you're in trouble," she once famously said. Helen Gurley Brown was perfectly incorrigible, and a lot smarter than anyone gave her credit for. In other words, a difficult woman at her best.

---

* "... though parts of her are considerably younger," according to the *New York Times*.

CHAPTER 13

EDIE SEDGWICK

Decadent

ONE DAY IN 1963, when Edie Sedgwick was 20, she invited her friends to lunch at the Ritz in Boston. Her father, she claimed, had an account there. The parents of the soon-to-be It Girl and muse of Andy Warhol lived on a ranch in the wilds of Santa Barbara, California; it seemed unlikely that Duke Sedgwick would have an account at this particular hotel.

At the time, Edie was a student at Radcliffe studying sculpture. Her friends were mostly young gay men on Harvard's arty fringe. At the extravagant meal, they guzzled as much expensive champagne as humanly possible; Edie ordered roast beef with Russian dressing. (This was her favorite dish, although she never touched it.)

All the young men had brought money to cover the bill in case Edie had simply made the whole thing up, which was a distinct possibility. (She was cherished, in part, because of her complete indifference to reality.) The bill came, and she signed for it. The waiter went away and returned with the manager. As the story goes, Edie's dining companions all sobered up fast, worried that their friend had been busted. They began reaching in their pockets for cash, and were prepared to make an apology on her behalf. But the manager just wanted to confirm that she meant to leave a 100 percent tip. The lunch was $250 give or take, and she had left an additional $250 for the waiters, who bowed their heads at her generosity. Edie celebrated by standing on the table and singing "Loads of Love," from a recent Richard Rodgers musical.

As for the tip, Ed Hennessy (who related the anecdote in Jean Stein and George Plimpton's classic oral history of Edie's life) discovered later that Edie had just been winging it. She didn't have a clue about tipping, and had never left one in her entire life.

Shortly after this episode, Edie ditched Radcliffe for New York, where in 1964 she met Andy Warhol, becoming his muse and "superstar" of his New York City studio, known as The Factory. She modeled for *Vogue* and was proclaimed the It Girl of 1965 before plunging deeper into drug addiction and dying in her sleep from an accidental overdose at 28. Bob Dylan's "Just Like a Woman" was said to be inspired by her. Robert Rauschenberg declared her a living work of art. Lena Dunham, another member of the It Girl sorority, occasionally posts pictures of Edie in her various iterations on Instagram—attracted, as we all were and are, to her insouciance and fatal charm.

I've read Stein and Plimpton's *Edie: American Girl* half a dozen times over the years. The first was in 1982, the month it was published. I was only a bit older than Edie was when she split for New York, and I was both enthralled and envious. Like Edie, I was a girl from Southern California who had also moved to New York for a time—but there the comparison ended. She was so pretty, so skinny, so glamorously messed up. That platinum hair with the intentional roots. The chandelier earrings and "anthracite eyes," a term coined by Diana Vreeland, editor of *Vogue* (see Chapter 23). I believed John Anthony Walker's poetic observation that Edie "had the capacity to create instantly the world around her." Of her he wrote, "You entered Edie's world and nothing tangential made any difference: everything else fell away and there Edie was in the middle of a pirouette."

Everything about Edie was mythic. She came from a great American family. The Sedgwicks were equal parts rich, influential, and eccentric since the founding of our nation. Along with the de Forests (Edie's mother's people), various Sedgwicks helped settle the Massachusetts Bay Colony, signed the Declaration of Independence, served as Speaker of the House under George Washington, founded colleges (Williams) and railroads (Southern Pacific), and created Central Park. Edie's fifth-great-grandfather, Judge Theodore Sedgwick, was the first in the country to win a case arguing for the freedom of an African-American woman. (And in case you were wondering: Kyra Sedgwick is Edie's first cousin, once removed.)

Edie was born and grew up on a 3,000-acre ranch in Santa Barbara, where she was homeschooled with her seven siblings. They had those rich people names: Saucie, Suky, Minty. They called their dad Fuzzy. There's a midwestern saying about people who migrate to the West Coast: If you tip America on its side and shake it up and down, all the nuts wind up at the bottom, in California. This was more or less the situation with Edie's father, Francis Minturn "Duke" Sedgwick, who was deemed by the more-staid Sedgwicks to be "arty" (code for a little crazy). At one point he was diagnosed with manic-depressive disorder and "nervous breakdowns."

Duke had a preferred psychiatric hospital, Silver Hill in New Canaan, Connecticut, where he also sent his children when they started showing signs of not being the people he wanted them to be. In 1962, when Edie was 19, she was sent there at her father's insistence to deal with her anorexia. It didn't work. Her older brother, Minty, was sent there when he came out of the closet and Duke disapproved. Later, Minty hanged himself with a necktie.

I'm not dismissing the severity of the Sedgwicks' mental illness. It was real and debilitating and caused a lot of genuine anguish. Still, right or wrong, for those of us who hail from the murderously dull middle-class suburbs, there is something enchanting about upper-class mental instability. (Maybe it's that their breakdowns always allow for plenty of time off, at a place with heavy plaid lap robes and a restful view.) We middle-classers also suffer nervous breakdowns, but they generally consist of taking a fake sick day from work, sitting on the couch in our sad coffee-stained bathrobes with a pint of ice cream, and binge-watching something mediocre on TV. The next morning we're back in fine fettle, because we have to be.

After she moved to New York in 1964, Edie drove a gray Mercedes-Benz, often on acid. When a friend of hers crashed it, she switched to a limo service. As her onetime flame, Bob Dylan crony Bob Neuwirth, said: "Edie went through limousine companies the way people go through cigarettes. She never paid her bills, so the limousine people would shut off her credit, and she'd switch to another company. The drivers loved her madly, because she'd dole out these 25- and 35-dollar tips."

I have always felt conflicted about adoring Edie. She was a fragile girl, wounded bird division. The kind of girl men rush in to protect, to rescue, to make excuses for, to celebrate. The exact kind of woman I normally struggle to wrap my feminist arms around.

And still, her March 1966 spread in *Vogue* is captivating. The camera loved her. Just try to take your eyes off of her.

Maybe we can't help but adore Edie. Maybe it's just not our fault. A wise philosopher friend of mine (literally, he had a Ph.D. in philosophy) once explained that girls have never been swept away by *Star Wars* because it doesn't tell the archetypal female hero's journey. The archetypal female hero's journey, according to my friend, is exemplified in *Dirty Dancing*. Specifically, the way nobody puts Baby in the corner. Women, according to my friend, want to be seen and appreciated for everything they are, *just* as they are. Edie lives on in our imaginations because she made a life out of doing nothing but being Edie.

NEW YORK IN 1965 was all about Edie. *Vogue* called her a youthquaker:

the perfect, awkward-in-retrospect descriptor for the times. Her love-fest with Andy Warhol, in which she starred in multiple underground films he directed, was surprisingly short-lived: Their association lasted only from 1965 to early 1966. People said that Andy believed Edie would be his ticket to Hollywood. Together they made 18 films, which are (in my humble opinion) total unwatchable crap. His first film with Edie, *Poor Little Rich Girl*, starred Edie being Edie (a great subject, as we know). Half of it was out of focus. I survived a semester of experimental film theory, and I can tell you there are genuinely bizarre and successful underground films *(Scorpio Rising, Pink Flamingos)*. But the Warhol oeuvre looks as if it came from a student auteur on the verge of flunking out of film school. Andy financed the movies from the sale of his paintings. He didn't pay Edie a penny, which (understandably) she began to resent.

Booze, coke, uppers, downers, and speedballs. These were the drugs that Edie took from morning till night. Sometime in 1967, *Vogue* stopped calling. There was some high-schoolish infighting between the Factory hipster crowd and Bob Dylan's hipster crowd—and when Edie took up with Bob Neuwirth, her time with Warhol was over. She moved in to the Chelsea Hotel, then accidentally set her room on fire when she nodded off holding a cigarette.

Here is something I don't understand: For all the great love people had for Edie, where were they when she began her slide into deep addiction? Where were the young men from Harvard's arty fringe? Where was Andy Warhol, who, upon hearing of her death in 1971, reputedly said, "Edie who?" The coroner's report listed the cause of Edie's death as undetermined/accident/suicide. It's tremendously sad. Still, the mystery suits her.

In 1969, after sustaining serious burns in the Chelsea Hotel fire, Edie went home to California to try to get herself together. She struggled to stay sober, and after an arrest in August of that year, she was admitted to a psychiatric hospital where she met her future husband, the dashing hippie Michael Post. They married in 1971, and their wedding picture shows Edie looking like the typical California girl she once was; her brown hair is shoulder-length, glossy, center-parted. She wears a white lace dress with bell sleeves and holds a white magnolia, still on its stem. Michael Post wears a fancy tux. They both grin into the sun.

Edie's death on November 16, 1971, came not on the heels of some major youth culture happening, but after a fashion show at the Santa Barbara Museum (how staid), where she drank too much. Afterward, she responsibly called her husband to pick her up. At home, Michael Post gave Edie some medication prescribed by her doctor. In the morning, she didn't wake up. She was 28 years old.

LISTEN, LADIES, we all do too much. I don't even have to know what you do to know that it is too much. We are exhausted—or at least I am—by the demands of American womanhood. Our contemporary It Girls and superstars work too much. Rather than exuding the languorous appeal befitting the hip, famous, and gorgeous, they always seem to be slaving away. They endure Navy Seal–level workouts, to which they submit daily before dawn, and special enjoyment-free diets. They live in a state of eternal, sexy selfie, red-carpet readiness, smooth, waxed, and starving, and tend their Instagram accounts with the obsessive attention usually reserved for rare orchids. Madonna once said, "I live a highly scheduled life. There's absolutely no time wasted. I'm very focused."

Edie's life, on the other hand, was unscheduled, wasteful, unfocused. She possessed the sexy louche aura of someone perpetually smoking a cigarette. Her idea of exercise was a few ballet stretches upon awaking, sometime around noon. She liked to lie around listening to opera. She showed up for fashion shoots in a T-shirt and a pair of black tights (which then became all the rage).

Can't we all be a little more like this? Sleeping in, eating something whenever, moving around when our bodies demand it, showing up for our appointments in whatever we feel like wearing? We might be viewed as being a little decadent, a little difficult. But let's agree not to care, shall we?

CHAPTER 14

ANGELA MERKEL

Inscrutable

THE BERLIN WALL CAME DOWN on November 9, 1989. It was a Thursday, and on Thursdays Dr. Angela Merkel left the Central Institute of Physical Chemistry at the Academy of Sciences, where she worked as a research scientist, to take a nice, long sauna. Here was a woman so disciplined and unflappable that even at a turning point in her country's history, she still wasn't about to miss out on one of the few joys of her week. While other East Germans rushed across the border into West Germany, Angela didn't see the need. "I figured if the wall had opened, it was hardly going to close again, so I decided to wait," she said later. Afterward, pink-cheeked and relaxed from the heat, she allowed herself to be swept over the Bornholmer bridge and into West Berlin, where she had a beer and then walked back home. After all, she had to work in the morning.

This anecdote is often trotted out in the press to demonstrate the stolid, methodical, and passionless nature of Germany's first female chancellor, a position Angela Merkel has held since 2005. According to this theory, Angela's celebrated steady-as-she-goes management style belies the fact that on a fundamental level, she is a little odd.* On this day, of all days, when the Eastern bloc was no more and Germany was reunited, how

---

* John Kornblum, the U.S. ambassador to Germany, who in 1999 reopened the American Embassy in Berlin after the reunification, called Angela's governing style "mashed potatoes"—meaning bland and boring. I don't know about you, but I love mashed potatoes, especially with garlic and butter.

could the woman who would in six short years become the leader of the nation, as well as the de facto president of the European Union, be so blasé? Why wasn't *she* weeping with joy and dancing in the streets and making out with strangers like other Ossis (as the "Easties" are called), drunk on liberty and newfound possibilities? People didn't understand her behavior, and so they didn't understand her.

Brilliant, introspective, and inscrutable, Angela Merkel enjoys a global reputation as an enigma—in part, because her personality belies the female stereotype. Angela isn't shrill, chatty, erratic, emotional, or frivolous, so no one knows what to make of her. And once you refuse to be pigeonholed—especially if you're a woman in power—you become known as difficult.

Angela doesn't *look* difficult. No one lays an eye on her and thinks, Here comes trouble. Her chancellor uniform consists of black pants, low heels, a bright jacket, and a necklace. Sometimes she goes a little crazy with the necklace and accidentally makes a fashion statement. She still wears her hair in the standard bowl cut she's sported since she was a girl—but lately she's added some blond highlights.

Saturday Night Live's Kate McKinnon, the show's utility player for all blond female politicians, portrays Angela as awkward and secretly in love with Barack Obama. McKinnon's German accent is good, and the impersonation hilarious—but it's not really spot-on. In private, peers say, Angela has a sharp sense of humor (she's an expert mimic of arrogant men in power). And it supposedly took her a long time to warm up to President Obama—in part because Obama is also cool, intellectual, and analytical. A political reporter for *Die Welt* once wrote they were like "two hit men in the same room. They don't have to talk; both are quiet, both are killers."

ANGELA KASNER was born in Hamburg, West Germany, in 1954. Her father, Horst, was a Lutheran pastor, and moved the family—her mother,

Herlind, a Latin and English teacher, and two younger brothers—to East Germany. Horst had been offered a pastorate in Templin, located in the Uckermark, a rural region known for its deep forest and cold lakes. They were moving against the tide of emigration. Other East Germans, fearing the repressive fallout of Soviet occupation, were moving west before a more liberated life was no longer an option. When Angela was seven, she watched the Berlin Wall go up, sealing her off from freedom, opportunity, and the free exchange of ideas.

Angela felt caged in but made the best of it, excelling in school and becoming a star of the Russian Club, a Soviet-backed educational program that encouraged the kids of its satellite states to master the mother tongue. Angela had a gift for pinpointing what she excelled in and forgetting everything else. As a girl she was gawky and uncoordinated, so sports were dead to her. She could manage a hike without tripping over her own feet, and grew to love the outdoors. At home, life was serious. Dinner conversation might involve drilling down into the arguments of Kant.

Hardships aside, young Angela was shielded from Western consumerism. The trade-off for missing out on shimmery pink lipstick, push-up bras, and miniskirts was a sense of herself as smart, competent, and powerful. This view was never undermined by the itchy insecurity advertisers work to instill in girls and women, convincing us from puberty onward that if only we buy this (fill in the blank), we would be slimmer, smoother, silkier, prettier, sexier.

If you raised a girl in a society where frivolity and consumerism weren't valued, where you were never told you would be prettier if you smiled or lost weight, where you were allowed to find the thing you were good at and zero in on it, you might grow up to be Angela Merkel.

IN 1973 ANGELA ENTERED Leipzig University, where she earned a degree in physics, then earned a doctorate in quantum chemistry at the German

Academy of Sciences in Berlin.* In 1977, when she was 23, she married another physicist, Ulrich Merkel. They divorced in 1982, after she became enamored of Joachim Sauer, a professor of theoretical chemistry. The Stasi (the East German secret police) noted they lunched together often when they were married to other people. Both scientists left their spouses and moved in together in 1988, eventually marrying a decade later, and they are together still.

When the wall fell in 1989, Angela was 35, the only woman in the chemistry department. Even though she appeared to be completely absorbed in co-writing papers with titles like "Vibrational Properties of Surface Hydroxyls: Nonempirical Model Calculations Including Anharmonicities," she remained alert to the seismic political changes afoot. Since she was 14, she'd followed politics (once hiding in the girls' restroom to listen to the returns from the West German presidential election), and she smelled opportunity in the reunification of the nation. In 1990 Angela was hired to be a deputy spokesperson for Lothar de Maizière, the first (and only) democratically elected president of East Germany. A year later, after the reunification, she ran for state representative to the Bundestag, the federal legislative body. In a scant year she had completely discarded her science career for one in politics, having become a minister in the new government of a united Germany.

I'm curious: Now that a businessman and reality show star has become president of the United States, will the ongoing consternation over why Dr. Angela Merkel, physicist and quantum chemist, so abruptly left science for politics subside? This 180-degree career switcheroo is yet another measure of how indecipherable she is said to be. But Angela was never anything if not ambitious, and in the German Democratic Republic (GDR), the sciences were a field in which a citizen could make her mark. (Also, gymnastics, but that was a complete nonstarter.)

---

* The layman's definition of quantum chemistry is quantum physics as applied to chemistry. So, basically, a lot of incomprehensible theories expressed as mathematical equations on a whiteboard.

Angela, with her analytic mind and deep, hidden well of ambition, saw the future. She may not have been dancing with a lamp shade on her head celebrating the fall of the wall—but she saw that radical change would be coming, and coming quickly. A situation this fluid and unstable offered opportunities—big ones.

Angela walked into the offices of the newly formed East German political party Democratic Awakening and asked for a job.** She started small, running for local offices and winning ever-larger elections until one day she caught the eye of Helmut Kohl, the stocky, unrefined chancellor who signed the German Reunification Treaty and was reelected in a landslide.

It was 1990. As the guy who oversaw the successful reunification of the nation, Kohl was in the market for an East German woman to serve in his cabinet. The unassuming Angela fit the bill nicely. "She looked like a typical GDR scientist, wearing a baggy skirt, Jesus sandals, and a cropped haircut," said Lothar de Maizière. She also smoked like a fiend and bit her nails.

It was nothing for Kohl to take her under his wing. Look at the broad-minded, influential West German man championing the poor, intellectual East German woman! Angela was quiet and frumpy and made for great optics. She was nonthreatening, with her bowl cut and complete disinclination to flirt or make small talk. He called her *mein Mädchen,* "my girl." In 1991, Kohl appointed her minister for women and youth, even though she expressed not a whit of interest in either women or children. Nor in clothes, shoes, handbags, makeup, sports cars, or any of the other things now available to her as a German politician. In 1994, she became minister for the environment and nuclear safety, a job she was better suited for, given her academic background. Secretly, she longed for more.

Meanwhile, Democratic Awakening had been absorbed into the Christian Democratic Union, the main right-of-center political party. With

---

** They gave her one that day—setting up the office computers.

my American binary political party brain, I cannot begin to parse the many parties of Germany—but for our purposes, it's interesting to note that Angela was never a natural fit with the CDU, which was Catholic and conservative and believed the role of women was limited to popping out *kinder*. She was the daughter of a Lutheran minister, a practicing Protestant, divorced, childless, and living with the man who wouldn't become her husband until 1998. She was a misfit in every conceivable way, and it's a measure of her instincts for politics that she was able to leverage the association.

Of the many weapons Angela Merkel possesses—her formidable intellect, her chess master's ability to see all the plays on the board, her patience—the greatest is her complete lack of vanity. She had no problem being treated like Helmut Kohl's pet for as long as it took to gain power. She allowed herself to be overlooked, underestimated, and mocked for lack of feminine appeal. Another woman might have left her husband for a movie star, written a children's book, launched a high-profile charity—*something* to show that she wasn't just chopped liver.

But being perceived as chopped liver is one of Angela's main plays. While no one is paying much attention to her, she quickly figures out her opponent's weakness, then waits until he makes a mistake. Usually, that opponent is a self-admiring man who believes himself to be smarter than he is—and always at his own peril. She was and is oh so difficult, but people are lulled into thinking otherwise because she is quiet and keeps her own counsel. Difficult women need not be tap-dancing, opinion-slinging extroverts.

In 1999, after eight years of being Kohl's girl, Angela made her move. Without telling anyone in the CDU, she wrote an op-ed for a conservative newspaper exposing Kohl's practice of putting campaign donations into a secret fund he'd then use to buy favors. She called for his resignation, as well as that of Wolfgang Schäuble, the man he'd handpicked as his successor. Many men were mired in the scandal, and thanks to her, they all went down. Remember the famous bloodbath scene at the end of *The*

Godfather, where the heads of the Five Families are taken out at once during the baptism of I can't remember which baby? It was a little like that, only German and political.

A year later, in 2000, Angela Merkel became the chairman of the CDU. The few men left standing after the ousters and scandal that followed didn't think she'd last two years. They plotted the best way to get rid of her behind closed doors. Still, they disliked each other even more than they disliked her, and could never agree on how to proceed with the coup—or even who to replace her with—and so she prevailed. She was much more popular with the German people than she was with her own conservative party members, and in 2005 was elected chancellor. On September 24, 2017, she was elected to her fourth term.

ANGELA MERKEL IS A METHODICAL and dull leader. Most Germans prefer this—or, prefer it enough to keep her in office, anyway. She cannot give a speech to save her life, and is proud of it. Her public speaking style is dedicated middle-school principal reading fire drill instructions. She doesn't believe in the power of charisma, because, as she likes to say, "you can't solve tasks with charisma." Germans still have the burn marks from their last charismatic leader. They're suspicious, and rightly so, of a politician who gives flamboyant speeches and is big on the theatrics of power: rallies, missile parades, and special salutes. They've had all that, and look where it got them.

There are very few people alive today who have lived under fascism. One of the last members of the Third Reich's inner circle, Brunhilde Pomsel, private secretary of Nazi minister of propaganda Joseph Goebbels, died in January 2017 at the age of 106. Germany has tried to move on—but even now, being called a Nazi remains one of the premier insults of the Western world. They cannot atone enough—but they can keep electing a woman who keeps the nation wealthy and drama-free.

By and large, many Germans also approve of the way their chancellor lives her life outside the spotlight. She and her husband live in a modest apartment with a single guard. She shops for herself and cooks dinner. The Merkel-Sauers' one extravagance is opera, for which they are season ticket holders.

Angela has survived two global calamities during her administration. The Eurozone crisis has been ongoing since the financial crash in 2008. Basically, the fun-loving, irresponsible southern nations (you know who you are) are spending a lot of money and failing to pay their debts, while the hardworking, fiscally responsible northern nations (Germany) support them, making the European Union like one big dysfunctional family out of a Sam Shepard play.

"If the euro fails, Europe fails," Angela said in 2011. Then, using her giant math brain and a bunch of charts and graphs she reads for fun, she whipped the EU back into economic shape—that is, enough to stagger forward for another few years. Rather than kicking the fun-loving countries to the curb, she authorized a bailout that passed through the European Parliament with a lot of grumbling. She also insisted the fun-loving nations cut back on their partying, and instituted a draconian debt repayment schedule, which was also not met with good cheer. She was successful because everyone on every side of the extremely complicated issue was unhappy to the same degree—and so the EU was saved. (In 2016, Britain voted in a special election to leave the EU. As of this writing, Germany's response to Brexit has been Don't let the door hit you on the way out.)

The Syrian refugee crisis is ongoing. In the summer of 2015, hundreds of thousands of migrants poured into Germany, seeking asylum. On September 4, in a move that was perhaps the most public display of passion in her life, Angela opened the German borders to 10,000 refugees stuck in Budapest. People were astounded. The woman who had no vision, no issue for which she was willing to become unpopular, no philosophical hill she was willing to die on, had taken everyone by surprise.

"The heart and soul of Europe is tolerance," she said in one of her usual lackluster speeches. "It has taken us centuries to understand this. We have laid our own country to waste . . . The worst period of hatred, devastation, and destruction happened not even a generation ago. It was done in the name of my people."

The other thing Angela Merkel has going for her is a long memory. She remembers being a girl living behind a wall. She remembers going to work every day, driving past the wall and wondering what was on the other side. She remembers being 20 and looking forward to the day when she was 60, the age at which East Germany would grant visas to citizens for nations in the West. (She planned to go to California.) She remembers what it's like to feel caged, to be without freedom. And she wouldn't wish that on anyone.

This is my optimistic view of Germany's chancellor. Many detractors believe her motivations are more nefarious—that she's working on some long play she's figured out in her head long ago. It's utterly possible. She's a difficult woman who can't be shamed for possessing more intelligence, drive, and discipline than most of the men around her. In her quiet, self-contained, confident way she keeps on keeping on without fanfare. Great news for the introverted would-be difficult women among us.

CHAPTER 15

BILLIE JEAN KING

Competitive

I ONCE HAD THE OCCASION to interview Billie Jean King for a magazine story about 20 female fitness icons. This meant contacting the representatives of 20 celebrities and almost-celebrities. Let me tell you, there were a number of women who were thrilled to participate—that is, if I could just guarantee they would somehow be featured above the others. If I could give them more words or a larger photo, they were in. Not Billie Jean. Her rep didn't even ask those questions. Billie Jean called me right up without fanfare and we talked for an hour.

She really is a one-for-all, all-for-one type of difficult woman. Since fifth grade, her desire for the world has been kitchen-sampler simple: equal opportunity for everyone. The moment she played her first game of tennis in 1953, at a country club where the family of her grade school chum were members, she thought: I'm *crazy* about tennis, but where is everyone else? Where are the poorer people, and where are the darker people? Battling to become number one and fighting for fairness became the twin goals of her young life.

BEFORE SERENA AND VENUS, before Monica and Steffi, before Martina and Chrissy, there was Billie Jean, generally considered to be the mother of contemporary women's tennis. Born on November 22, 1943, she grew up playing on the public courts of Long Beach, California.* She would go on to win 39 Grand Slam titles, including 12 singles, 16 women's doubles, and 11 mixed doubles. The list of wins on her Wikipedia page is six and a half inches long. (I know, because I measured it.) In 1972 she was named the *Sports Illustrated* Sportsman of the Year.** In 1987 she was inducted into the Tennis Hall of Fame, and in 2009 President Obama awarded her the Presidential Medal of Freedom.

I'm a generation younger than Billie Jean. But we grew up about 25 miles away from each other in Southern California, and I recognized her species of jokey, nonchalant girl-jock cool right away. She told me a story about how, in 1959 when she was 15 and already playing on the pro circuit, she needed to get out of a class early to make a big tournament. But her teacher said if she left, he would give her a zero (worse than an F). She said, "But you let boys go early for basketball and football games all the time." He said patiently, as if she were stupid: "That's completely different. They're boys." Billie Jean is in fact not stupid, and she heard him loud and clear: Even if females are playing a sport at an elite, professional level, they don't matter. (Her parents permitted her to skip class that day, and true to his word, her teacher gave her a zero.)

At Wimbledon in 1961, Billie Jean and doubles partner Karen Hantze Susman pulled off a jaw-dropping upset, becoming the youngest players to win the women's double title. Billie Jean was 17. For the next several years her performance was spotty, and she realized that if she wanted to be the best, she'd have to practice longer and harder than everyone else. Five years later, her work paid off. In 1966 she won her first singles title, at Wimbledon, and by 1967 she was ranked the top women's player in the world.

In 1965 at the age of 21, she married Larry King, whom she'd met at

---

* As I grew up playing on the public courts of Whittier, California, I can assure you that they were crowded, with torn nets and faded lines and mediocre players like me on the next court, swearing loudly and hitting a nonstop stream of wild balls into the middle of her game.

** She shared the award with basketball great John Wooden; the award is now known as the *Sports Illustrated* Sportsperson of the Year Award.

California State University, Los Angeles, where they were both students.*** "We got married so we could have sex!" she admitted. (Clearly she was not one of the millions who purchased *Sex and the Single Girl*.) Billie had no clue that she was attracted to women. Her family was homophobic, she was homophobic, and in those days, suburban Southern Californians rarely gave a thought to the nuances of sexuality. Anyway, Larry was Ken doll-handsome and supported her tennis career. What wasn't to like?

As Billie Jean blossomed, so did the women's movement. If Gloria Steinem (see Chapter 3) was the voice of the feminist revolution, Billie Jean King was the body. The female body in motion: running, jumping, swinging, thwacking, and holding that giant Wimbledon serving platter—trophy thing over her head.****

Before Billie Jean, most people believed the whole point of "professional" women's tennis was providing spectators with the sight of comely women prancing around gracefully in very short skirts. When they fluidly reached up to tap the ball, and the skirts got even shorter, the sport of women's tennis got even better. But Billie Jean was a competitor. She wasn't there to provide a floor show. She was quick, and cultivated a wicked net game. She wasn't afraid to get in her opponent's face. She was outspoken, and back-talked when she received a lousy call from the line judge. The fact that Billie Jean took her game seriously and was there to win made her, in the minds of sports commentators of the time, extremely difficult.

She *really* had no sense of humor when it came to unfair awarding of prize money. In 1968, she won the Ladies' Singles at Wimbledon and earned £750, while Rod Laver, the men's champ, took home £2,000. At the 1970 Italian Open, men's winner Ilie Năstase won $3,500, while Billie Jean won $600. As the seasons passed, and as tennis became more

---

*** Not *that* Larry King. This one was a law student who also played tennis on Cal State L.A.'s champion men's team.

**** The Ladies' Singles trophy is a salver that bears the mystifying name The Venus Rosewater Dish. If there isn't an all-girl punk band called Venus Rosewater Dish, there should be.

popular, male winners won increasingly bigger pots, while female champs were paid less and less. At one point the ratio of prize money was 12:1, for no good reason other than the United States Lawn Tennis Association (USLTA), the governing body of professional tennis, simply wasn't interested in equity, and the male players had no interest in sharing the pot.

Together with eight other female players, Billie Jean quit the USLTA in protest. The Original Nine, as they were dubbed, signed on to the Virginia Slims Circuit for a token dollar bill.* They hustled like crazy, selling tickets, doing interviews, playing at whatever venue could guarantee an audience. Eventually, Virginia Slims would become the Women's Tennis Association, today the primary organizing body of women's tennis, founded by Billie Jean. At the time, however, male players—as well as the women players who stuck with the safety (and discrimination) of the USLTA—thought the Nine were nuts to risk their careers. But sometimes, you have to choose nutty. Sometimes, you have to walk away and risk everything. It would have been impossible for Billie Jean to continue to tolerate the inequity, and she had no choice but to make the leap.

In 1973, onetime U.S. men's champion and self-proclaimed male chauvinist pig Bobby Riggs challenged Billie Jean to a "Battle of the Sexes."** Riggs was hoping to make a buck, while also stemming the tide of so-called "women's libbers" blasting "I Am Woman" on their car radios and refusing to be ordered around by their husbands like the family dog. That he was 55 and Billie Jean was 29 mattered not to him. He was a huckster and hustler, crude and rude, a proto-troll in the era before the Internet, and he targeted Billie Jean because of her feminist activism. He would tell whoever would listen that women should stay in the bedroom and the kitchen—and that he could handily beat any woman because females lacked emotional stability.

---

* They were Billie Jean King, Rosemary Casals, Judy Tegart Dalton, Nancy Richey, Peaches Bartkowicz, Kristy Pigeon, Valerie Ziegenfuss, Julie Heldman, and Kerry Melville Reid.

** It was such a momentous historic occasion that A-listers Emma Stone (as Billie Jean) and Steve Carell (as Bobby Riggs) starred in the 2017 movie.

Billie Jean declined the challenge, fearful that the cause of women's equality—and her fledgling women's tour—would be endangered if she lost. But things were changing for women, and they were changing fast. In February 1972, the U.S. government began accepting the honorific Ms. on official documents. In June 1972, the Supreme Court passed Title IX.*** On January 22, 1973, women were granted the right to choose whether to terminate a pregnancy. When Australian Margaret Court accepted Riggs's challenge on Mother's Day, 1973, and was thoroughly trounced, Billie Jean felt she had no choice but to play Riggs when he challenged her for a second time.

On September 20, 1973, 30,000 spectators at the Houston Astrodome and 90 million viewers around the world watched as Riggs entered the stadium surrounded by a gaggle of cheerleaders he called "Bobby's Bosom Buddies." When King entered, carried by the Rice University men's track team on a litter like Cleopatra, the announcer opined that King was ". . . a very attractive young lady, if she would ever let her hair grow." (For the record, she wore her hair in a stylish shag.)

As for "emotional stability," Riggs could hardly know how wrong he was. Billie Jean was holding it together like a boss. In the bathroom stall before the match, she heard women standing at the sinks talking about how they'd just placed bets *against* her. Not only that, but her personal life was in turmoil. After years of trying to convince herself otherwise, she was in the process of accepting that she was gay. She continued to love her husband, Larry, but she was *in* love with her secretary, Marilyn Barnett. They would go on to have a clandestine relationship that lasted seven years.

Still, King steeled herself and beat Riggs like grandma's old rug, in straight sets 6-4, 6-3, 6-3.

Upon his defeat Riggs jumped over the net, shook her hand, and said "I underestimated you."

*** No person in the United States shall, on the basis of sex, be excluded from participation in, be denied the benefits of, or be subjected to discrimination under any education program or activity receiving Federal financial assistance.

Why yes, Bobby. Because men like you always underestimate women.

BILLIE JEAN WAS NOT ONLY an advocate for women's equality. In April 1981, she also unwittingly became one of the first pioneers of gay rights. The love affair with Marilyn had run its course. Marilyn, apparently unhappy that she'd invested so much in Billie Jean and her career with nothing to show for it, slapped her former lover with a palimony suit, which also outed Billie Jean as gay.

In early May, just three days after the news broke and against the advice of both her publicist and attorney, Billie Jean held a press conference and admitted to the affair. "I've always been aboveboard with the press, and I will talk now as I've always talked: from my heart," she said. "People's privacy is very important, but unfortunately someone didn't respect that. I did have an affair with Marilyn, but it was over quite some time ago."

I wish I could say that speaking her truth set Billie Jean free—that within weeks of being outed, she was hitting the gay bars and linking arms with iconic feminist writer Andrea Dworkin. But it wasn't that easy. In footage of the press conference, you can see that her beloved parents are stunned. Her mother is both scowling and tearful. Within 24 hours, Billie Jean lost all of her endorsements. Within five years, she and Larry were divorced, about which she felt terrible. In the movies, she would have been rewarded for her courage in confessing the truth. In the real world, she suffered for quite some time. Then she picked herself up and went on.

WHEN I ASKED BILLIE JEAN KING what she wanted to be remembered for, she cited World Team Tennis. Founded with her ex-husband Larry in 1973—the same year she beat Bobby Riggs—WTT is the only pro tennis league where men and women, privileged and not, play on the same team, together.

"Equal pay, equal treatment, equal respect. Equal everything, you see?" said King.

She made it sound so easy; it was anything but. Still, it's easier to be difficult when you know in your heart that you're right. Billie Jean was and is, and so she continues to fight.

CHAPTER 16

JANE GOODALL

Determined

AS A CHILD, I'd idolized her. Jane Goodall, "the girl who lived among the wild chimpanzees," was blond and looked smart in her khaki shorts as she walked on thick jungle branches in her bare feet and play-wrestled with baby chimps. I'd seen her in *National Geographic,* which I would avidly page through before I could even read. We lived in the L.A. suburbs, and even though we had a swimming pool, I was aware that my life was sadly lacking in adventure. Once, inspired by Jane, I asked my mother if we might go camping. She blew smoke out of her nose and told me we weren't the camping types.

Jane Goodall is best known for her 26-year study of the chimpanzees in Gombe Stream National Park, located on the eastern shores of Lake Tanganyika in Tanzania. In 1960, while visiting a friend in Kenya, she met celebrated anthropologist Louis Leakey, who obtained a grant for her to collect data on chimps in the wild to study their similarities to humans. There, she made several groundbreaking discoveries that secured her position as one of the greatest field scientists of the 20th century. She was 26 years old.

In 1962, Dutch wildlife photographer Baron Hugo van Lawick filmed *Miss Goodall and the Wild Chimpanzees.* It was the first documentary produced by the National Geographic Society, and it made Jane Goodall a star. Also, a wife, and then, mother. She married van Lawick, and in 1967 gave birth to a son, Hugo Eric Louis, known as

Grub. She is the author of dozens of books on chimp and animal behavior, as well as on the critical role of conservation. In 1977, she founded the Jane Goodall Institute, a nongovernmental organization devoted to protecting the rapidly disappearing chimp habitat. In 1995 she was made a Commander of the British Empire, and became Dame Jane Morris-Goodall, DBE.

BORN VALERIE JANE MORRIS-GOODALL in London in 1934, her father, Mortimer, was a businessman; her mother, Myfanwe (Vanne) Morris Goodall, was a novelist and looked after her family. The expectations for Jane were standard issue for the time: a marriage to a nice, responsible man, followed by a few children. To her credit, her mother never discouraged her interests: animals, the natural world, and above all, the wildlife of Africa. Once Vanne discovered that little Jane had brought a handful of earthworms to bed; rather than shrieking, she explained that her new little friends needed the soil to live, and together, they took them back to the garden.

Jane was a quiet girl, a bookworm who adored Doctor Dolittle and devoured the Tarzan novels. Reading did its usual stealthy, life-changing thing: Jane developed a deep love of animals and a longing to go to Africa and live among the wild animals. But World War II was raging, and her family had little money. Instead of university, Jane enrolled in secretarial college, graduating in 1952.

Meanwhile, one of Jane's school friends had moved to Kenya and invited her to come for a visit. Jane was working in London selecting music for advertising films at the time. In a move that seems so very right now, she moved home and worked as a waitress to finance the trip. When she had saved enough, she quit her job and off she went.

By which I mean she took an exciting, month-long journey from

England, around the Cape of Good Hope, to Mombasa, eventually making her way to Nairobi. There she met Dr. Louis Leakey, the great archaeologist and paleoanthropologist who traced our human origins to Africa.* Leakey was charismatic, influential, and, at the time, a curator at Nairobi's natural history museum. He offered Jane a job there, then invited her to come along on a dig at Olduvai Gorge. She spent three glorious months immersed in painstaking tasks: removing dirt from a fossil with a dental pick no bigger than your pinkie finger, or digging gently with a hunting knife. Leakey saw in her a person who was patient and thorough: one who could survive long stretches of isolation, who could sit and watch and learn. In sum, she was the perfect candidate for his latest project—observing primates in the wild—and when he asked whether she would be interested in setting up camp at Gombe Stream on the shores of remote Lake Tanganyika, she didn't hesitate for a moment.**

Since women have entered the workforce, it's been noted that we tend to apply only for positions for which we possess the correct qualifications. If a job description lists the ability to juggle an egg, a flaming torch, and a chain saw, and we can only juggle oranges, we don't bother applying. Men, on the other hand, feel confident applying for jobs they believe they can do, regardless of their education or previous experience. They send in their résumé, figuring they'll delegate the juggling once they're hired.

Jane's credentials were: I love animals. What's ethology? Still, she didn't care. She was focused on her improbable life goal, and presumed herself to be qualified and capable of doing things that the world insisted she had no business doing. She gave herself over to learning what needed to be done.

---

* This was easier than you might expect: Expats tend to stick together and run in the same circles in very foreign lands.

** He'd already tried to enlist his secretary for the primate-observing fun. After four months in the wilds of Uganda, she fled.

JANE ARRIVED AT Gombe Stream Game Reserve on July 14, 1960. Lake Tanganyika is a vast inland sea, the longest and second-deepest deepwater lake in the world. It borders Tanzania (then called Tanganyika), the Democratic Republic of the Congo, Zambia, and Burundi. Leakey would not be joining her on the expedition, and the government, worried about a young white woman camping in the bush by herself, ordered Jane to bring a companion. Her mother volunteered, which was probably not what the government had in mind. The two women had a used army tent, some tin plates and cups, and the services of an African cook named Dominic.

At first, Jane hiked around and looked. Really, it was days and days of marching through the rain forest with a pair of second-hand binoculars. The only thing she saw, at first, was a flash of dark against the greens and golds of the forest: the back of a chimp, running away from her. They could not get away from her fast enough.

In case you think this is even remotely romantic, I'm here to tell you it wasn't. When I was 18 and a sophomore in college, I spent a few weeks in East Africa, part of a student study-abroad program.

Tanzania and Kenya are as spectacular as they look in the documentaries. But one thing you don't see is the lung-squeezing, brain-boiling, itchy, rash-inducing heat—nor the stupendous bugs and insects, pretty much all of which can be described as "the size of your fist." Picture it: moths, spiders, roaches, beetles, and millipedes—all the size of your fist. Common dung beetles are smaller than your fist—but they are all over the place, and the giant balls of dung they roll, eat, breed in, and live on *are* the size of your fist. Possibly larger.

I'm not particularly high-maintenance (a form of difficulty, as we know), and I'm not unnerved by rats, mice, or snakes. But the dung beetles—the males have horns!—were too much for me. Every time I see a picture of

Jane squatting in the dust next to chimps,* I always worry that a dung beetle was seconds away from rolling a manure ball over her foot, or a giant centipede was on the verge of crawling up her shorts.

Then there are the diseases. Before my trip, I was required to be vaccinated for cholera, typhoid, smallpox, and yellow fever. None of this prevented me from getting sick; like Jane, I came down with malaria (though my case was considerably milder than hers).

"The more I thought of the task I had set myself, the more despondent I became," Jane wrote in her first book, *In the Shadow of Man.* "Nevertheless, those weeks did serve to acquaint me with the rugged terrain. My skin became hardened to the rough grasses of the valleys and my blood immune to the poison of the tsetse fly, so that I no longer swelled hugely each time I was bitten." (See?)

Note, please, that she didn't say, "What in the hell am I doing here? I'm a fraud. I don't have the proper training. Leakey never should have sent me." She didn't question her competence just because her mission sometimes seemed bloody impossible.

CHIMPANZEES —*Pan troglodytes*—are our closest evolutionary relatives. We share about 98 percent of our DNA with them.** Genetically, we are more like chimps than mice are like rats. Their similarity to humans was Leakey's primary interest. But Jane studied them for the sake of studying them, fascinated with their family and clan relationships. She let her intuition guide her.

For two months, the chimps fled when they heard her coming. Then, one day, a huge male sauntered into camp, climbed a palm tree, and

---

* That woman was limber. If I met her, I would ask her how her knees are holding up because she was a pretzel in her youth.

** The chimpanzee genome was sequenced in 2005.

ate a few nuts. A while later, he came into camp and stole a banana off a table. Eventually, he allowed Jane to offer him one. She called him David Greybeard, for his jaunty white goatee.

Naming animals was scoffed at among the scientific community as being amateurish and silly. Serious scientists, "real" scientists, assigned the subjects numbers. But David Greybeard signaled to the rest of the community that Jane was not as scary as they had thought. Consequently, she became acquainted with (and named) Goliath, Humphrey, Rodolf, Leakey, and Mike. There was Mr. McGregor, a cranky old male. There was the alpha female Flo, and her offspring, Faben, Figan, and Fifi. She observed them kiss, embrace, pat each other on the back, shake their fists at each other. She watched them act pretty dang human.

One day, moving quietly through the jungle in search of the chimpanzees, Jane came upon a large termite mound. David Greybeard sat beside it. She watched as, over and over again, he poked long, sturdy blades of grass into a hole, withdrew them, and plucked off the termites with his lips. After he was finished with his meal, Jane inspected the mound, and the grass blades he'd left behind. She poked one in the hole and withdrew it. A dozen or more termites clung to the stem. Yum. A few weeks later, she would watch the chimps *make tools*, breaking off small leafy twigs from trees and stripping the leaves, before poking them in the termite mound holes.

At that time—the 1960s—the defining characteristic of man was that he alone, among all the creatures on God's green Earth, made tools. We called ourselves Man the Toolmaker, and that skill allegedly distinguished us from every other living thing. I find this odd. You would think biologists would have focused on something there was no chance of any other creature ever mastering. Why were we not Man the Terrible Joke Teller? Or Man the Insufferable Fishing Trip Yarn Spinner?

In any case, Jane's discovery was the talk of the scientific world, causing Leakey to proclaim, "Now we must redefine 'tool,' redefine 'man,' or accept chimpanzees as humans." Harvard's Stephen Jay Gould would call her observation "one of the great achievements of twentieth-century scholarship."

Already a legend at the age of 27, Jane would go on to make more discoveries. That chimps were not the benign vegetarians we thought them to be, but omnivores, like us. And also (somewhat sadly), they were wagers of war. Jane's first article was published in 1963 and was featured on the December 1965 cover of *National Geographic*. Since then her work has appeared there more often than any other scientist. Even her mentor, Louis Leakey.

A MERE WOMAN, and one without any credentials, had redefined what it means to be Man. Louis Leakey believed that Jane's discovery should earn her acceptance into the Ph.D. program in ethology at Cambridge—despite the fact that before becoming, in a few short months, one of the most important field biologists on Earth, she'd never been to college. Leakey knew she would need a degree if she wanted to be taken seriously, and so he used his influence to convince the dons of her worthiness. It was no small feat: Jane was only the eighth person in the history of the university to enter a doctorate program without a degree.

When the bigwigs in the ethology department at Cambridge learned what she'd been up to, they were appalled. Discovery notwithstanding, Jane was guilty of the most heinous crime in the kingdom of science: anthropomorphizing, or attributing human traits to animals. Naming the chimpanzees! Describing their behavior and interactions in humanlike terms! Could anything be sillier? Plus, it was plain old bad science, according to the thinking of the day, which prized cold, hard objectivity. I can just imagine a faculty meeting, wherein the grizzled old sexists pooh-poohed Jane's work with barely disguised glee. Her first book, *My Friends, the Wild*

Chimpanzees, was published before she finished her dissertation, and one of the Cambridge dons nearly gave himself a heart attack: "It's—it's—it's for the general public!" For that intellectual crime, she was nearly kicked out of the program.

In fairness, Robert Hinde, her direct adviser, took Jane's achievement seriously. She praised his influence in a 2017 blog post, saying she could never thank him enough for teaching her to think critically. He was assigned to her, it appears, because he had been studying a colony of rhesus monkeys and he, too, had seen fit to name them. I'm presuming that none of his colleagues thought he was ridiculous or amateurish for doing so.

Can you imagine yourself in this situation? Some of the most esteemed thinkers in your field at one of the most esteemed universities on the planet criticize your methodology. They probably have a point because your methodology, insofar as you had one, was Make It Up As You Go Along. Plus, these men are brilliant and powerful. I don't know about you, but my knee-jerk reaction would be to cede them their point—or at least pretend to hear them out, then call my girlfriends and complain about being misunderstood.

Jane Goodall not only did *not* go along with their assessment, she told them they were straight-up wrong. She was soft-spoken, but she refused to back down. She didn't cite her thousands of hours of current research with chimpanzees, which gave her at least some ethological cred; instead, she referenced a relationship she'd had with her childhood pet, a black mutt named Rusty. "Fortunately, I thought back to my first teacher, when I was a child, who taught me that that wasn't true," she wrote years later. "You cannot share your life in a meaningful way with any kind of animal with a reasonably well-developed brain and not realize that animals have personalities."

It's breathtaking, really, the way Jane stood her ground and wouldn't let her superiors talk her out of her own experience and what she knew to be true. Every time I know I'm right about something, but begin to feel as if it would make life easier to simply pretend to believe that the other person (usually, a man) makes a good point, I remember Jane Goodall in this moment. So genteel, yet so impressively difficult.

IN 1986, AFTER PUBLISHING *The Chimpanzees of Gombe*, which summarized 25 years' worth of research, Jane concluded her life in the field and became an activist. Her marriage to Hugo van Lawick had ended in 1974; a year later, she married Tanzanian Parliament member Derek Bryceson. Her new husband was also director of national parks and helped preserve the integrity of Gombe, keeping it wild and isolated from animal-loving tourists and well-meaning supporters. As a result, when Jane departed, Gombe was thriving, and continued to thrive. It had evolved into a flourishing research station staffed primarily by native Tanzanians.

Jane had spent enough time in Africa to experience the chimpanzees' diminishing habitat firsthand—channeling the same zeal with which she threw herself into studying the chimps, she now devoted herself to their conservation. She's still at it today, still wearing slacks and comfortable shoes, her blond hair gone gray and still held back in its low ponytail. Her look has changed very little in 50 years. She's simply older, but no less beautiful and intimidating.

When *Seeds of Hope: Wisdom and Wonder From the World of Plants* appeared in 2014, Jane was interviewed on both *The Colbert Report* and *Last Week Tonight With John Oliver.*

It's not as if Jane Goodall doesn't have a sense of humor. In 1987, celebrity cartoonist Gary Larson drew a comic that showed two chimps sitting on a branch. One pulls a long, clearly human, hair off the back of the other and says, "Well, well—another blond hair. Conducting more 'research' with that Jane Goodall tramp?" The Jane Goodall

Institute quickly shot off a letter of objection, without stopping to think that Jane might find it hilarious, which she did.*

Still, her dry sense of humor can sometimes be misinterpreted. During a 2014 interview with comedian John Oliver she simply refused to give in. He tried to lure her into admitting that during her time at Gombe she was tempted to dress a chimp up like a butler. She said no. He kept pressing her in his faux hard-hitting journalistic way, and she neither smiled nor acquiesced. Though in the end, she rewarded him with a few chimp gestures that had the audience roaring.

Jane was polite and utterly unmovable. It was as if Oliver was trying to get her to mock her family, and she was not about to do that. It's a terrific, awkward moment of television where a woman refused to smile, become giddy and jokey to relieve a tense moment and make everyone feel better. It would have been so easy for her to go along with the joke, to make light of her life's work. But being difficult, she wasn't about to give in. Difficult women aren't all swashbuckling extroverts who shoot off their mouths and shout down their adversaries. Sometimes they just sit quietly and refuse to pretend to be agreeable.

Jane Goodall's life story inspires me still—perhaps even more than when I was a girl. Back then, I thought if you were the right kind of girl (who got to go camping), you could find the path to an incredible life and hike straight to the top. I didn't understand the concept of female self-sabotage. I had no idea that brilliant, capable women might hobble themselves by indulging in self-defeating ambivalence, chewing their cuticles with self-doubt. Unlike many accommodating women I know (me), difficult women don't gum up the works with second-guessing, a terrible and counterproductive habit that generally goes something like this: Make decision, regret decision, beat self up

---

* Later she would write the introduction to *The Far Side Gallery 5*, and Larson donated the profits from a T-shirt with the cartoon on it to the Jane Goodall Institute. Later still—and this may be apocryphal—Larson visited Gombe and was attacked by Frodo the chimp.

for making wrong decision in the first place, further beat self up for regretting having made wrong decision in the first place. Drink too much wine. Sleep it off. Do nothing.

Jane, with her calm, steady ways, sat in that jungle—frustrated at first, but moving forward, trusting that she'd made the right choice. She always seemed to trust herself, which made her a difficult woman.

CHAPTER 17

VITA SACKVILLE-WEST

Self-Assured

IN MY EARLY 20s I worked as a secretary at a talent agency on Sunset Boulevard. My job consisted primarily of getting yelled at by my boss for failing to answer his endlessly ringing phones fast enough. Rather than being an entrée into the glamorous world of Hollywood, the experience plunged me into despair. I distracted myself from my misery by assigning myself a task: reading Virginia Woolf's entire oeuvre, including the five volumes of her diaries and the six volumes of her letters.* As I would discover, the most flamboyant and desperately glamorous character in Virginia's life was the aristocratic Vita Sackville-West: popular novelist, poet, gardener, and wife of writer Sir Harold Nicolson, with whom she enjoyed what would become an open marriage for the ages.**

Vita was self-assured. Vita was magnetic. Vita was gender-fluid, as we call it in our time, known for stirring up passions people didn't know they possessed. In an oil portrait of her painted in 1910, when Vita was 18, she resembles a handsome musketeer in puffy shirt and jaunty velvet Edwardian hat. London's infamous literary clique the Bloomsbury Group—of which Virginia (and tangentially, Vita) were a part—spent most of their time

---

* Why Virginia Woolf? The reasons are lost to time. Escapism, intellectual pretensions, bragging rights: I've read all of Woolf, even *The Waves*.

** Vita would be disgruntled that I'm mentioning her books, and only the best known at that, in a footnote. They are *The Edwardians* (1930) and *All Passion Spent* (1931); her travel memoir *Passenger to Teheran* also holds up well. Though intrepid in matters of the heart, she was dull on the page. Her poetry was better, and in 1927 she won the Hawthornden Prize, the oldest major British literary award, for her pastoral epic *The Land*. She won it again in 1933 for her *Collected Poems*.

discussing the Meaning of Art and engaging in secret trysts with other members of the group. Next, they'd scamper back to their desks to scribble madly in their diaries, put forth some steamy love letters, and then work up a novel with the secret lover as the main character. The greatest piece of literature to emerge from all of this carrying-on was the satirical romp *Orlando,* Woolf's most accessible and popular novel. Vita served as the inspiration for the eponymous Orlando, a handsome British nobleman born under the reign of Elizabeth I who mysteriously changed into a woman at age 30, then lived for another few centuries without aging a day. (Oh, if only.) Vita's son, the writer Nigel Nicolson, would call *Orlando* "The longest and most charming love letter in literature, in which [Virginia] explores Vita, weaves her in and out of the centuries, tosses her from one sex to the other, plays with her, dresses her in furs, lace and emeralds, teases her, flirts with her, drops a veil of mist around her, and ends by photographing her in the mud at Long Barn, with dogs, awaiting Virginia's arrival the next day."

VITA'S FULL NAME WAS the Honourable Victoria Mary Sackville-West, Lady Nicolson. Born in 1892, at the end of the Victorian era, she was the only child of Lionel Edward Sackville-West, third Baron Sackville, and his cousin, Victoria Josefa Dolores Catalina Sackville-West, Baroness Sackville (who was the illegitimate child of the second Baron Sackville-West, also called Lionel, and the notorious Spanish flamenco dancer, Pepita).

Vita was born at Knole, in West Kent. The estate is one of the largest houses in England. Elizabeth I bequeathed it to some earlier Sackville cousin, and the family had lived there since 1603. With 365 rooms, 50 staircases, and many courtyards, towers, and battlements, all set within a thousand-acre park, the house makes Downton Abbey look like a split-level in Teaneck.

Vita loved her home the way other young girls love ponies. But because she was an only child, and female, the house and the title that went with it was passed on to her father's nephew. Even though I've suffered some not-

females could certainly love other females? Or did misogyny render the idea inconceivable: How could a lowly woman possibly prefer another woman when a man was around?

In a basic cultural sense, then, lesbianism wasn't even a thing when Vita was sorting herself out. It would be like standing in your bedroom as a teenager, staring at yourself in the mirror and thinking, maybe I really am a mermaid. Yet Vita thrashed on ahead, desiring, feeling by turns ashamed, embarrassed, confused, rapturous, and content. It wasn't easy, but it was who she was. It would be a betrayal of her fundamental self to pretend otherwise. She refused to be trapped by the mores of the day, which made her difficult.

Violet Keppel was another girl at Vita's school. Her beauty was delicate, and oddly modern. In pictures and portraits, Vita looks of her time. But Violet looks as if she could guest star on *Girls*. They met in 1904, at the bedside of another girl who'd broken her leg. Both of their mothers had pressed them to visit. Afterward, in the hallway, Violet gave Vita a kiss. Vita was 12 and Violet, 10.

Vita was always a terrible snob, and might have looked down on Violet as being "bedint," or tasteless (as was anything not of the aristocracy). But her mother, Alice, was King Edward VII's favorite mistress, which earned Violet the necessary upper-class cred.

The love affair of Vita and Violet lasted for more than a decade, through their teens and into both of their marriages. They would meet in London, where Violet lived with her mother in Portman Square (Alice had been installed there by the king), and exchanged hundreds of sweet, urgent letters. (I'm a little sad that letters don't fly back and forth between lovers anymore. Snapchat, I'm sorry to say, is just not the same.) Vita called Violet an "unexploded bomb." Violet said she loved Vita "because you have never yielded in anything; I love you because you never capitulate. I love you for your wonderful intelligence, for your literary aspirations, for your unconscious coquetry."

Despite her love for Violet, Vita never expected to forgo marriage. She was too snobbish, too attached to her station in life and privilege. In any case, her mother—the battle-ax Lady Sackville—would have had her

dissimilar ridiculousness—years ago my stepbrother was made trustee of our parents' living trust because he was male, and not in the arts—it's hard to feel too bad for the extremely wealthy, privileged, well-connected Vita. On the other hand, what the hell? I don't blame her for being pissed, and carrying the scar from this injustice for her entire life.

Vita was lanky and dark-haired, with dramatic, hooded eyes. In some photos she looks not unlike Oscar Wilde. Indeed, despite my fascination with her, I've sometimes mistaken her for Wilde (especially in one picture, where he sports center-parted hair and chin-length curls). Vita thought of herself as ugly, "rough and secret." She was gawky, and lonely in her huge house that was as big as a town. Her favorite companion was a giant tortoise, his shell monogrammed in diamonds, who slowly roamed the long halls.

Vita knew she loved women from an early age—and also, that she loved them with a distinctly male attitude. No cuddling and sharing girlish secrets for her, although she settled for that more than once. At Helen Wolff's School for Girls in Park Lane, she fell hard for a classmate, Rosamund Grosvenor. Rosamund was a standard-issue society girly girl of the time, feminine and kittenish, without a thought in her head. Vita was madly attracted to her, even though she wasn't much interested in engaging her in conversation.

She was a woman with urges, and she was determined to indulge them. This was a radical act for a female born in the Victorian era, when one's success as a woman could be measured by the degree to which she was able to keep basic human yearning under wraps. When it came to sex, most well-bred girls only received the memo about the calisthenics to come on their wedding night.

A little context: Being a person who loved someone of their own gender wasn't merely a scandal in England, it was also illegal. We're not talking community service for a sex act in a public restroom: Oscar Wilde did two years of hard labor in prison for "gross indecency." Homosexuality remained illegal in Britain until 1967. Even then, the Sexual Offences Act only applied to decriminalizing sex between *men*. I've never understood this. Were men simply unwilling to extrapolate that if males could love other males, then

daughter's head on a pike to even suggest such a thing. In March 1913, Vita married writer and diplomat Harold Nicolson, son of Arthur Nicolson, first Baron Carnock, at the Knole chapel. (Vita's parents opposed the union because Nicolson earned only £250 a year, and his father had only been made a peer under Queen Victoria—practically trailer trash.)

Nicolson was charming, winsome, and clever. The first words Vita ever heard Harold say were "What fun," in response to an unheard question the hostess of the party posed. He was also gay, but this was a detail men kept to themselves. Vita also didn't mention her predilection for women, or her love for Violet. As repressed and pathetic as this sounds, this secretiveness was perfectly in keeping with the times.

Over the next four years, Vita would give birth to two sons, Benedict and Nigel. But she never gave up on Violet. During World War I, when Harold was busy at the Foreign Office in London on war matters and the boys were with their nanny, Vita and Violet would go to Paris, where they sometimes posed as a hetero couple on vacation: Julian and Eve. Vita, as Julian, made a handsome man, at once rakish and soulful. She felt bold and liberated by her attire. As Julian, Vita called herself "a person translated." Given Vita's *No Sex Please: We're British* upbringing, the courage it took to "translate" herself into someone who felt true to who she really was took a lot of guts. Not because other people might discover her predilection—although of course there was that—but because it would put her in deeper touch with her true self. And let's face it: That can be downright terrifying.

November 11, 1918: Armistice Day. Harold was still working overtime at the Foreign Office in London, now busy brokering peace. In early 1919, he sent Vita off with Violet to Monte Carlo, where they spent several months swimming in the sea and gambling.* Vita couldn't have been happier. Boys safe in Kent with their minders, husband safe in London working his head off, none the wiser, and Violet here with her. They got carried away and

---

* Have you ever noticed how long vacations were back in the day? Vita and Violet never seemed to go away for less than three months at a time.

engaged in some public displays of affection; rumors of their indiscretion shot back to England and straight into the ears of their mothers—Lady Sackville, the aforementioned battle-ax, and Alice Keppel, the favored mistress of the now-late king. Harold also managed to look up from his work long enough to register that Violet was trying to lure away his wife. None of this would do, *at all*.

Denys Trefusis was a handsome, diffident soldier in the Royal Horse Guards who'd taken a fancy to Violet. She couldn't have been less interested, but once her mother got wind of the shenanigans with Vita in Monte Carlo, she ordered Violet to accept Denys's marriage proposal. When Vita saw the engagement announcement in the paper in March, instead of flying into a jealous rage as most of us would, she thought this would make their lives *easier*. She and Violet would make a pact—no sex with their husbands, and as many holidays as Julian and Eve as possible, taking care not to start another scandal.

Meanwhile, Harold had begun his own affair, with fashion designer Edward Molyneux. He didn't see any reason he and Vita couldn't be allowed the occasional fling—which completely underestimated the depth of Vita's feelings for Violet. Because who had ever heard of such a thing as two women deeply in love? (No one, as we know.) There were bitter rows between Vita and Harold, between Vita and Violet, between Violet and Denys. Diaries filled up. Letters were posted, sometimes two and three a day. (Violet was also a writer—did I mention that?) In the end, Vita got wind of the fact that Violet had, in fact, had sex with her husband (because, duh), and she flew into a jealous rage; the relationship careened downhill from there. Vita ended it in late 1921.

Vita would fall in love with many more women, and Harold many more men. But after the Violet "muddle" (as they referred to their infidelities), they refashioned their wedding vows to reflect what worked for them: to honor each other in a sex-free union, bound by mutual respect, shared intellectual interests, and warm companionship. They didn't want to be unmarried. They enjoyed being husband and wife, even though they liked having sex with other people of their own gender. Was it a sham marriage?

Or was it the perfect solution to a problem that remains intractable to this very day: maintaining a long-term happy marriage to someone you don't want to have sex with, but whom convention insists you're supposed to pretend you want to have sex with forever and ever? In any case, they made it work for them. How much better our intimate relationships would be if we fashioned them to suit ourselves, and not the expectations of our times?

One thing's for sure: Their arrangement reduced marital quarrels and allowed for a steady production of novels from both wife and husband. In 1930, Vita and Harold purchased Sissinghurst Castle in Cranbrook, Kent. There, they worked together to create one of the most epic contemporary gardens in the world, now in the British National Trust. As someone who is pained to tug a weed, I find Sissinghurst to be no less an artistic achievement than the Sistine Chapel. Designed as a series of "rooms," each garden is flat-out breathtaking: the cottage garden, the white garden, the blue flower bed. So vast is Sissinghurst that in 2009, BBC Four found enough material to fill an eight-part documentary detailing its evolution.

BY THE TIME VITA MET Virginia Woolf in 1922, she and Harold had been married for 13 years, and had found their marital groove. Vita was free to pursue Virginia to the degree she wished to be pursued. Vita wrote to Harold: "I've rarely taken such a fancy to anyone, and I think she likes me. At least, she asked me to Richmond where she lives. Darling, I have quite lost my heart."

Virginia was married to Leonard Woolf, a graduate of Cambridge and former civil servant. Theirs was a great marriage of minds. They were a two-person literary band: Not only did they preside as de facto king and queen of the Bloomsbury Group, but in 1917 they founded the Hogarth Press, which published the writings of the group members (as well as an English version of Dostoyevsky's *The Devils,* translated by Virginia, and the first edition of T. S. Eliot's *The Waste Land*). When she and Vita met,

Virginia was absorbed in her work and—as she would throughout her life—struggling with depression.

Virginia's first great literary success, *Mrs. Dalloway,* was still several years in the future. She was 40 and set in her ways, equal parts attracted to and frightened of the whole sexy, eccentric, androgynous Vita Sackville-West package.

Vita wrote to Virginia from Milan on January 21, 1926: "I am reduced to a thing that wants Virginia. I composed a beautiful letter to you in the sleepless nightmare hours of the night, and it has all gone: I just miss you, in a quite simple desperate human way."

Virginia wrote to Vita, on January 26: "And ever since [Vita left] nothing important has happened—Somehow [it's] dull and damp. I have been dull; I have missed you. I do miss you. I shall miss you. And if you don't believe it, you're a long-eared owl and ass."

Then, on October 5, 1927, Virginia made a note in her diary about a new book: "And instantly, the usual exciting devices enter my mind: a biography beginning in the year 1500 and continuing to the present day, called *Orlando:* Vita; only with a change about from one sex to the other." The book was a critical and popular success, and for the first time in their lives, Virginia and Leonard Woolf were financially stable.

On the day *Orlando* was published, Vita received a package from Virginia. It contained a copy of the novel, fresh off the press, and the original handwritten manuscript bound in Niger leather, Vita's initials tooled on the spine.

The love affair with Virginia (Vita seemed to have a weakness for women whose names began with V) lasted until 1935. Apparently Virginia got fed up with Vita's libido and general promiscuity. In an essay examining the effect of the relationship on the literary output of the two women, scholar Louise deSalvo wrote "neither had ever written so much so well, and neither would ever again reach this peak of accomplishment."

UPON VITA'S DEATH IN 1962, her son Nigel, whom Vita had named her

literary executor, went through her papers in her office at Sissinghurst. He found 40 boxes of letters carefully stored in pinewood boxes, her own diaries, and the diaries of her mother, Lady Sackville. He found every letter his father had ever written his mother. He also found, in a corner of the room, a locked Gladstone bag. He sliced open the leather and inside discovered a notebook, in which Vita had written the story of her desperate love affair with Violet Keppel. It was roughly 80 pages long, written for future readers, for a time when "the psychology of people like myself will be a matter of interest."

Nigel Nicolson sat on the manuscript for a while, waiting until he felt the time was right. In 1973 he published *Portrait of a Marriage,* a biography of his parents' life together, with Vita's story of her love for Violet at its center. "She fought for the right to love, men and women, rejecting the conventions that marriage demands exclusive love, and that women should love only men, and men only women. For this she was prepared to give up everything . . . How could she regret that the knowledge of it should now reach the ears of a new generation, one so infinitely more compassionate than her own?" he wrote in the preface.

I read *Portrait* during my mad Virginia Woolf phase. Descriptions of the intoxicating Vita appeared throughout the letters and diaries, and *Orlando* was my favorite of Virginia's novels so I had to read more. I remember thinking how modern it felt, and how adventuresome and daring Vita seemed, even then. It shouldn't be an amazing act of courage for a woman to strive to be fully herself—and yet time and time again, we see that it is. Really, we shouldn't be so timid. Look at Vita. Like us, she was a victim of the times in which she lived. But that didn't stop her from trying again and again to understand and express her needs and desires. Still, she wound up with a marriage for the ages, a son who had nice things to say about her after she was gone, a world-renowned garden and refuge of stupendous beauty, and a sense of having really, truly lived. Not too shabby, that. And a legacy that only a difficult woman could produce.

CHAPTER 18

ELIZABETH WARREN

Persistent

LAST WEEK MY Elizabeth Warren tribute T-shirt arrived: *"Nevertheless, She Persisted"* emblazoned on the front. It's one of the great things about the digital age: Someone, somewhere makes an incendiary remark, and an hour later the phrase appears on mugs, stickers, lawn signs, baseball caps, and fitted tees. I ordered mine in February 2017, about seven seconds after Senate Majority Leader Mitch McConnell muzzled Elizabeth for violating Rule 19 during the confirmation hearings for Attorney General Jeff Sessions.

What, you may ask, is Rule 19? Technically, a little-used conduct rule employed to prevent senators from "impugning" one another. In this case, a little-used rule employed to get Elizabeth Warren to shut the hell up.* At least McConnell went to the effort of pretending there was an official reason for interrupting Elizabeth; mere months later when California Democrat Kamala Harris questioned Sessions before the Senate Intelligence Committee (that guy gets around), she was interrupted twice during the handful of minutes she had the floor. This time the unstated reason was: You're a woman and you're being annoying by being articulate and assertive.**

---

* My own senator from the great state of Oregon, Jeff Merkley, also read a portion of Coretta Scott King's letter, but no one said boo.

** If your blood pressure can take it, check out Susan Chira's piece in the *New York Times*, "The Universal Phenomenon of Men Interrupting Women."

Elizabeth, the pugnacious junior senator from Massachusetts, had been reading a 1986 letter, written by Coretta Scott King, in opposition to the nomination of then Judge Sessions to the federal bench in Alabama. The nine-page letter doesn't have many flattering things to say about Sessions when it comes to his attitudes about voter equality. McConnell told Elizabeth to stop, but she kept right on going, forcing McConnell to proclaim, in an exasperated, superior tone: "She was warned. She was given an explanation. Nevertheless, she persisted."

(McConnell's tone was so familiar. It was patronizing, but also reminded me of how I address the dog when I discover that yet again she has gotten into the recycling, strewing scrap paper and take-out containers around the house. It's a daily occurrence, and really, by this time the dog should know better.) Does it go without saying that women who keep talking after they're "warned" are difficult? I'm saying it anyway.

Sessions was easily confirmed by the Republican majority, but the kerfuffle in the press caused King's letter to go viral. Millions of people who would otherwise never have paid attention wound up reading the letter online, and Elizabeth's Facebook Live reading of the letter received six million views. When Trevor Noah of the *Daily Show* asked if she'd realized in the moment how much McConnell had inadvertently helped her cause, Elizabeth dodged the question, as she often does. "What it's done is to help us have a better democratic conversation," she observed diplomatically.

Elizabeth Warren had never planned on becoming a politician, but here she is, kicking ass and taking names. Mother of two, grandmother of three, former Harvard law professor, she is the author of 11 books, including the 2017 best seller, *This Fight Is Our Fight: The Battle to Save America's Middle Class*. She's also one of those intensely charismatic public speakers who makes you want to go out and join up.

ELIZABETH HERRING was born in 1949 and grew up in Norman, Oklahoma. Her father sold carpet at Montgomery Ward and her mother stayed home and took care of Elizabeth and her three older brothers. They were a typical, post–World War II middle-class family; as long as nothing bad happened, they got by. Crossed fingers are not and have never been a safety net, and when Elizabeth was 12, her father had a heart attack. After he recovered, his old job had been filled. The medical bills piled up. The family station wagon was repossessed. Elizabeth's mother, wearing her one nice dress, interviewed for a job answering phones at Sears. It paid minimum wage, but it kept the family afloat. Elizabeth babysat, waitressed, sold hand-sewn dresses, and even bred the neighbor's elegant black poodle to her own dog and sold the puppies. The experience forced her to grow up there and then: She realized a person could work as hard as she possibly could and still never get ahead.

Elizabeth's brothers went into the military; she was expected to find a husband. When she mentioned college, her mother said that money aside (they didn't have any), a college education would make her less marriageable. I have no doubt her mother said this out of love, but it's a good thing Elizabeth (then as now) persisted. She pretended to listen but went to the library and began researching colleges, and secretly sent away for admission packets.

Anyone who's watched five minutes of Elizabeth on C-SPAN or read a day's worth of her tweets won't be surprised to learn that she was the star debater on her high school team. After being named "Oklahoma's Top High School Debater," she won a full debate scholarship (who knew that was a thing?) to George Washington University in 1965.

Culture shock followed on the heels of her arrival at Foggy Bottom. As she writes in her memoir, *A Fighting Chance:* "I had never been north or east of Pryor, Oklahoma. I had never seen a ballet, never been to a museum, never ridden in a taxi." After two years, she reconnected with Jim Warren, her old high school boyfriend; when he proposed, she said yes and promptly dropped out of college.

In 1968, not every young person was turning on, tuning in, and dropping out. Janis Joplin's "Piece of My Heart" may have been blasting out of every car radio (see Chapter 27), but for a small-town Oklahoma girl like Elizabeth, chucking your scholarship to a prestigious university to marry literally the first guy who asked was a sensible move.

Jim Warren was an upstanding engineer. When he landed a job at NASA, the couple moved to Houston. For someone else, this might have been the Happily Ever After. But Elizabeth had a sharp, active mind and still wanted to finish college. After enrolling in the University of Houston, she graduated in 1970 with a bachelor of science degree in speech pathology. They moved to New Jersey soon afterward—again for Jim's job. Elizabeth dutifully got pregnant, but after the baby was born, she simply wasn't content to stay home. On some level, she knew that motherhood is not a one-size-fits-all situation. She loved her baby but was also a smart, ambitious young woman who longed to make her mark.

Elizabeth applied for and was accepted into Rutgers Law School. Difficult woman–style, she accepted her feelings of guilt and marched on anyway. After she graduated in 1978, she began lecturing at Rutgers. Then, when Jim was transferred back to Texas, she found a similar position at the University of Houston.

The law is lousy with women these days, but when Elizabeth began lecturing at the UH Law Center, she was "mistaken for a secretary, a student, the wife of a student, a lost undergrad who had wandered into the law school by mistake, and a nurse (blood drive day)." But she was too exhilarated by her life to get waylaid by stupid sexism. She had a husband, a pair of healthy, beautiful kids, and a challenging and fulfilling career. Without knowing it, Elizabeth was a Having It All trailblazer.

Her husband never complained, but it was clear as the years passed that having a working wife wasn't what he'd signed on for. Even though she continued to do it all, when dinner was late, he would pointedly look at his watch. In 1978, they divorced amicably. Two years later, in a match that reflected her academic passions, she married law professor and legal historian Bruce Mann, who presumably does not look pointedly at his watch under any circumstances.

IN THE 1980S AND '90S, Elizabeth became an expert in bankruptcy law. It was an arcane (boring) field in which legal scholars and change makers had little interest. Common wisdom held that only deadbeats who blew their paychecks on blow, strippers, and muscle cars were forced to declare bankruptcy. Elizabeth had other ideas, formed in her childhood, that made her think maybe things weren't always that cut and dried. She launched an investigation into who, exactly, benefited from bankruptcy protection laws. She and her team interviewed bankruptcy court judges, attorneys, and debtors to discover, lo and behold, that many people who went bankrupt had jobs, sometimes two, and tried to pay their bills on time. She proved what we know today to be true: People in the middle class are all one job loss, divorce, or catastrophic illness away from bankruptcy.

In 1995, Elizabeth took a position lecturing at Harvard Law. The same year she advised the National Bankruptcy Review Commission, working to fight legislation restricting bankruptcy protection for consumers. She wrote extensively about income equality and the threat of predatory lending, long before it was on the national radar. She became the avowed enemy of the protective laws enjoyed by big banks and large financial institutions that allow them to squeeze middle-class families to improve their profit margin.

In the summer of 2007, in an academic journal called *Democracy,* Elizabeth published a think piece called "Unsafe at Any Rate." It revealed the danger of subprime mortgages, the coming financial collapse, and the need for government oversight. (The subtitle was: "If it's good enough for microwaves, it's good enough for mortgages. Why we need a Financial

Product Safety Commission.") Remarkably, politicos read the piece and saw it as part of the solution to the problem of big banks gone wild. In 2011, the Consumer Financial Protection Bureau was signed into law. "Nobody's responsible to the American consumer, no one's looking out for American families; we started that," Elizabeth told ABC News.

Let's stop for a moment and appreciate how rarely this kind of thing actually happens. Scholars are always publishing think pieces and op-eds about solutions to the world's thorny problems—but mostly they're writing for each other, and 37 other nerds. The creation of the CFPB is the equivalent of sending an idea for a great feminist anthem to Beyoncé, and then having her record it and sing it at the Super Bowl. Still, the experience wasn't all high fives and ticker tape parades; then President Obama refused to nominate Elizabeth for the position of director, worried that with her passion for equity and unwillingness to soft-pedal her opinions, she would never win the approval of Republicans.[*]

Elizabeth Warren was crushed. She was down but not out. So in 2012, at the age of 63, she found another way to contribute: She ran for and was elected as the first female senator from Massachusetts, smoking the competition by eight points. Her campaign promise was that she did not intend to go to Washington to be polite and go along to get along.

Her second act is a wonder to behold. She's got her public style down pat. Blond bob, frameless glasses, minimal makeup. For appearances she usually sports black pants and a bright, stylish jacket. Not quite a pantsuit. More frisky. Maybe because she didn't intend to be a politician, or maybe once a star debater always a star debater: Either way, she doesn't seem to see any point in measured speech.

Like Donald Trump, Elizabeth is an ace tweeter (though more articulate, with a larger vocabulary and an ability to spell). During the 2016 election the two went back and forth like a pair of high-profile table tennis champs. After Trump defended his middle-of-the-night rants,

---

[*] And right he probably was, given that Republicans love Elizabeth Warren only slightly more than they do Hillary Clinton (see Chapter 26).

Elizabeth observed: "You never tweet at 3am with ways to help students getting crushed by debt or seniors struggling on Social Security."

Of course, Elizabeth Warren has been called too angry—but my bet is that she doesn't much care. She *is* angry. This is what makes a woman difficult: She not only refuses to change her behavior when she is called a name—but she keeps right on doing it, with verve and conviction. If that's difficult, I'll have what she's having.

CHAPTER 19

MARGARET CHO

Unrestrained

IN 1999, I WAS IN NEW YORK for one reason or another and a friend
whose name I cannot recall—in those days she would have been
called an acquaintance, but since the advent of Facebook, that term no
longer exists—came down with something or other and gave me
her ticket to an off-Broadway show to see a one-woman act by someone
I'd never heard of. My memory is pretty good, but Margaret Cho blew
my mind to such a degree that nothing associated with how I wound
up in that theater seat exists. I laughed so hard my mascara tears
left black stains on the front of my T-shirt. A bisexual Korean American—former phone sex operator, former sitcom star, daughter of a
disapproving Asian mother whom she imitates brilliantly with equal
parts scorn and love—Margaret Cho was a revelation. The show, *I'm
the One That I Want,* went on to become a hot concert film and best-
selling memoir. In 2002, her next show, *Notorious C.H.O.,* would sell
out Carnegie Hall.

Margaret was 31 years old in 1999, and "Hollywood obese" (that is,
a normal-size female). She wore a pink skirt over pink pants, and very
tall black platform shoes. Her set pieces included riffs on race, fag-
haggery (her term), sexuality, eating disorders, and the reason men in
straight porn are always so unattractive. She had just put herself back
together after having barely survived the trauma of starring in her own
sitcom, *All-American Girl.* The show came and went in 1994, leaving

her devastated, suicidal, and with a shrink's filing cabinet worth of material to be mined.

She was born in San Francisco in 1968, at hippie ground zero. Her father, a writer of joke books, also owned Paperback Traffic, a gay bookstore in the Castro. She went to elementary school on Haight Street, at home among the aging flower children, druggies, and drag queens. It may have been the peace and love 1960s, but the kids at school were as mean as snakes. Margaret was bullied mercilessly. She tells the story of a time she was ganged up on at summer camp. She was told she looked like shit, and then one night someone stuffed a handful of dog poop into her sleeping bag. "I had to empty it myself in the dark forest and still sleep in it, smelling that shit all that night and for weeks after, because my family was too poor to afford a new one."

In 1984, at the age of 16, Margaret started doing stand-up at a club near her father's bookstore. School was not really her thing. She skipped classes, got lousy grades, was expelled from one high school, and barely graduated from another. She lied about being in college when she entered a local college comedy contest. The winners were awarded the chance to open for Jerry Seinfeld. Margaret was one of them, and after her set, Seinfeld took her aside and told her she should just drop out of college and work on her stand-up full time. She was thrilled, since she'd already done just that.

Amy Schumer wasn't even born when Margaret was landing sex-positive jokes about her lady bits.* In the early 1990s, she was the most popular act on the college circuit, booking upwards of 300 concerts a year. Roseanne Barr, another Edgy Female Stand-up, was starring in a smash sitcom based on her comedy. Hollywood rounded up all the successful Edgy Female Stand-ups like wild mustangs and, eager to duplicate Roseanne's success, handed out production deals. That Korean-American Margaret Cho's comedy was bawdy, groundbreaking, and difficult to categorize made no difference. She, too, was given her own show.

---

* Kidding, actually she was in high school.

All-American Girl was the first sitcom centered around a Korean-American family. The network, in its wisdom, cast actors of Chinese and Japanese descent. Margaret was the only Korean American.** You can imagine how well this went over with Asian-American viewers. It also turned out that Margaret wasn't supposed to be genuinely edgy, but fake TV edgy. Also, fake TV Asian American. It turns out girls born in San Francisco to immigrant parents can be pretty American. (Because they are.) ABC, having no clue how to "fix" her, hired an Asian consultant to offer instruction. "Use chopsticks, then put them in your hair," was one piece of advice.

Margaret was also—wait for it—too fat. I'm sure you're surprised. A dietitian and personal trainer were quickly dispatched to whip her into shape. She lost 30 pounds in less than a month. She had a bit in her stand-up routine during this time about how, when she first saw *Jesus Christ Superstar,* she could only focus on how many calories Jesus burned hauling that giant cross uphill. Eventually, she was hospitalized with kidney failure. She was also told there was an issue with "the fullness" of her face. Meaning, her Korean-American face.

The entire experience, from being discovered to cast aside, was due to all the ways in which Margaret wasn't right. On YouTube, you can see her doing a short set at the Montreal comedy festival Just for Laughs, the same year she was trying so hard to be some studio executive's idea of a perfect Asian-American sitcom star. Her voice is high and a little breathless. She's very put together in all black, with a slash of red lipstick and styled hair. The real Margaret is still under wraps.

MARGARET CHO IS ONE IN A long line of boundary-busting female comedians—Phyllis Diller, Joan Rivers, and Wanda Sykes come to mind—who has figured out how to be her own woman, involving herself

---

** None of the producers, directors, or writers were Korean American.

in pretty much everything that catches her creative eye. Her interests are far-ranging, and she explores them all. In addition to acting in a burlesque-style variety show, creating albums supported by music videos (some of which she's directed), and starting a clothing company, she took up belly dancing, developed a line of belly dancing belts, and co-wrote and starred in a sitcom (it was not picked up). She got a hankering to do some funny animated rap videos, so that happened as well. In 2010, she was on *Dancing with the Stars* (this girl says yes to everything); she and her partner were voted off the third week. She's cohosted a podcast, and also currently cohosts E!'s *Fashion Police*.

Everything about Margaret Cho's persona is difficult. She's sweary. She's not afraid to talk about or imitate oral sex, gay sex, threesomes (insofar as one person can imitate a threesome). In recent years she's amassed dozens of tattoos: beautiful peonies and, weirdly, portraits of Presidents Washington and Lincoln, one on each knee. "I wanted to be in a one-man band, that's my idea," she told the *Today* show by way of explanation. "So I was going to put knee cymbals so I could bang their heads together. I just thought that it would be good to keep the beat and stay patriotic."

DIFFICULT WOMEN WHO HAVE this much access to their rage tend to put people off. The world doesn't seem to know what to do with women who insist not only on talking about their sexual abuse and anger but then converting it into comedy. Margaret was Jerry Seinfeld's guest on his web series *Comedians in Cars Getting Coffee*, and cracked him up with a display of her mother's feeling about her molestation. "I know he's a rapist because he's already raped your aunt. You're not special. Also, he very old. He gonna die soon. So why don't we do this? We can cremate him and I let you flip the switch."

What Margaret does best and most consistently is give us a glimpse at what it's like to walk in her Korean-American shoes. Once, when she was out promoting *All-American Girl,* she was a guest on a local talk show, and the host wanted her to say something in her native tongue. She looked into the camera and spoke in clear, West Coast–accented English. Her hilarious impression of the obsequious, bowing, tiny step–taking, Asian flower girl sends up our expectation that she or anyone like her would ever behave that way. In 2015, she made a cameo at the Golden Globes as a Korean army general and expert on pop culture. She stood between Tina Fey and Amy Poehler in their sexy gowns opining about *Orange Is the New Black.* Was it just hilarious, hilarious and offensive, or hilarious and racist? A million think pieces bloomed in the coming days; she was lambasted as engaging in "minstrelsy" by journalist Kai Ma in *Time.* But this is all part of the Margaret Cho terrain. "I take issue when PC culture works against me," she says. "When it works to silence me, *then* it's racist."

She's certainly had her flops. She's always playing on the edge, and sometimes she falls off. In her most recent show, *Margaret Cho: PsyCHO* (2015), political rants take center stage. And you know, I can do that for myself.

But I'm still with her. She set the bar high all those years ago—and if I'm not weeping with laughter, that doesn't mean I love her any less. It's instructional that when Margaret was trying to contort herself into Hollywood's vision of herself, people turned away. Now she's freely mouthy, angry, and unrestrained. And as a difficult woman extraordinaire, she's earned our respect.

CHAPTER 20

AMELIA EARHART

Adventurous

ON JUNE 17, 1928, WHEN FAMED aviatrix Amelia Earhart made her first transatlantic flight, she was a passenger, not a pilot. Amelia already knew how to fly. She'd had her pilot's license for five years, but her expertise mattered not; a transatlantic flight was presumed to be too stressful and terrifying for a member of the fairer sex. She went along with it, because she was passionate about flying—and being the first woman, even if she wasn't in control, was nevertheless awesome. She was stowed in the back of the *Friendship,* which wasn't much larger than a Chevy Suburban, behind pilot Wilmer "Bill" Stultz and co-pilot Louis "Slim" Gordon. Amelia, who did nothing but endure the discomfort of the 20-hour, 40-minute flight from Trepassey Harbour, Newfoundland, to Burry Port, Wales, nevertheless became an instant celebrity: the serious, pretty, female face of this newfangled thing called air travel.*

When she returned to New York, Amelia was thrown a ticker tape parade. Afterward, a limo had been hired to take her to another appearance. It was a scorching day, the traffic thick. Automotive air-conditioning had yet to be invented. Amelia took one look at the car and imagined being stuck in the backseat in a pool of her own sweat. But then she spied an empty sidecar attached to the motorcycle ridden by one of her police escorts. Without a thought, and without asking any of her minders' or

---

* She was well aware that she hadn't done any of the heavy lifting, and in every interview about the flight she credited Bill Stultz and Slim Gordon.

managers' permission, she hopped in. The cop flipped on his lights and siren, and away they roared.

This is classic Amelia: She went along with the program, allowing herself to be celebrated for something she didn't believe she deserved—I should have been *flying* the *Friendship*, not sitting in it like a sack of potatoes! But when the moment arose to escape, she took it without looking back.

The traditional difficult woman is generally outspoken, opinionated, and headstrong. She likes to shoot her mouth off, and has little interest in avoiding conflict; indeed, she finds it stimulating. Apple carts? She lives to upset them. For those of us who wish to be difficult but are introverted and see no reason we shouldn't keep our opinions to ourselves, Amelia Earhart is our girl. Gracious and somewhat shy on the outside, she was willful and independent on the inside: polite, yet freewheeling, a person who answered to no one. She took the position that adventure is a worthwhile pursuit in and of itself—a radical stance for a woman.

Born on July 24, 1897, in Atchison, Kansas, Amelia was always an adventuresome girl, bombing down hills on her sled in the winter and hunting rats with a rifle she'd pilfered from some male relative in the summer. She maintained a scrapbook of magazine stories and newspaper clippings about women with exciting (male-dominated) careers: film directors, engineers, attorneys. In 1920, at an airshow in Southern California, pilot Frank Hawks was offering 10-minute flights for 10 bucks. Amelia, always restless, always eager to *go*, took him up on it and was hooked. In the summer of 1921, she bought a used Kinner Airster biplane. In 1923, she became the 16th woman in the world to receive her pilot's license.

After her celebrated transatlantic flight aboard the *Friendship* in 1928, Amelia vowed to use the money she made with celebrity appearances, lectures, and best-selling memoirs to finance her *own* solo trip across the pond. On May 22, 1932, she took off from Harbour Grace, Newfoundland, landing 15 hours later in Londonderry, Northern Ireland. More records followed. She was the first woman to fly solo across the United

States, east to west, and the first woman to fly solo from California to Hawaii. In the early 1930s, Amelia set seven solo women's records, for both time and distance, before setting off, in 1937, to become the first person, male or female, to circumnavigate the globe at the Equator. (Others before her had completed a northern route.)

PART OF AMELIA'S INDEPENDENT nature was inborn. When she was a toddler, she once told her mother, "If you are not here to talk to, I just whisper into my own ears." When she was seven, the family visited the 1904 St. Louis World's Fair. Amelia asked if she could ride the roller coaster, and her mother declined. So the child went home and built her own: a death trap made of a pair of two-by-fours, nailed to the edge of the toolshed roof with a wooden crate and roller skate wheels attached. She was the first to test it, and the wipeout at the bottom—busted lip, torn dress—deterred her not at all. "Oh, Pidge," she said to her sister, "it was just like flying."

Amelia's home life was complicated. Her father, Edwin, was an alcoholic. An attorney of some promise, he had no trouble landing jobs but could never seem to keep them. Her mother, Amy (also an Amelia), came from a prominent Atchison family; Amy's father was a former federal judge and a bank president. She lived in a constant state of disappointment and low-grade fury that married life had left her struggling for money and prestige. The family moved around as their fortunes rose and fell and fell: Des Moines, St. Paul, Chicago. Amelia and her sister were parked at the home of their grandparents for long stretches of time while her parents tried to work things out.

From her very proper grandmother—yet *another* Amelia, who disapproved of her granddaughter's tomboy high jinks—Amelia learned a very valuable skill (and one my own mother subscribed to): Tell people what they want to hear, then do whatever the hell you want. From her frustrated mother, Amelia learned the price a wife pays for relying on her husband for her happiness and financial well-being.* From her charming father, Edwin, she learned to do whatever made her happy. (Yes, he was *that* parent.)

In 1920, when Amelia was 23, she and her father took in an air show in Long Beach, California. At that time, aviation was all the rage. Fighter pilots who'd perfected their skills and daring during the First World War barnstormed around the country, showing off their barrel rolls and loop-de-loops. Air shows garnered as much buzz then as the Super Bowl does now. Still, the whole business was insanely dangerous. Engines dropped out of planes at a moment's notice, propellers ceased turning for reasons no one could explain. Because formal runways were things of the future, landing in a field that looked flat from the air but was in fact studded with gopher holes could spell death. In 1920, 40 pilots had been hired by the government to deliver "aerial" mail, and by 1921 all but nine of them had died. Amelia was undeterred; the risk inherent in flying was part of the magic. Her father paid for her 10-minute introductory flight, and five minutes into the spin around the Southern Californian sky, she knew she had found her passion.

Before that, Amelia hadn't found anything that compelled her. She was tall and a little nerdy, had excelled at math and science, and had toyed with a career in medicine. But she was pathologically restless. She enrolled in and dropped out of college several times. She completed a course for ambulance drivers. She flitted. She was the original One Thing Leads to Another Girl. Then she discovered flying, a profession that required and burnished her essential character traits: determination, bravery, calm in the face of danger. How lucky it was for her to find an avocation that didn't force her to tamp down who she knew herself to be.

Her mother—grateful, I suppose, that her daughter had found an outlet for her restless tomboy nature—helped pay for her first flying lessons. Her first flight instructor was also a woman, Anita "Neta" Snook. She was not

---

* Sometime in the 1930s, in response to a reporter's remark that "I still think the smart woman is the one who can get some man able and willing to provide for her," Amelia snapped back, "Why should marriage be a cyclone cellar into which a woman retreats from failure in other spheres?"

pretty—then as now, a feminine sin that's very hard to overlook. Neta was gruff, smelled of engine oil, and was a little weird, living and breathing for this kooky new mania called flying. Amelia showed up for her first lesson in her horseback-riding outfit. The jodhpurs, leather jacket, and boots would become the foundation of her signature style.

By the time Amelia was 24, she had a plane of her own and a series of odd jobs to support her habit. She worked at the phone company, then drove a gravel truck. She took up photography as a sideline, and developed an interest in photographing garbage cans. She wrote, "I can't name all the moods of which a garbage can is capable."

Meanwhile, she flew whenever she could. At an air derby in October 1922, she set her first record: the woman's altitude record, 14,000 feet. She was stubborn, virtually penniless, without a husband or proper career, and completely smitten with flying. It was all she thought about. She taught herself airplane mechanics, read everything she could about airplanes and flight, and hung out at the airfield.

Still, passion doesn't put pork chops on the table, and in 1925, as Amelia was rounding the bend to 30, she discovered social work. So-called settlement houses, where new immigrants were assisted in transitioning from poor, scary foreigners into respectable middle-class Americans, were considered cutting-edge. The most famous settlement house was Jane Addams's Hull House in Chicago. (Addams would go on to win the Nobel Prize and write the middle school reading list staple, *Twenty Years at Hull-House*.) Amelia was hired by Denison House, in Boston. She loved her work, but it didn't pay much; she ran out of money and was forced to sell her plane.

Then, something life-changing fell into her lap.

After Charles Lindbergh made the first solo nonstop flight across the Atlantic in 1927, it was only a matter of time before a wealthy woman of means wanted in on the glory. (Back then, you had to have means if you were going to do something as serious and treacherous as attempt to fly across an ocean; you needed the best plane, mechanics, pilots, navigators, and underwriters.)

Amy Phipps Guest, a freewheeling middle-aged heiress and daughter of Henry Phipps, Jr., Andrew Carnegie's business partner, was worth literally billions. She fancied herself an adventuress and saw no reason she shouldn't be the first woman to fly across the Atlantic. She leased an at-the-time elite plane from Donald Woodward, heir to the Jell-O fortune, hired a couple of pilots, and then succumbed to family pressure that the whole enterprise was simply too dangerous. Guest was 55, and aviation was the province of the young and strapping (difficult to imagine when you think of the near-comatose state required to enjoy flying today). She was also the mother of three grown children, including a son fresh out of Columbia Law School. Poised to take the bar exam, he told his mother he would certainly fail if he was forced to spend time worrying about her crashing into the North Atlantic.

Here's the thing: No one flew anywhere of note in those days without making a big to-do about it. Certainly not across an ocean. We great anonymous flying hordes cruising along on the giant, invisible conveyor belt across the sky, gorging on tiny bags of snack mix, were far, far into the future.

Through her connections, Guest reached out to renowned publisher George Putnam, and brought him on board as one of the project coordinators. Also a genius promoter and publicist, George Palmer Putnam was tall and dark haired, old-style handsome in the Don Draper mode. He was the grandson of G. P. Putnam, founder of venerable G. P. Putnam's Sons, and a self-professed adventure addict. He'd already carved out a niche for himself commissioning expeditions for world-famous adventurers, who would then bang out their tales of mountain climbing, deepsea diving, and yes, flying, in follow-up memoirs. Putnam had published "*We*": *The Daring Flyer's Remarkable Life Story and his Account of the Transatlantic Flight That Shook the World* by Charles Lindbergh (and in one stroke cornered the market on the aviation adventure genre).

Guest and Putnam assembled a list of surrogate women for the flight. Guest required "the right sort of girl." Here is where the Neta Snooks of the world—the ornery, greasy, whiskey-swilling, fingernail-biting female pilots who were brave and willing—simply wouldn't do. Amelia's reputation as an up-and-coming star of aviation, with more than 500 hours in the air under her belt and no serious accidents, preceded her. Also, and equally important, her daredevil tomboy soul was hidden beneath a soft-spoken, ladylike exterior. She sported a tousled head of blond curls (although her hair was actually board-straight; her look of weather-beaten aviatrix chic required that she curl her hair daily), along with a sprinkling of freckles and a friendly gap-toothed smile. More important, perhaps critically, her body was the body of the times; she was built like a flapper: tall, flat-chested, reed-thin. She wore pants—not to be contrary, but to hide her fat ankles—her only serious figure flaw.*

Then came the triumphant flight of the *Friendship*. When the plane landed in Wales on June 18, 1928, Amelia was instantly famous. In New York, the *Times* banner headline read: "City Greets Miss Earhart; Girl Flier, Shy and Smiling, Shares Praise With Mates."

That summer of 1928, after the flight that put her on the map, Amelia moved into George and Dorothy Putnam's home in Rye, New York. The professed reason was so that she and George could work together on her book, *20 Hrs., 40 Min.: Our Flight in the Friendship,* but there was also romance in the air. George was smitten with Amelia, and presumably she felt something similar, even though she was a woman who kept her cards close to her chest. Amelia wrote all day, every day, while George focused on promoting her and the forthcoming book. Meanwhile, Dorothy secretly pined for her much-younger lover, George Weymouth, a sophomore at Yale. It was commonly believed that Amelia stole George out from under Dorothy's nose. But even Sally Putnam Chapman, the granddaughter of Dorothy and George, and author of *Whistled Like a Bird: The Untold Story of Dorothy Putnam, George Putnam, and Amelia Earhart,* says "This was simply not the truth. In fact, quite the opposite; Amelia gave [Dorothy] the excuse she needed [to divorce George]."

---

* She got bonus points for worrying about this alleged flaw. It made her seem like every other woman, vain and a little silly, and that reassured everyone.

In December 1929, Dorothy moved to Reno and filed for divorce, and George persuaded Amelia to marry him. It took some doing. Since girlhood, she hadn't thought much of the institution. She suspected that unless she took care, she would fall into the same bad situation as her mother. The couple took out a marriage license in November 1930, and on February 7, 1931, Amelia submitted to a no-muss, no-fuss ceremony, wearing one of her usual brown suits with no hat, her dark blond hair carefully tousled in its usual way.

I once knew a woman, a professional BASE jumper, who would rather literally jump off a bridge than hazard the big risks of marriage and motherhood. She was cut from the same cloth as Amelia, who found marriage to be much scarier than flying. On the morning of their marriage, full of fear and dread, Amelia presented George with a letter that read in part:

> *You must know again my reluctance to marry, my feeling that I shatter thereby chances in work which means most to me . . . On our life together . . . I shall not hold you to any midaevil code of faithfulness to me nor shall I consider myself bound to you similarly . . .*
>
> *Please let us not interfere with the others' work or play, nor let the world see our private joys or disagreements. In this connection I may have to keep some place where I can go to be myself, now and then, for I cannot guarantee to endure at all times the confinement of even an attractive cage.*

It was addressed to GPP and signed A.E. In it, she also promised to do her best to make the marriage work in every way. This letter is so perversely pragmatic, it's a wonder the union survived. But George Putnam was just the man to receive such a letter (it's always important to know your audience). He read it repeatedly, then tucked it away. Only after Amelia's death did he reveal its existence, calling it evidence of his late wife's "gallant inward spirit."

It was the perfect marriage of promoter and promotee.

George worked long hours "growing the Amelia Earhart brand," as we might describe it today. Cast as "Lady Lindy" by a cagey photographer who snapped her in her aviatrix duds and made her look like Charles Lindbergh's sister (which she didn't), Amelia had proved able to compete in the he-man's world of aviation without appearing in any way threatening. She looked swashbuckling and chic in her breeches and leather jacket, and had a face made for a leather aviator cap (you can't say that about most people). But whenever the newspaper ran a picture of her, George always made sure it ran alongside another photo of her in elegant flapper attire, complete with fetching cloche hat (again with the hat), an elegant long-waisted dress, and a strand of pearls.

Amelia was a traditionally feminine woman who could nevertheless get in an airplane and fly away. Men remained unthreatened, and women—most of whom are reluctant to completely smash the patriarchy and give up their affection for pretty underwear—were encouraged and inspired. How could they not be?

The same preternatural patience and stamina that allowed Amelia to sit for many long hours in the cockpit of a plane made her a self-promotion warrior. In the early 1930s, she devoted herself to advocating for women in aviation (once, she gave 13 speeches in 12 days), served on committees, gave more speeches, served on more committees, wrote letters on behalf of this, that, and the other aeronautical whatnot. She founded the Ninety-Nines, an organization for female pilots, and her own clothing line. She was made an honorary major of the U.S. Air Service and given a pair of silver wings, which she often wore with her pearls. She struck up a friendship with Eleanor Roosevelt. The first lady had an adventurous streak herself, and was keen to take flying lessons. Amelia hooked her up, but the president vetoed it as too dangerous, even as he was publicly saluting Amelia's efforts to convince the country that air transportation was the wave of the future.

On May 20, 1932, five years to the day after Lindbergh made his historic transatlantic flight, Amelia Earhart finally made her own solo flight across the pond. During those five years, many women had taken up flying, and a lot of female pilots were angling for the record. Ruth Nichols, owner of both the altitude and speed record in 1931, announced her own plan to attempt to fly across the Atlantic. She took off in June amid much media hysteria, only to crash during her refueling stop in New Brunswick, wrecking her plane and smashing five vertebrae. Laura Ingalls, an aerialist who held the record for uninterrupted barrel rolls, and 20-year-old Elinor Smith, briefly famous for having flown beneath all of Manhattan's East River bridges, also had their eyes on the prize.

Amelia, not wishing to alert the press, prepared for her own attempt in secret.

Days before her flight, she puttered around the house with George. She raked leaves (her sole form of exercise). She went over the proofs of her next book, *The Fun of It*. They invited Ruth Nichols, in a back brace and still recovering from her crash, for a leisurely dinner, and in general behaved as if nothing out of the ordinary was afoot. Bernt Balchen, one of her flight advisers, busied himself every day at the private New Jersey airport Teterboro, prepping her Lockheed Vega; the press reported he was borrowing the plane to fly to the North Pole. Then, on the morning of May 20, 1932, Amelia moseyed over to the airport, hopped in her plane, and took off alone across the ocean, headed for Paris.

The sky was clear. She flew northeast, stopping to refuel at Harbour Grace, Newfoundland, before continuing along the polar route. She flew at 12,000 feet, sipping hot soup from her thermos. Hours passed. Below, icebergs drifted past, pink in the setting sun. Then the altimeter went on the fritz. She wasn't too worried. There were a few scattered low clouds, and she was confident she could estimate her altitude as long as she could still see the water. A bit later she glanced out the window and spied a tiny blue flame near the exhaust manifold. She was at that point where turning back was as treacherous as continuing on.

The visibility began to deteriorate. Suddenly, she was flying through dark, many-storied thunderheads, the kind every modern-day commercial pilot is routinely ordered to fly around, or risk upsetting the drink service. There was nothing for Amelia to do but fly through them, jouncing around in the wind and rain, continuing along her fixed-compass course. Soon the rain turned to ice, and the controls froze, sending her tiny plane into a spin. As she hurtled toward the green-gray whitecaps, the ice melted, and she was able to regain control. But minutes after she regained her cruising altitude, the rain turned to ice again, the windshield frosted over, the gears froze, and the plane spun. Once again, she plummeted toward the sea, the ice again melted during the descent, and she flew low over the churning sea until she hoped it was safe to ascend once more. As the sun rose, she found herself on the other side of the storm, gliding into the dawn. All the unanticipated descending and ascending had used up fuel; she flipped the switch on an auxiliary gas tank, only to feel fuel trickling down the side of her neck from an invisible leak overhead.

She had been headed for France, but once she saw green hills beneath her she thought better of it, given the frozen altimeter, the fire in the exhaust manifold, and the leaky auxiliary gas tank. At 13:46 GMT, she landed in a pasture on a farm outside Londonderry, Ireland. The flight had lasted 14 hours, 56 minutes. A farmer came running as she crawled out of the cockpit. "Have you flown far?" he asked. She said, "From America." If she was frazzled and freaked out, you'd never know it. Amelia could be as laconic as a cowboy. Even though she didn't make it to Paris, as Lindbergh had done, the world saluted her achievement. Amelia received a Gold Medal from the National Geographic Society, and Congress presented her with a Distinguished Flying Cross.

MOST WOMEN ARE WARY OF indulging their difficult side. Oh sure, we may have managed to convince our friends—even our mothers and sisters—that we're feisty or kickass. We tell stories about hurling F-bombs, how we carried on at Burning Man, or rocked some inappropriate outfit at a friend's wedding. We smoke, even though we know it's going to kill us! But when it comes to putting ourselves and our own needs above those of people we love, we are wary. We've been bred to worry that only a woman who's prepared to wind up alone insists on the primacy of her own needs. We're afraid that if we honor and express our true selves, and if that true self is not as self-sacrificing as society demands of women, we will chase everyone we love away.

But Amelia was true to herself, and George did not run away. She followed her heart—not his heart—and he only loved her more. He loved her enough to help her prepare for her greatest flight, the one that would take her from him.

AMELIA'S GREAT DREAM was to fly around the world. "Women, like men, should try to do the impossible," she said by way of explanation. The proposed flight wasn't exactly impossible, but it was complicated and expensive. The risk was off the charts, the kind of chance that only difficult women take. Amelia couldn't have been more exhilarated. Flying with navigator Fred Noonan, she took off on May 20, 1937, from Oakland, California, heading east. Across the United States, down the east coast of Central and South America, across the Atlantic, Africa, the southern edge of Arabia, India. Amelia and Noonan reached Lae, New Guinea, on June 29. The only leg left was a final 7,000 miles across the Pacific. They took off on July 2 for Howland Island, her Lockheed Electra groaning with enough fuel to get them to the next stop on their round-the-world flight.

Howland Island is a 1.7-square-mile amoeba-shaped dab of featureless earth in the middle of the ocean, 2,556 miles northeast of Lae. To give you a sense of the challenge of trying to find and land on teeny Howland using only compass navigation: Imagine standing atop the Empire State Building and trying to hit a bull's-eye on a dartboard hanging on the Statue of Liberty, five miles away.

The Coast Guard cutter *Itasca* was moored off Howland, belching a thick column of black smoke into the air: a signal for Amelia. As she made her approach, the *Itasca* received a few radio transmissions from her, but the Electra never arrived. It has never been found, and the boundless curiosity about Amelia's disappearance continues to this day. As of this writing another search party has departed for the South Pacific, equipped with the usual high-tech search and rescue devices, as well as a few rescue dogs trained to sniff out bone fragments.

So many theories, one more romantic than the next. That Amelia was a spy, tasked with mapping the Pacific for her good friend President Franklin D. Roosevelt, and was captured and killed by the Japanese. Or that she was rescued from the crash and, in some kind of nonsensical famous person protection program, sent to live out the rest of her life as a banker in New Jersey. The most likely of the unlikely explanations is that she crashed on Nikumaroro Island, a few hundred miles southeast of Howland, where she and Fred lived as sexy tropical island castaways until they perished.*

Every time there's a new Amelia book or movie, people get whipped up all over again about her disappearance. There are think pieces about her character: America's sweetheart was not as pure of heart as we once imagined, but selfish and self-aggrandizing. Or she took that last, fatal flight *for her own pleasure.* Or she enjoyed self-promotion a little too much. And what about her very modern marriage? There are stories about the obsessives who've devoted their lives to "finding" her, and updates on how the latest in advanced technology can be employed in the ongoing search. (If we can't find Malaysia Flight 370 with all the goodies in the search and rescue box, I think it's unlikely anyone will find the 80-year-old Electra.)

Though Amelia has been gone all these years, her difficult woman philosophy lives on. "Adventure is worthwhile in itself," she said. Men have always done things because it gave them pleasure and a sense of achievement. So why shouldn't women be granted the same privilege?

---

* The telltale artifacts, including skeletal fragments, parts of shoes, and a box that looked as if it might have contained a sextant, used for celestial navigation, were discovered in 1940, then somehow misplaced. In 2014, a square of metal from the alleged wing of Amelia's alleged plane was found on Nikumaroro.

CHAPTER 21

FRIDA KAHLO

Fervid

LEGENDARY ARTIST FRIDA KAHLO spent most of 1950 in a hospital bed in Mexico City, recovering from a series of spinal surgeries. Her recuperation involved bed rest, during which her torso was immobilized in a heavy plaster cast. In a telling contemporary photograph of the painter and future global feminist icon, she is propped up against her pillows, embellishing the front of her latest plaster corset with the aid of a hand mirror and a tiny brush. Her pointy nails are lacquered with dark polish. Her center-parted hair is pulled back neatly. A pile of satin ribbons and flowers adorns the crown of her head. She sports dangly earrings, chunky rings on every finger, and a pair of bracelets.

Regardless of the degree to which she was suffering, Frida Kahlo always enjoyed the spectacle of herself. She was a playful exhibitionist, a fervid and erotic provocateur dispatching updates from the land of female suffering. It was part of what made her difficult: She forced people to look at her, to share her feelings, when they would prefer to look away.

Magdalena Carmen Frieda Kahlo y Calderón was born in Coyoacán, a tidy suburb of Mexico City, in July 1907. Until the day Frida (she dropped the "e" in 1922) was hit by a streetcar—literally, at the age of 18—nothing in her upper-middle-class background would disclose her future: that she would one day become Mexico's most celebrated painter, a sexy international art megastar and pop icon who would produce unnerving masterpieces that would hang in the world's major museums.* Or that she would "enjoy" a passionate, tumultuous marriage to Mexico's most famous muralist and womanizer, Diego Rivera. Frida and Diego married for the first time in 1929, divorced in 1939, remarried in 1940, and remained wed until Frida's untimely death in 1954, at the age of 47. Years after both artists were dead, a travel squib appeared in the *New York Times,* which included the sentence: "Though they created some of Mexico's most fascinating art, it's the bizarre Beauty-and-the-Beast dynamic that has captivated the world and enshrouded both figures in intrigue."

It's often said that girls who grow up to be women at ease with themselves had loving, nurturing relationships with their fathers. To be appreciated and accepted by the first man in our lives gives us confidence to march that self out into the world, to feel that we will not be shunned for being both a woman *and* a complex human being. Frida's father, German-born Guillermo Kahlo, was one such dad. Among his five daughters, Frida—high-spirited, clever, and entertaining—was his favorite. Frida would steal fruit from a nearby orchard in lieu of attending catechism class, or sneak up on her sisters when they were using the chamber pot and shove them off. But these high jinks ended when she contracted polio at age six.

Frida was confined to her bed for nine months—an eternity for an active six-year-old. Her father tended to her with care, and when she was finally given the go-ahead to return to school, Guillermo prescribed sports. Frida excelled in soccer, swimming, roller-skating, and boxing. She grew stronger, but her right leg remained puny and withered. She was ostracized at school for her "peg leg." To help compensate for her loneliness, her father,

---

* Also inspiring cultlike devotion and the manufacturing of any number of decorative mugs, key chains, T-shirts, socks, sweatshirts, swimsuits, leggings, paper dolls, earrings, bedding collections, curtains, throw pillows, rubber stamps, coloring books, bottle openers, umbrellas, nail decals, cell phone cases, aprons, floral crowns—and of course, tote bags.

who believed her to be the most like him of all his daughters (smart, artistic, strong-willed—practically a son!), gave her books from his library and taught her how to take and develop photographs.

Frida's relationship with her mother, Matilde, was fraught—as is generally the case with clever daughters poised to escape the limited existence of an older generation who played by the rules. Beautiful, pious, and illiterate, Matilde had dutifully married a man with "prospects," managed the household, and kept the babies and delicious meals coming. Frida dared to hope for a bigger life.

When she was 15, Frida was enrolled in the prestigious Escuela Nacional Preparatoria, where she focused on biology with the hope of one day becoming a doctor. Still shy about her smaller right leg, she wore extra pairs of socks to help disguise it. But she seemed to have more or less recovered. She was bright, engaged in her studies, and a star of the *Cachuchas,* an elite club of brainiacs and mischief makers. She had a popular boyfriend, Alejandro Gómez Arias.

On September 17, 1925, Frida and Alex were riding home from school on the bus when it was T-boned by a streetcar. She was impaled by a handrail that entered her just above her left hip and exited through her vagina. Her back and pelvis were each broken in three places. Her collarbone was broken. Her withered, polio-afflicted leg was fractured, her smaller foot dislocated and mangled. Someone at the scene thought it was a good idea to pull out the handrail before the ambulance arrived. Frida's screams, and the sounds of bones cracking, were louder than the approaching sirens.

Alex, who suffered only minor wounds, recalled it this way: "Something strange had happened. Frida was totally nude. The collision had unfastened her clothes. Someone in the bus, probably a house painter, had been carrying a packet of powdered gold. This package broke, and the gold fell all over the bleeding body of Frida. When people saw her, they cried, '*La bailarina, la bailarina!*' With the gold on her red, bloody body, they thought she was a dancer."

For a month, Frida lay in a plaster body cast. No one expected her to survive. When she was released from the hospital, the treatment was bed rest—at first, months of bed rest. Then, two solid years of bed rest. Gone was Alex the boyfriend, gone were Frida's dreams of becoming a doctor. The medical bills piled up, and her father mortgaged the house to pay them. Her life of chronic pain began. The next year, a new set of doctors examined her spine and realized the first set of doctors had failed to see that several vertebrae had healed incorrectly. This would become a running theme, new doctors shaking their heads at the ineptitude of previous doctors. The solution: another plaster body cast and more bed rest.

"I never thought of painting until 1926, when I was in bed on account of an automobile accident," she wrote to gallery owner Julien Levy before her 1938 show. "I was bored as hell in bed . . . so I decided to do something. I stoled [sic] from my father some oil paints, and my mother ordered for me a special easel because I couldn't sit down [the letter was written in English; she meant sit up], and I started to paint."

Frida's letter was crafty, disingenuous. After the accident, flat on her back in bed, painting presented itself as one of the only activities available to her. She pretended not to care about the quality of her work, but in 1927, once she was up and around, she sought the professional opinion of the celebrated artist Diego Rivera. As popular lore and the 2002 biopic *Frida** would have it, she cornered the artist one day while he was atop a ladder working on a mural; she demanded he come down, have a look, and tell her straight out whether she was good enough. "Look, I have not come to flirt or anything, even if you are a woman-chaser," she told him. "I have come to show you my painting. If you are interested in it, tell me so; if not, likewise." (More likely, Frida met Diego at a party hosted by photographer and activist Tina Modotti. But the story of tracking him down and challenging him from her place beneath the ladder better suited her sense of self-drama.)

---

* Directed by Julie Taymor, starring Salma Hayek and Alfred Molina.

Rivera and Frida were both members of the Mexican Communist Party, and Rivera was captivated by Frida's bohemian élan. She was one of those tiny women who could drink men twice her size under the table. She lived on a diet of candy, cigarettes, and a daily bottle of brandy. When this diet (and, presumably, casual dental hygiene) caused her teeth to rot in early middle age, she promptly ordered two sets of dentures: one solid gold, another studded with diamonds. As anyone who's ever purchased a Frida tote bag, postcard, coffee mug, or T-shirt knows, she was proud of her unibrow and her mustache, which she kept neat with a small comb reserved for that purpose.

On a sweltering August day in 1929, Frida and Diego were married, to the consternation of her family and friends. Frida was a somewhat sheltered 22—she had spent three of those years bedridden—and Rivera was a 43-year-old man of the world, an established artist whose murals celebrating the 1910 Mexican revolution had made him famous. He came equipped with two ex-wives and three daughters; when he and Frida first fell in love, he was still married to wife number two.

People are rarely surprised when a beautiful woman marries an average-looking man. Even so, people were mystified by Frida's adoration of and devotion to Diego Rivera. I'm reluctant to objectify Diego in the same way men routinely objectify women, but despite some fairly extensive research I've been unable to find a single photograph of the great muralist in which he isn't completely repulsive. "Twenty-one years older, 200 pounds heavier, and, at more than six feet, nearly 12 inches taller than she, Rivera was gargantuan in both scale and appetites," wrote Amy Fine Collins in *Vanity Fair*. "As irresistible as he was ugly, Rivera was described by Frida as 'a boy frog standing on his hind legs.' "

(It's safe to say that of all the traits men possess that are catnip to women—sense of humor, great hair, nice shoulders, lead guitar player in a band—"boy frog standing on his hind legs" rarely makes the average woman's must-have list.)

There was a window of time during the first years of their marriage when Frida, more or less recovered from her accident, happily and with fervor performed the role of exemplary wife. She devoted herself to cooking for her husband, fussed over his clothes and comfort, gave him his nightly bath in which she floated bath toys for his amusement. Her 1949 painting "The Love Embrace of the Universe, the Earth (Mexico), Myself, Diego and Señor Xólotl," in which she cradles a naked Diego in her lap while she is in turn cradled by Aztec Earth Mother Cihuacoatl, pretty much sums up the way she viewed their marriage: Her husband was a giant baby.

In 1930, Frida traveled with Rivera to San Francisco, where he'd been commissioned to paint a mural for the San Francisco Stock Exchange Luncheon Club.* This required him to seek out a female model that would represent the essence of California womanhood. He was put in touch with international tennis star Helen Wills. She was the real deal, having won 31 Grand Slam titles and two Olympic gold medals. In the name of making a "study" of Wills for the mural, Rivera disappeared with her for a few days.

Frida wept at Diego's endless extracurricular canoodling, which he had no intention of giving up despite the anguish he caused. He would explain patiently that for him monogamy was simply out of the question, and that he viewed sexual intercourse as essential and uncomplicated as taking a piss. Frida would howl in fury, hurling the occasional ceramic plate against a brightly painted wall, then lock Rivera out of her bedroom. He would retaliate by throwing himself into his latest mural commission, and maybe take on another mistress or two. Sometimes, upon discovering the identity of the new mistress, Frida would enjoy a little spicy revenge by seducing the woman. Then they would have another argument in which Frida hurled another ceramic plate, and so on and so forth.

---

* American capitalists, taken with the prestige of having a Rivera mural grace the side of their building, turned a blind eye toward his radical left-wing politics.

Frida's hot temper was the most generic aspect of her difficult nature, handily reinforcing the stereotype of females as prone to hysteria. A teary, pissed-off woman slouched on the sofa eating a pint of Ben and Jerry's is exhausting and irritating, but acceptable—in part, because a weeping woman doesn't have to be taken seriously.

Consider this: A recent study of jury dynamics conducted by the journal *Law and Human Behavior* found that although an angry man can influence the feelings and opinions of his fellow jurors, the same is not true for women. In fact, the angrier a woman gets, the more jurors were convinced their own opinions were correct. The more furiously a woman juror behaved, the less anyone listened to her. Translated into the domestic realm, this means that husbands don't actually mind the type of behavior Frida often displayed. It turns their woman into someone they don't have to take seriously, and it also allows them to do something they rather enjoy, which is to throw up their hands, go to their local bar, order a stiff drink, and complain with other men about the impossibility of women.

But Frida had other, less predictable traits. She could be sly and misleading. A now-infamous 1933 profile in the *Detroit News*, headlined "Wife of the Master Mural Painter Gleefully Dabbles in Works of Art," was written during the couple's sojourn in Detroit that year (Diego was painting "Detroit Industry," a celebration of the city's workers). The accompanying black-and-white photo shows Frida at the easel, her head turned toward the camera at an angle that mirrors exactly the one in the self-portrait she's painting. She wears an apron tied around her waist, as if she's come straight from the kitchen. Regarding hubby Diego, her quote reads: "He does well for a little boy, but it is I who am the big artist."

She was being facetious—something that was lost on the writer, who wasn't prepared for Frida's wit. But the joke contains the beating heart of her ambition. Frida may have started painting to amuse herself during her convalescence, but by the early 1930s she was determined to make her mark. During her time dabbling in Detroit, she painted two pictures that would one day be considered masterpieces: "Henry Ford Hospital" and "My Birth." The latter depicts a woman, presumably Frida, giving birth to herself. The picture is startling, even today. The figure on the bed is covered by a white sheet from the waist up. Her legs are splayed open, and a full-grown female head bearing the distinctive unibrow protrudes from her vagina. Pop icon Madonna currently owns the painting. In an interview in *Vanity Fair*, Madonna said, "If somebody doesn't like this painting, then I know they can't be my friend."

IN THE SUMMER OF 1938, at the age of 31, Frida made her first sale. The actor Edward G. Robinson was also an art collector, and while he was in Mexico City he purchased four little pictures, for $200 apiece. French artist André Breton also discovered her work, and heralded it as surrealist. Her paintings, he enthused, were like "a ribbon around a bomb."

You might imagine that after laboring in the shadow of her husband for almost a solid decade, Frida would be thrilled and even grateful to be tapped for inclusion in a big-deal art movement that included powerhouse painters Max Ernst, Marcel Duchamp, and René Magritte. But she wasn't much interested. She found the French to be insufferable, cold, and bourgeois. And anyway, she was her *own* movement.

In the fall of that year, Frida traveled to New York for her first solo exhibition, at the Julien Levy Gallery. Clare Boothe Luce, wife of *Time* magazine magnate Henry Luce, was enjoying a moment with her hit Broadway play *The Women* and attended the opening. Frida was notoriously charming, even among the capitalist gringos she disparaged. She and Clare hit it off, and by the end of the evening Clare had commissioned Frida to paint a portrait. The subject was the late Dorothy Hale, a depressed young socialite and friend of Clare's who had lived beyond her means in an upper-floor apartment at the newly opened Hampshire House on Central Park South. Key details that will become important: On the night before she died, Dorothy threw herself a farewell cocktail party. After the last guest left, she put on her favorite black velvet dress and a corsage of tiny yellow roses. Then, at 5:15 a.m. or thereabouts, she threw herself out the window.

Clare and Frida had both known Dorothy and agreed that the situation was tragic. Clare also felt guilty. Her relationship with Dorothy had been complicated by money; Clare would loan her rent money, and Dorothy would spend it on a cocktail dress. Dorothy was *that* annoying friend. At some point Clare had cut Dorothy off. And now she was dead. To help assuage her guilt, and as a kind gesture, Clare intended to give Frida's beautiful portrait of Dorothy to Dorothy's bereaved mother, as a remembrance.

Time-out for a thought experiment: You are Frida, perpetually strapped for cash. Your marriage is shakier than usual. You also have an ongoing cavalcade of medical problems. You are beginning to gain an audience for your paintings, and the only way you can or want to earn some extra money is by selling them. Clare Boothe Luce is rich and powerful, and if she's happy with the picture she has commissioned, she will tell her rich and powerful friends, who then might also commission a picture from you. You know this is how it works. It's the golden rule: He who has the gold, rules.

What do you do? Do you give Clare Boothe Luce what you know she wants—a pleasant, decorative picture to present to her friend Dorothy's grieving mother? Or do you respect your own talent and vision and give her the shocking "The Suicide of Dorothy Hale," as well as a near heart attack?

Unlike Frida, I have been permanently scarred by the number one rule drilled into my head at every retail and fast-food job of my youth: Customer satisfaction is our number one goal. In other words, like many women (like you?) I was conditioned to please from a young age. I would have been delirious with joy to have received a commission from someone like Clare Boothe Luce. Keeping in mind that I was painting the portrait for Dorothy's poor mother, I would have made Dorothy look even prettier than she had been in real life. My goal would have been to make everyone weep with joy, including the spirit of Dorothy herself.

But then, I'm not difficult. Frida was.

In the center of the painting, behind what appears to be a feathery layer of cirrus clouds, the cream-colored Hampshire House rises up with its many small windows and mansard roof. In the background, a tiny figure plummets past the upper stories. In the middle ground there is another, larger falling woman, clearly Dorothy Hale, her arms extended, her skirt billowing around her knees. In the foreground, resting on the brown earth is Dorothy in her black velvet dress and yellow corsage, her neck clearly broken. The banner running along the bottom of the painting says, *In the city of New York on the 21st day of the month of October, 1938, at six o'clock in the morning, Mrs. DOROTHY HALE committed suicide by throwing herself out of a very high window of the Hampshire House building. In her memory [a strip of missing words] this retablo, executed by FRIDA KAHLO.* Blood flows from beneath Dorothy's head and dribbles onto the banner and frame.

Horrified does not begin to describe the reaction of Clare Boothe Luce. "I will always remember the shock I had when I pulled the painting out of the crate," she wrote later. "I felt really physically *sick*. What was I going to do with this gruesome painting of the smashed corpse of my friend, and her blood dripping down all over the frame?"

Clare Boothe Luce's first impulse was to cut up "The Suicide of Dorothy Hale" with a pair of shears. But at the last minute she called an illustrator friend who did covers for the *New Yorker*. Intrigued, he rushed over and took it off her hands.

Currently the picture hangs in the Phoenix Art Museum and is routinely cited as one of Frida Kahlo's masterpieces.

Frida may have been thrilled to receive a commission, but her gratitude didn't poison her vision. Frida obeyed her own heaving feelings, always, and could only paint what they dictated. If people were alarmed, so much the better. She wasn't about to make an exception, thinking, "I'll hold off doing my wacky Frida thing just this once." Nope. Frida expressed what was in her heart with every brushstroke, and what was in Frida's heart that fall of 1938 was despair. Her marriage was over. The final straw had been Diego's latest affair. Of all the women available to Diego in Mexico City—and according to historians, that would have been all the women in Mexico City, so charming and irresistible was he—his choice for an extramarital affair was Frida's sister, Cristina.

In 1939, Frida and Diego Rivera were divorced. Perhaps they would have remained forever estranged, if not for the assassination of exiled Russian communist leader Leon Trotsky.

Several years earlier, while Frida and Diego were still relatively happy, Trotsky and his wife arrived in Mexico City to live with them, having been expelled from the Soviet Union. The short version of the Trotskys' time with the Riveras: tequila, tequila, tequila; Trotsky and Rivera argue politics; Trotsky and Frida have a fling, sending Madame Trotsky into an understandable depression; Trotsky escapes several assassination attempts by Stalinist operatives dispatched from the Soviet Union, only to be murdered on August 20, 1940, by a demented local man with an ice ax. Frida and Diego, now living separately, were both suspects! Rivera fled to San Francisco, while Frida was taken into custody for questioning. She was released after a few days, and also left for San Francisco to consult Dr. Leo Eloesser about some kind of chronic fungal infection; Eloesser had treated her for various maladies in 1930, and had become a trusted friend.

So devoted was Frida to "doctorcito," as she liked to call him, that she painted two pictures for him: "Portrait of Dr. Leo Eloesser" (1931), a somewhat straightforward and inexpert rendering of the good doctor standing with his elbow on a high table in front of a sailboat

(Frida was never as good painting other people) and "Self-Portrait Dedicated to Dr. Eloesser" (1940), which displays her trademark nightmarish razzle-dazzle. She captures herself in her favorite three-quarter angle, looking straight at the view from beneath her infamous unibrow. Dangling from her one visible ear is a golden ear-ring of an open palm. A choker of thorns digs into her neck, drawing a few drops of blood.

In San Francisco Frida and Diego got back together. Perhaps the calamity of being persons of interest in Trotsky's homicide reunited them. Or maybe the romance of the City by the Bay was just impossible to resist. In any case, they remarried in 1940 at a small civil ceremony. Trying to parse the logic behind their reconciliation is above my pay grade.

DURING FRIEGO 2.0, Frida painted most of her masterpieces.

Inspiration is mysterious in its complexity. What fires up any given artist is as unique as a fingerprint. Frida seemed to require a carefully titrated mixture of despair at Diego's disappearing acts, loneliness, and active engagement with her own broken body. To date, her complete medical history remains unknown. She is said to have had 30 surgeries over the course of her lifetime, most of them attempts to repair the damage from the bus accident she'd suffered at 18. She saw a round of doctors, most of whom contradicted each other. Mexican doctors once declared she had "a tuberculosis in the bones" and wanted to operate; Dr. Eloesser disagreed. In 1944 her chronic back pain worsened (treat-ment: steel corset prescribed to reduce "irritation of the nerves" that she wore for five months).

In the first part of 1946, she sought out a "high-up doctor of Grin-golandia" to perform a complicated surgery in which four vertebrae were fused using bone from her pelvis. The operation was performed in June. Her recovery was a success, but eventually she suffered again from shooting pains. A new doctor in Mexico examined her and claimed the New York doctor had performed the fusion on the wrong vertebrae. But there's another version of this story: The fusion was a success and Frida made a full recovery. Then one night Diego didn't come home, and in a fit of rage and frustration, she either opened her own incisions or else threw herself on the ground and compromised the barely knitted bones.

Frida's bone grafts developed infections, requiring exquisitely painful injections. Her circulation suffered so much from inactivity and a terrible diet that one day she woke up to find that the tips of the toes on her right foot were black. Eventually, they were amputated, followed by her leg, amputated below the knee in 1953, a year before she died.

Diego's love for Frida seemed directly related to her invalidism. The worse his wife's pain—the more she suffered—the less Diego philandered. He would sit beside her bed and read poetry aloud, or hold her as she fell asleep. When the pain became manageable (often with the aid of heavy-duty meds to which she would eventually become addicted), he would go back to work, become distracted by a new lover, and leave her alone. Again.

Then, she would paint. Some of Frida's most arresting work—her certifiable masterpieces—come from this period. "The Broken Column" (1944) shows her naked form split jaggedly in half, her skin pierced with nails. Inside her open body, crumbling steel replaced her spine, her torso held together by the white straps that run under and above her pretty breasts. In "The Wounded Deer" (1946) her face, in its standard three-quarters angle, has been placed atop a wounded deer running in the forest. Antlers extend from either side of her head, and nine arrows pierce the deer's body. Her anguish at being force-fed what was essentially baby food is on display in "Without Hope" (1945). She lies in a four-poster bed in what appears to be a postapocalyptic landscape; a wooden frame looms over her, holding a funnel overflowing with fish heads, a strangled chicken, some kind of offal, and a skull. She gazes at the viewer with her classic stare, tears on her cheeks, the end of the funnel pressed between her lips.

The degree to which Frida helped facilitate her own misery will forever remain a mystery. Her questionable medical care is inferior only in retrospect. Her doctors were for the most part top-notch, practicing the most up-to-date methods of the time. But regardless of how she came by her suffering, Frida wasn't about to do it in silence. She wasn't interested so much in communicating her situation as expressing it. This is how it feels to be in this broken female body. This is how it feels to be alone and without my beloved. This is how it feels to be me. I dare you to look—and once you look, I'm going to make sure you cannot look away.

"I recommend her to you, not as a husband but as an enthusiastic admirer of her work," Diego once wrote to Picasso. "Acid and tender, hard as steel and delicate and fine as a butterfly's wing, lovable as a beautiful smile, and profound and cruel as the bitterness of life."

When Frida died in 1954 at the age of 47, she was known primarily as Diego Rivera's exotic little wife. The rise of feminism in the late 1970s brought with it the question "Hey, where are all the women artists? Where are all the women of color?" and the answer was the rediscovery of Frida Kahlo.

In 2016, Frida's 1939 painting "Two Nudes in the Forest (the Earth Itself)" sold at Christie's for a record eight million dollars—the most expensive Latin American art piece sold at auction to date. A small, somber oil on metal, the painting depicts one naked Frida resting her head in the lap of another naked Frida, amid the thick vines and heavily veined leaves of a voluptuous jungle that existed only in her mind.

Fifty-five of Frida Kahlo's 143 pictures are self-portraits. Many of them depict the woes of living in a human female body, including the mess of female reproduction and its sometime failures. Metal hospital beds, bloody instruments, a snarl of internal organs she seems to be vomiting in despair. A delicate, anatomically correct image of her own heart beating inside her chest, her naked body splayed open, giving birth to her mustachioed adult self. The female nude, so beloved of fine artists, had never been nude like this.

Then as now, it's a well-known truism that men are uncomfortable when women cry. One can only imagine how squirmy they must have been—how squirmy they are—in the presence of Frida's pictures. But Frida was a woman comfortable among the chaos of her feelings. She never denied them, never dialed them down. It made her strong. Or, in the view of some—difficult.

CHAPTER 22

NORA EPHRON

Exacting

NORA EPHRON WAS THAT RAREST of difficult women: the lovable bitch. I'm not disrespecting the dead. I've had a girl crush on Nora since I first read *Heartburn* in 1984. The rainy afternoon I finished her best-selling, lightly fictionalized memoir, I took the bus downtown to the library where I spent the afternoon reading her as-yet-uncollected magazine and news-paper pieces (she wrote many memorable pieces for *Newsweek, Esquire, New York* magazine, and many others, before going on to become a best-selling author and one of Hollywood's most successful directors). These days, that kind of devotion would violate stalking laws.

Years later I met her at a party in New York. It was perhaps the late 1990s. She was enrobed in her usual black finery. Her hair was a little fluffy—I don't think she was getting it blown out weekly yet. I shook her very slender hand, felt myself blush, and whispered, "So nice to meet you." The only other option was to weep with love and throw myself on her narrow, polished black shoes. She said, "So nice to meet *you*." She may have been mocking me. I then turned to feign interest in the drinks table, because I feared I might further embarrass myself. Behind me I heard her ask someone, "Who was that again?"

This wasn't why Nora was a bitch. (She had every reason to wonder whether I'd actually been invited to the party or had recently escaped from the closest minimum-security facility.) She was bitchy because she was exacting and perfectionistic—and because even though she was a woman who reveled in her femininity, she refused to be mawkish or sentimental. She called it as she saw it, and her prose was so sharp you could cut yourself. In a 2010 piece for *Slate,* "Who Gets to Be a Feminist?" the other esteemed authors dutifully weighed in on this very serious matter. Nora wrote: "I know that I'm supposed to write 500 words on this subject, but it seems much simpler: You can't call yourself a feminist if you don't believe in the right to abortion." Take that, Earnest Content Providers.

Nora was born to a couple of screenwriters on May 19, 1941. Henry and Phoebe Ephron were theater people who liked Hollywood money, and moved their family to Beverly Hills. After graduating from Beverly Hills High in 1958 and breezing through Wellesley, graduating in 1962, she returned to New York, where she went on to become the new and improved Dorothy Parker. (With respect to Mrs. Parker, Nora was consistently funnier on more topics, and never stank up the joint with her self-pity. Nora didn't believe in self-pity.)

She started in the mail room at *Newsweek,* then moved to the *New York Post;* her career caught fire in the late 1960s. By 1972 she had a regular column in *Esquire,* writing personal essays about the Beatles, the small size of her breasts, a silly feud between Gloria Steinem and Betty Friedan. She was called one of the early practitioners of New Journalism, but claimed not to know what that meant. "I just sit here at the typewriter and bang away at the old forms," she observed. She was all about women power, but wasn't above poking fun at the parts of the women's movement she found to be ridiculous. That impulse to point out the ludicrous aspect of things she generally approved of was part of her exacting nature. She wasn't one to let anyone get away with anything if she could help it. She could be both ally and merciless critic.

In 1976, Nora married Carl Bernstein, the hotshot *Washington Post* reporter who, along with Bob Woodward, broke the Watergate scandal and brought down down the Nixon presidency. Nora and Carl were a Washington, D.C., writer power couple. (Such a thing no longer exists.)

They had a son, Jacob. Then, when she was very pregnant with a second child, she discovered Carl was cheating on her with a friend.

One of the great advantages of having a smart, sophisticated screenwriter mother is that the kind of wisdom passed down to you is not how to fold a fitted sheet but that everything is copy. Phoebe taught Nora that everything that happened to her in life could be transposed for fun, profit, and revenge, into art. In 1983, Nora published the aforementioned modern classic, *Heartburn,* the blistering roman à clef about the end of her marriage to Bernstein. It became a best seller, and in 1986, Jack Nicholson and Meryl Streep starred in the movie version, for which Nora wrote the screenplay.

(Things turned out less well for Bernstein. He went from superstar investigative journalist to gossip column fodder, which led to a rank-and-file position at ABC News. In 1987, he was not invited to *Washington Post* editor Katharine Graham's 70th birthday party. He consoled himself by dating Bianca Jagger. I don't want to make you feel too sorry for Carl. Everything *is* copy, and who knew that better than Carl Bernstein?)

A year later, in 1987, Nora met screenwriter Nicholas Pileggi. They adored each other; she was more delightful under Nick's devoted eye. When asked to contribute to an anthology of six-word memoirs, Nora wrote: "Secret to life: marry an Italian."

In 1992, Nora directed her first film, *This Is My Life,* from a screenplay she co-wrote with her sister, Delia, based on the novel by Meg Wolitzer. It was a flop. Nora hated failing. She did not take flops in stride. She was not philosophical about them. "Flops stay with you in a way that hits never do," she wrote. "They torture you. You toss and turn. You replay. You recast. You recut. You rewrite. You restage. You run through the what-ifs and the if-onlys. You cast about for blame."

But in 1993 came *Sleepless in Seattle.* Nora made directing seem effortless—but then as now, Hollywood was the consummate boys' club. She had begun directing because as a child, she'd seen firsthand how poorly the film business treated writers (which probably contributed to her parents' steep slide into alcoholism when she was a teenager). Also, she enjoyed directing because she was exacting. She was famous for firing people. She fired *children*.

Nora became famous primarily for her trinity of old-fashioned romantic comedies: *When Harry Met Sally . . .* (1989, directed by Rob Reiner); *Sleepless in Seattle* (1993); and *You've Got Mail* (1998). The more recent *Julie & Julia* (2009) is a valentine to both Julia Child and Nora's love of cooking. Modern classics though they may be, the "Nora edges" were by necessity rounded off in the Hollywood router. Her writing is much bitchier, and thus better, all the way around.

DURING THE FILMING OF *Julie & Julia* in 2008, Nora was already sick. In 2006 she had been diagnosed with acute myeloid leukemia, a cancer of the bone marrow. She told her family and swore a handful of intimates to secrecy, but otherwise continued on with her life. No one—close friends who'd produced her movies, editors, not even Meryl Streep, who played Nora in *Heartburn*—had known.

Nora wrote no witty novel about dying, no sly rom-com screenplay or slim book of perfect, hilarious essays. In her last days, she was working on a play called *Lucky Guy,* set in the late 1980s, about a tabloid newspaper reporter. She, who had written frankly about her nutty parents and their mad drinking, her famous husband's adultery, her shame over her sagging neck, wrote nothing about dying. She wasn't having any of it—in part, I'm going to presume, because she found the experience to be both tedious and not something she could control. And above all, Nora liked to be in control.

I, who have read every syllable she's written, suspected something was up when *I Remember Nothing*, published in 2010, failed to live up to the million-copy best seller *I Feel Bad About My Neck,* published in 2006, but written before her diagnosis. "*I Remember Nothing* is fluffy and companionable, a nifty airport read from a writer capable of much, much more," wrote Janet Maslin in the *New York Times*. Maybe, I thought, all that *Huffington Post* blogging was making her sloppy. But of all the things Nora Ephron was—domineering, persnickety, warm, generous, judgmental—sloppy she was not.

Maybe she didn't tell people she was sick because her great mantra was to be the hero, rather than the victim, of her own life. It was something she told the Class of 1996 when she gave the commencement speech at Wellesley that year. She also wrote about it in *I Remember Nothing*. "When you slip on a banana peel, people laugh at you; but when you tell people you slipped on a banana peel, it's your laugh. So you become the hero, rather than the victim of the joke."

Nora kept a picture of mobster John Gotti on her desk to bolster her during her post-flop moments. It was taken on the way out of the courthouse on the day he was handed a sentence of life in prison. He wore an excellent, well-cut suit. He looked terrific. I imagine Nora was thinking that she wanted to go out like John Gotti. She didn't want to be a dying person dispensing wisdom. She despised complaining—it was one thing she hated about feminism, all that kvetching. "All those women-in-film panels!" she once said, throwing up her hands. One night she appeared with Arianna Huffington at an Advice for Women event (that was literally the name) about the "myriad challenges women face today." Her best advice: Be in denial.

Upon Nora's death on June 26, 2012, Lena Dunham (see Chapter 28) wrote in a tender remembrance for the *New Yorker*: "Nora introduced me to, in no particular order: several ear, nose, and throat doctors; the Patagonia jackets she favored when on set because they were 'thinner than a sweater but warmer than a parka' . . . the photography of Julius Shulman; the concept of eating lunch *at* Barneys; self-respect; the complex legend of Helen Gurley Brown; the Jell-O mold; her beloved sister Delia."

Nora introduced me to the concept that a woman could be opinionated, witty, exacting, and still beloved. In a word: difficult.

CHAPTER 23

DIANA VREELAND

Outlandish

MY GRANDMOTHER LUNA was born in Warsaw in September 1903—the same month of the same year that the *très difficile* fashion magazine queen Diana Vreeland was born in Paris.

Luna was a couturiere in Hollywood in the '60s. She made fancy gowns for the wives of movie moguls and kept a small family of cross-eyed Siamese cats. She gave me my first issue of *Vogue* (setting me up with the fashion bible was the only activity she could think of to occupy me while I was under her care). I would sit under her big cutting table and drink it in, page by page, while she worked. She waved away my mother's justifiable concerns (I saw my first naked boob in *Vogue*) by saying the magazine was "educational."

Like Diana Vreeland, Luna had dark hair, hooded eyes, and an exacting, imperious European manner. Both women used cigarette holders and had bright red polished nails. There the comparison ended. But somehow, for most of my life, I've conflated them, believing irrationally that maybe Diana Vreeland *was* my grandmother. A lifelong practitioner of "faction" —a cross between fact and fiction—Diana would understand and probably applaud this urge.

Diana was the most inspired, outlandish fashion editor of the 20th century. When she assumed the post at *Harper's Bazaar* in 1936 (a position she held until 1962), the job was mostly one of glorified wardrobe mistress. Diana transformed it into a position for an artist with a great eye, great style, and an ability to predict (and create) trends. In 1963, at the age of 60, she became editor-in-chief of *Vogue*. At 69, in 1971, she began her final, glorious third act as a consultant at the Metropolitan Museum of Art's Costume Institute. Pre-Vreeland, it was a sleepy department of the museum, of interest only to scholars. Diana single-handedly revitalized it, mounting 14 dazzling exhibits in 14 years and making the museum a pile of money. La Vreeland also injected new life into the Met Gala, transforming it from an obligatory overcooked chicken Kiev fundraiser attended by dutiful museum-supporting dowagers to a fashion-forward star-studded event tied to the opening of her brilliant exhibitions. *Vogue* editor-in-chief Anna Wintour took over the hosting honors in 1999, and the Gala (as it was now simply known) became the most sought-after social ticket in the known world, a gathering of every celebrity you love, and love to hate, all spiffed up in over-the-top avant-garde. It always feels fresh, exciting, and outlandish; not to take anything away from Anna Wintour, but it's the spirit of Diana that energizes the evening.

Diana Dalziel was the daughter of an American socialite mother and British stockbroker father. (Her difficult name was pronounced Dee-AH-nah Dee-EL. You may have no need of this information, but in the event you're ever sipping champagne at a fancy party and the subject turns to Diana Vreeland née Dalziel, I've got you covered.) The catastrophe and (eventual) blessing of her life was not being born beautiful.* Her mother, Emily Key Hoffman, was very beautiful, and Diana's younger sister, Alexandra, took after her. Diana's father, Frederick, was tall, dashing, and responsible for the Dalziel nose. Diana inherited this spectacular appendage—something her mother never let her forget. She called her "my ugly little monster." Really, how does a girl survive this? By taking a page from Diana Vreeland, and becoming outlandish.

---

* You would think her mother, being so well traveled and cultured, would have more imagination when it came to female allure. Most people found Diana to be rakish and fascinating, with charisma to burn.

Before the outbreak of World War I, the Dalziels moved to the Upper East Side from Paris, where they had lived on the avenue du Bois-de-Boulogne since before Diana was born, and became titans of New York society. Diana spoke no English, and lasted at the Brearley School for three months before leaving to study dance with a Russian ballet master who she would always claim taught her discipline. In 1919, when she was a 16-year-old debutante, she determined that the only way she could compete with the other girls was through stylish theatricality. Diana may have had no formal education—something she would feel insecure about all her life—but this was a truly inspired idea. "You don't have to be born beautiful to be wildly attractive!" she would say one day. Of all her celebrated expressions, this is one of the best. What Diana meant was: Be singular, be interesting, find what works for you and never stop working it.

Life began looking up when Diana discovered makeup—red lips, nails, a defiant slash of red rouge on each cheek—and caught the eye of Thomas Reed Vreeland, a tall, handsome bank trainee. They met in Saratoga, at a party (where else?). Vreeland was lanky and handsome—the young Gary Cooper comes to mind—and the best-looking guy in the room. Another woman might have set her cap for someone richer, but Diana was swept off her feet. They married in March 1924, quickly produced two sons, Thomas Jr. and Frederick, and zipped off to London, neatly dodging the U.S. stock market crash in 1929. Diana had inherited some money from her maternal grandmother, allowing the Vreelands to live a joyously decadent life in a fancy flat on Hanover Terrace, near Regent's Park. They bought a Bugatti and employed a young driver. Diana took rumba lessons in her dining room, painted bright yellow. She was in heaven.

The Vreelands ripped through her inheritance, and when they returned to New York, they needed money. Reed, as it turned out, wasn't a terrific businessman. There was also the matter of his wandering eye, and the money he spent on his mistresses. Reed was Diana's weakness. She would go on to be demanding and uncompromising in her professional life, but she would always give Reed a complete pass. He is rumored to have asked for a divorce, but she refused. She would adore him for the duration of their 42-year marriage.

Meanwhile, fate intervened in the form of Carmel Snow, the fierce editor-in-chief of *Harper's Bazaar*. Snow glimpsed Diana at a party, dancing on the roof of the St. Regis Hotel in a white lace Chanel dress, roses pinned in her black hair. She called her up the next day and asked whether she wanted a job.

Diana's first move as *Bazaar*'s fashion editor was to conceive and pen "Why Don't You . . . ?"—a *monthly* "advice" column that proffered no genuine advice but gave readers a shot of fizzy fantasy—a welcome diversion in the middle of the Depression. Why don't you . . .

. . . Find one dress that you like and have it copied many times? You will be much more successful than if you try to produce the same effects each evening. (I've totally done this.)

. . . Rinse your blond child's hair in dead champagne to keep it gold, as they do in France?

My favorite for sheer cheeky lunacy is: "Why don't you . . . have every room done up in every color of green? This will take months, years, to collect, but it will be delightful—a mélange of plants, green glass, green porcelains, and furniture covered in sad greens, gay greens, clear, faded and poison greens?" First, please note the sentence construction: *have* every room. As in, that's not going to be you at the paint store collecting chips and buying brushes, but some servant or hired decorator. For years. It will be so delightful for you to watch him work. And not only will he be painting, he will also be collecting green porcelain. I don't even have to know anything about green porcelain to know that it wasn't something you picked up at the five-and-dime. I will leave the thought of having furniture covered in "sad green" with you.

The column was an instant hit; people adored its crazy extravagance.[*] For 25 years Diana came up with this squirt of pure fantasy every month, and for 25 years people loved it.

---

[*] So popular was this column that *Harper's Bazaar* brought it back in 2014. The 21-century iteration is less preposterous and far too useful.

"I think part of my success as an editor came from never worrying about a fact, a cause, an atmosphere," she said. "It was me—projecting to the public. That was my job. I think I always had a perfectly clear view of what was possible for the public. Give 'em what they never knew they wanted."

The stories of Diana's fashion triumphs at *Bazaar* are legendary. In 1943 she discovered Lauren Bacall, and jump-started the career of celebrated photographer Richard Avedon. She was a blistering, dizzy fashion force. But in the end, when it came time for Carmel Snow to retire, Diana was passed over for the job in favor of Snow's niece, Nancy White. Diana was mortified. "We needed an artist and they sent us a house painter!" she cried. (Truth be told, Diana was the artist—but let's face it, the artist should never be put in charge of the budget.)

Five years later, at the age of 60, Diana had the last laugh and became the editor of America's foremost fashion bible: *Vogue*. She was high-handed and tough to please. She spoke in riddles and koans. Clarity in communication meant nothing to her. When photographer David Bailey was off to shoot the Italian collections, her marching orders were "plenty of wops."**

Perhaps because she had been born and bred in Paris, her sensibility was essentially French. She was drawn to people she felt were interesting, rather than conventionally attractive. Her models weren't the usual pretty faces. Pale-eyed amazon Veruschka, alien-looking Penelope Tree, and Edie, with her anthracite eyes and bony hips (see Chapter 13). A full-faced and very young Mick Jagger. Lauren Hutton. Cher. Anjelica Huston.

Under her direction, *Vogue* became the magazine that enchanted me as a little girl. Tahiti, the pyramids, Veruschka in Japan in the middle of winter in all those furs. It was like a very fancy *National Geographic,* and this was probably what my grandmother meant when she said it was educational.

Diana Vreeland in her 60s, in the '60s, was a woman in full. I could chronicle her outlandish eccentricities all day long. She chain-smoked

---

** This directive predated political correctness but was considered offensive even then.

Lucky Strikes in a holder and didn't get dressed until noon. She liked to take her phone calls in the bathroom, from a phone mounted on the wall. Her usual ensemble consisted of black trousers and a black cashmere sweater. Her usual lunch consisted of peanut butter and a shot of Scotch. She typed all her memos on onionskin with a carbon. They were as mysterious as her verbal directives. "I am extremely disappointed to see that we have used practically no pearls at all in the past few issues," she wrote on December 9, 1966.

The year 1966 was a bad one for Diana, though you would never know it. Reed died of esophageal cancer that year. Her determination to be positive and *up up up!* was exhausting to those who knew her well. She never let on her heart was broken then—or five years later, in 1971, when she was let go from *Vogue*. Her fundamental lack of respect for the budget played a role, but so did the changing times. Feminism was on the rise—a concept she wasn't interested in and claimed not to understand—and collectively, the country seemed to have sobered up. Suddenly the extravagant fashion shoots—models in bikinis at the pyramids, or wandering through the Amazonian jungle in evening gowns—seemed a little crazy.

If we need any evidence that our final professional acts can be our best, consider Diana's showstopping stint at the Metropolitan Costume Institute. Jackie Onassis pressed to have her hired, and in the same way she completely revamped her role as fashion editor at *Harper's Bazaar*, she redefined the term "consultant." Brought on as a favor to Jackie, Diana was tasked with "raising awareness" of the institute, and perhaps pressing her rich friends to donate. Her first exhibit, showcasing couturier Cristóbal Balenciaga, blew the collective minds of New York society. The museum fathers were expecting a row of mannequins fitted with nice outfits. They never expected art installations in the true sense of the word. Dramatic lighting, mood music, fragrance pumped in for maximum ambience. And the glow from the stars who showed up: Bianca Jagger, Paloma Picasso, Halston, and Jackie O, of course.

What have we learned from Diana Vreeland? That being outlandish—her particular form of difficult—is a strong, smart way to navigate life. According to her, to be chic is to be interesting and original—and these qualities, truth be told, are far more compelling than being beautiful. Beauty, after all, is an accident of birth, rather than an act of imagination and creativity. "There's only one very good life," Diana wrote. "And that's the life you know you want and you make it yourself."

CHAPTER 24

KAY THOMPSON

Incorrigible

UNLESS YOU'RE A total musical comedy nerd, chances are you know Kay Thompson only (only!) as the creator of *Eloise,* the six-year-old heroine of children's literature who lived at the Plaza with her pug, Weenie, her turtle, Skipperdee, and no adult supervision, save the boozy Nanny. If that's the case, please go straight to YouTube and watch "Think Pink!" Kay's show stealer from *Funny Face,* one of the great (by which I mean totally campy) films of Hollywood's golden era. She costars as eccentric magazine editor/despot Maggie Prescott, who calls in her army of assistants to proclaim, in song, that pink is the new black. ("Red is dead / blue is through / Green's obscene / brown's taboo.")

That's Kay Thompson.

Brazen, cheeky, and flamboyant, Kay is arguably the most gifted song-and-dance woman of the 20th century. Genius lyricist, gifted choreographer, agile pianist, superb voice coach, sparkling actress and comedienne, Kay was the mad scientist responsible for the DNA of the classic Hollywood musical. All those performance conventions we don't even think about—the saucy gestures made by the diva as she struts around the stage, the stars belting it out and dancing *at the same time,* the chorus singing nonsense syllables that make them sound like musical instruments—they all came from the fantastically creative musical mind of the complete nut job Kay Thompson.

BORN CATHERINE LOUISE "KITTY" FINK in St. Louis, Missouri, on—well, no one is quite sure when she was born, because she lied strenuously about her age for the majority of her life.* We'll go with November 9, 1909, because that's the official date on IMDb. Her father, Leo, ran a pawnshop but called himself a jeweler; her mother, Harriet, was vivacious and musical and poured all her talent into raising her four children.

Oh, it was the usual thing. Kitty Fink had three attractive siblings—a brother and two sisters—but she was the one with "personality." That personality was rowdy, distinctly unfeminine, and prone to hijacking attention by acting out, pulling pranks, and behaving in a bratty manner that would, decades later, be celebrated as Eloise-esque. Her avid mother, eager to find something in which Kitty might excel, started her on the piano at age three. Even then, she had a gift for music, and by 16 she was playing Liszt with the St. Louis Symphony Orchestra. But she had no interest in classical music, she liked to say, because it would have required her to cut her fingernails.

Kitty Fink was a mediocre student at best. She graduated in the bottom third of her high school class and quit college to pursue a singing career on the radio. During the Depression and early 1930s, the radio was *it*, home entertainment–wise; the top shows were as beloved as whatever we're currently obsessing about on HBO or Netflix.

In the late 1920s, CBS affiliate KMOX was the number one radio station in St. Louis. Kitty showed up at manager George Junkin's office claiming she had a nonexistent appointment, also informing his secretary that she was in a tremendous hurry and was squeezing him into her schedule. Both the secretary and Junkin fell for her act; Junkin thought he must have met her at a party somewhere and asked her

---

* I've never understood the point of lying about your age. Does it really make any difference to anyone whether you're 55 or 50? In Kay's case it came back to bite her in the ass: Her *New York Times* obituary reported her age as between 92 and 95 when she died and she was only 88. Ha!

to come in.** She sang for him, emulating the blues singers she loved. He offered her $25/week; she demanded the amount he paid his other torch singers. He lowered his offer to $20. He was impressed with her voice—it was deep, smoky, even soulful—but not her brash attitude. Kitty was unconcerned. Even then, she knew that management came and went, but no one had a voice like hers.

She got the job, but then didn't bother to take it seriously. One hot spring afternoon in 1931, she was at a lake party, enjoying the sunset with some beau, when she remembered that she was supposed to work that night. She had also apparently forgotten to rehearse, so when she and her date roared up after the broadcast started, she had to wing it—and was fired. Oops!

In July of the same year, she found her way to L.A. (where it was all happening anyway) and immediately landed a job singing on KFI. She was 22, and fell into the trap that a lot of young people encounter by overspending their first paycheck before they've even started the job. A few years earlier she'd had a nose job; there was apparently more work than a plastic surgeon could manage in one go, so now she sprang for another one.*** She also had her teeth capped. Why not! And rented a ritzy apartment not far from the swanky new art deco Wiltern Theater on Wilshire Boulevard. She was ready for her career to take off!

At this stage, Glenn Dolberg, the KFI programming director who'd hired her, conducted a routine background check. Who knew that everyone knew everyone in radio? Dolberg called George Junkin, who advised him to steer clear of the gifted but unreliable Kitty Fink, and so she was fired. Again. Her solution was not to become less cagey but to change her name to Kay Thompson. Really, the woman was incorrigible. She viewed rules as suggestions, and I see no reason why we

---

** Totally excellent way to get your foot in the door. You go, Kitty!

*** It may be easy for me to say this as a relatively small-nosed person, but the only thing wrong with Kay's nose is that it was strong and straight and maybe a little prominent. It wasn't huge. It wasn't even ugly. There was just rather more of it than we consider feminine in our narrow-minded culture.

shouldn't see her as an inspiration to do the same. Cut loose, cut corners, have some *bazazz* (a word Kay coined to explain one of her many admirable qualities).

In the late 1930s and early 1940s, when Kay was working her way up the ladder from staff singer to featured singer to headliner, performers pretty much sang a song as it was arranged for the orchestra that accompanied them. Kay wasn't having any of that. She was drawn to jazz, swing, and scat singing when it was still considered the provenance of stoned beatniks and blues singers in dingy clubs in the bad part of town. She could never resist her impulse to bust a song out of time-signature jail and make a run for it. She became a singer's singer, a vocal arranger's arranger. The musical titans of the time—George and Ira Gershwin, Cole Porter—worshipped at the altar of her crazy innovation. My interpretation of a classic Kay Thompson arrangement of "Pop Goes the Weasel" might go like this:

All around, yes ALL around!, the mulberry bush
The monkey, the monkey, that silly old monkey, cha-cha-chased
the we-a-zel
The monkey stopped to pull up his sock, his soca-soca-sock
quelle belle sock!
Pop, pop-poppity pop goes that crazy ol' weasel.

DESPITE THE nose jobs—before she threw in the towel, she had had five—Kay looked like a man. I don't mean sort of winsome and androgynous like David Bowie or the latest Slavic supermodel; more like a leading man along the lines of Gary Cooper. But even Gary Cooper (those eyelashes!) was daintier than Kay. She had a long face, large eyes that shone with an anarchistic gleam, and a chiseled jaw. She was five feet five and a half inches and rail-thin. She favored six-inch spike heels and, when on stage, employed a lot of theatrical gestures that incorporated shooting straight up into the air her very long arms, at the end of which were very long hands, at the end of which were very long nails painted murder red. Despite the heels and the nail polish and the long mink coat she wore everywhere, her energy was decidedly male—whip-smart, authoritative, and in your face. Bazazz!

Kay was queen of playing both sides against the middle. She also subscribed to the adage that it's easier to ask forgiveness than permission. In 1934, she was contracted to appear on two music shows in San Francisco, on the radio station KFRC. Always eager to have 47 irons in the fire, she also accepted a gig at the Palace Hotel with Tom Coakley, a popular local bandleader. As it happened, Coakley had his own radio show, on KFRC's rival station NBC. Forgetting the fine print on her contract (if she ever read it at all), she started singing on Coakley's show. Her boss at KFRC ordered her to cease and desist. Her solution? Change nothing but her name. Even though her voice was as recognizable to listeners as that of Mick Jagger during his heyday, she became Judy Rich. Once again she was promptly canned.

But her scheming eventually paid off. At one point in 1935, through more of her usual slightly shady finagling, she had eponymous music shows on both CBS and NBC. She had assembled an all-girl chorus to back her up on CBS's *Fred Waring–Ford Dealers Radio Show*—but an old flame named Don Forker launched the *Lucky Strike Hit Parade* over on NBC, and promised her the moon. She shanghaied her all-girl choir without telling Fred Waring; he threatened to sue her but settled for sharing her. Everybody wins! Especially Kay.

She continued to experiment. She lived in fear of boredom and routine. She and her orchestra leader, Lennie Hayton, coaxed Fred Astaire, on the road promoting his new movie *Top Hat,* to come on the show and tap-dance on a wooden platform with table microphones at his feet. Listeners found her to be intriguing but were challenged by her music, which was more progressive than crowd-pleasing.

At the pinnacle of her radio career, Kay Thompson ruled on the top-rated *Chesterfield Radio Show*. By that time, 1936, and at the age of 27, she was a master of swing, jazz, and pop. She could play it, sing it, and arrange it for choirs large and small. She also liked to amuse herself by sprinkling in the occasional silly song that relied on sound effects and nutty fake foreign accents. Her one concession to the powers that be at Chesterfield was to hide the Camels she chain-smoked in Chesterfield packages.

IN JANUARY 1937, Kay eloped with jazz trombonist Jack Jenney. They were devoted to: (1) their careers, (2) boozing, and (3) each other. Pretty much in that order. Jack had alimony payments and a wandering eye. Kay dealt with his infidelities, both rumored and genuine, by launching an affair of her own with Dave Garroway, a page at NBC who was a diehard fan, and who would go on to make his mark in television with the *Today* show. For two years, Jack and Kay tried to make a go of it, but neither seemed particularly interested in sacrificing anything for the other. Then there was the business of Jack hocking Kay's jewelry to keep himself in cocktails. "I'm the dumb cluck who is always getting drunks out of scrapes and lending them money that I never get back," she remarked.

Still, Kay was the kind of woman who stayed friends with her exes. Down the road she would pull strings to get Jack a gig playing trombone on a big Judy Garland record. Not long afterward, he died, at age 35, of complications during a routine appendectomy.

MOST OF THE HOLLYWOOD STORIES we know well are variations on the rise-to-fame narrative. The big star-to-be lands the role of a lifetime—or if not of a lifetime, big enough to draw attention to her screen presence and charisma. She steals the show, and is set on her road to greatness. The more common showbiz story is the one Kay suffered for the first part of her career. Though she was already a well-known radio and music star, she had the usual acting aspirations—and offers that didn't pan out. But then one day in 1937, she was cast as herself in *Manhattan Merry-Go-Round,* a comedy about a New York mobster who busts his way into the music business, pressuring top recording artists—like Kay Thompson!—to join his label. She was happy to play herself but refused to make life easier for the producers and director by accompanying Joe DiMaggio on the piano. She was determined to be seen as a star, not an accompanist to a baseball player who couldn't even get through his few lines.

Later that year, director Vincente Minnelli tapped Kay to star in his new Broadway antiwar musical *Hooray for What!* She would do the vocal arrangements for the entire production but also play one of the leads: a femme fatale whose mission was to seduce a top-secret formula out of a hapless nerdy scientist. The part of Stephanie Stephanovich would be her big break! But actress Vivian Vance employed some strategic seducing of her own and wrested the role away from her; Kay was replaced without warning in previews. The press was told she resigned because she was having trouble with her throat—a complete lie that may have been belied by the fact that people heard her shrieking and wailing in her dressing room after she got the news. If her throat wasn't troubling her before, it surely was after all that carrying-on. Still, the play did well. A producer at MGM, the granddaddy of the movie musical, took note and hired her to be the head of the studio's vocal department.

AROUND 1942, Kay and her boyfriend (and eventually, second husband) Bill Spier moved from New York to L.A. Their new home was the Garden of Allah, the happening residency hotel at the east end of the Sunset Strip.

It was also ground zero for Hollywood hipsters. F. Scott Fitzgerald and Robert Benchley lived there during their Hollywood screenwriting days. Humphrey Bogart (Kay called him Humpy Bogus) lived across the swimming pool, and Frank Sinatra lived next door. He used to come over to Kay and Bill's at night and they'd sing around the piano, in exchange for homemade spaghetti. You know that distinctly Sinatra-esque phrasing where he sings just a little behind the beat? He learned that from Kay. Because she was under contract at MGM, helping Sinatra was a conflict of interest—but you know how she felt about contracts. Hedda Hopper got wind of Kay's informal coaching and reported it in the *LA Times*. Yeah, so?

Name any MGM musical from the 1940s and rest assured that Kay Thompson had a hand in it. Most actors couldn't sing or dance—and they really couldn't sing *and* dance. They couldn't sell the lyrics. Kay worked people until they wept. She had a huge set of pipes, and she assumed everyone else did too.

In 1945, at the age of 36, Kay fell in love with Judy Garland. Not in *love* love (although there were plenty of rumors). Assumptions were made because Kay did not fit the traditional female mold. There were the pants, the confidence, the big gestures, the wisecracking wit—and the overall sizzle that was not sexual, but something else. If there is one great lesson we can learn from Kay Thompson, it's that going for it in the manner she went for it carries its own madcap appeal.

Judy had been under contract at MGM since 1939, when she starred in *The Wizard of Oz* at age 16. Kay took Judy under her wing six years later, when Judy was in her failing first marriage and already struggling with the uppers, downers, and diet pills prescribed by studio doctors as a condition of work. Judy needed someone like Kay, and Kay needed to be needed. She needed to be the expert, the one who could control and fix everything. She achieved this by arranging Johnny Mercer and Harry Warren's "On the Atchison, Topeka, and the Santa Fe," expressly for Judy. It became one of Garland's signature songs, won the Oscar for Best Original Song that year, and sold millions in records and sheet music.

Producers now stood in line to employ Kay to arrange their songs and train their stars. She even worked with the voice doubles who stood in for stars incapable of even talk-singing, Kay's solution for people who couldn't hold a tune. But they were still reluctant to cast her. It drove her mad with resentment. "MGM was the biggest whorehouse in the world," she once said. A month didn't go by without some big director or producer "discovering" a starlet they'd been sleeping with and sending them to Kay for coaching, which devolved into teaching them how to lip-synch. Every so often, the muckety-mucks would throw Kay a bone—you can be the sassy old-maid orchestra leader who sings a comic ditty with the male star!—but it was insulting, truly. She passed. She would always pass. She couldn't possibly disrespect herself that much. She would always say no when her gut told her something was beneath her (and so should we).

In the mid-1940s, while Kay was still carrying the weight of the entire MGM musical juggernaut on her razor-sharp shoulders, her health began to fail. She began suffering from migraines and chronic intestinal misery. She was reduced to eating baby food (an improvement on the Fig Newtons and booze she had previously subsisted on). She was skeletal; her collarbone looked like a weapon. Friends urged her to seek medical help, but she had perhaps a little too conveniently become a Christian Scientist, fully embracing the faith's disinclination to seek any medical aid aside from "healing." (This didn't extend to plastic surgery; in 1947 she had her third nose job.)

By then Judy Garland's drug problem was large and in charge. During the filming of *The Pirate* with Gene Kelly (songs by Cole Porter), Garland missed 99 out of 130 shooting days due to "illness" (sleeping it off). Kay worried about her friend, and was one of the few people who confronted Garland and confiscated her pills when she found them. There was nothing for it. Judy continued to be "ill," and *The Pirate,* released in 1948, came and went—the only Garland MGM musical that tanked.

Meanwhile, Kay's five-year marriage to Bill Spier was unraveling. Spier was a gifted pianist, and a producer of *Suspense,* arguably the greatest drama on the air during the golden age of radio. It ran for 20 years, featuring every great star of the era playing against type, and would serve as a prototype for the great television anthology shows, including *Alfred Hitchcock Presents* and *The Twilight Zone.* In other words, Bill Spier was kind of a big deal in his own right. Kay and Bill drank and they argued. They argued and they drank. One day, during a particularly vicious spat, he said, "After all, who are you but a vocal coach for Judy Garland?"

"Exhaust pipe!" That was what Kay Thompson said when she was fed up and *done.*

In those days, to get a quickie divorce, you had to move to Nevada and take up residency for six weeks. Kay parked herself in Las Vegas. She was distraught the marriage hadn't worked out, but she also knew she didn't have it in her to be the sort of accommodating wife someone with an ego the size of her own would require. Whether she also grieved the lost opportunity to become a mother is unknown.

We must pause here for a life lesson. Kay was approaching 40. Trust me when I tell you that in 1947, that age was not the new 30. Kay was alone. She had worked herself to the bone helping to make less talented, would-be entertainers famous. Was she depressed at this juncture? Perhaps. But she was like a shark, and could only swim forward. She could only keep working and creating.

Back in L.A., Kay did just this. She was one of those people who could labor into the wee hours of the night, arise at the crack of dawn, and without so much as a piece of dry toast, log another 20 hours of singing, dancing, coaching, choreographing, lyric writing, and score arranging, all while tossing off one-liners. When she wasn't working, she threw lavish, star-studded parties in which there were usually two pianos but no food. At one point, she weighed 100 pounds.

The amphetamines helped. Kay was a patient of Dr. Max Jacobson, an Upper East Side purveyor of miracle vitamin "cocktails" to the rich and famous. The list of stars who regularly partook of Dr. Feelgood's zippy meth-based "B$_{12}$" concoction is long and varied. Marlene Dietrich, Lauren Bacall, and JFK. Truman Capote, Marilyn Monroe, and Mickey Mantle. In the same way that Kay's embrace of Christian Science didn't apply to plastic surgery, it also did nothing to discourage her from seeking frequent and regular injections—some shot directly into her vocal cords.

While she served her time in Vegas waiting for her divorce to come through, Kay entertained herself by pulling together a new nightclub act. She knew the four Williams brothers—Dick, Don, Bob, and Andy—from her days at MGM, and conned them into rehearsing together without any clear idea of what the future held. She taught them how to sing and move. This was, again, revolutionary. In those days, singers were tethered to a standing mic. The most action you could hope for was some swaying and finger snapping. Kay pressed her sound engineers into figuring out how to suspend microphones from the ceiling, thus giving her and the brothers room to dance.

She believed that part of their appeal was that she was so tall and they were so short. In fact, they were all about the same height, but she appeared to loom above them, a human skyscraper in high heels and shimmering white pants. The brothers looked like cleaned-up quadruplet bear cubs in their matching dark suits and ties. When it came time to open the act, Kay drove a hard bargain. She was never afraid to overestimate her worth—something for which you've got to admire her. Someone suggested a name for their act: The Williams Brothers, featuring Kay Thompson. Ha ha. No way. They made their debut as Kay Thompson and the Williams Brothers. Kay insisted on a 50/50 profit share, leaving each of the brothers a meager 12.5 percent.

They opened in Vegas at El Rancho, moved to the Flamingo, and then on to Ciro's on the Sunset Strip. It was *the* place for Hollywood A-listers, many of whom had been schooled by Kay. At first, audiences came because it was Ciro's, and anyone who was anyone went to Ciro's. But they came back because no one had seen anything like Kay Thompson and the Williams Brothers. They became the hottest nightclub ticket in town, then the nation. In September 1948, they landed a three-year, million-dollar deal with the Kirkeby hotel chain. It was the country's biggest nightclub contract to date. Getting a ticket to see them was on a par with current efforts to get a ticket for *Hamilton* without having to take out a home equity loan. Stars who thought they could just sashay in and take a table near the stage were turned away.

Kay was delirious with self-satisfaction. At the end of every performance she gave a deep, heartfelt bow, then refused an encore. She would never mix with the audience, believing it was always best to maintain an aura of mystery. Now, the offers came rolling in. Every radio station wanted to give her a show. Broadway producers who'd never given her the time of day were appearing with hats in hand. Perhaps the most personally satisfying development was that after *Daily Variety* chided MGM for failing to give her a vehicle in which she could display her many superb talents, the studio came sniffing around, seeing whether she would come back to work for them.

Ha. Ha. Ha. (She did return for a screen test, however.)

Meanwhile, the icing on the cake: Kay and Andy Williams, the youngest brother, fell in love. She was 38; he was 20. Did either of them care? They certainly did not. They tried to keep it a secret, sort of. They lived together off and on, vacationed on Nantucket. The romance lasted much longer than anyone would have imagined.

THE OFFICIAL AND COMPLETELY untrue story about the birth of Eloise holds that Kay was late for a meeting (a photo shoot, a rehearsal) with the Williams Brothers—and when she finally rolled in, her non-excuse was offered in the squeaky voice of a little girl. "I am Eloise and I am six!"

In truth, Eloise had always been one of Kay's personalities. In her early 20s, when she was a counselor at a swanky camp for girls on Catalina Island, she routinely disciplined rowdy campers in her Eloise voice. Later, during her radio days, she would occasionally be paralyzed by stage fright, and her preperformance ritual included a shot of whiskey and an Eloise impersonation or two. At MGM, she swanned around the commissary in her trademark long mink coat and entertained the stars she lunched with by becoming Eloise. Kay didn't think there was a book in Eloise. That imperious, squeaky voice was just something she did. D. D. Ryan, a junior editor at *Harper's Bazaar*, thought differently, and in 1954 introduced Kay to a young and gifted illustrator, Hilary Knight.

At first, the collaboration was fruitful and joyous. In between her nightclub gigs, Kay made notes and Knight managed to capture the perfect Eloise (strawlike hair, tiny gut hanging over her waistband) in a Christmas card. "I took three months off and wrote it. I holed in at the Plaza and [Hilary and I] went to work . . . We wrote, edited, laughed, outlined, cut, pasted, laughed again, read out loud, laughed and suddenly we had a book."

Published in November 1955, *Eloise: A Book for Precocious Grown-Ups* initially had a print run of a modest 7,500 copies. Then *Life* magazine featured the book in its December issue, and *Eloise* took off. Kay took up permanent residence in the Plaza straightaway. She was a guest on all the talk shows. She was over the moon—until a review in the *New Yorker* appeared, mentioning that half of the book's charm was due to Hilary Knight's perfectly adorable illustrations.

In his biography of Kay, Sam Irvin makes a case for the many little girls who may have inspired the final iteration of Eloise: Kay's goddaughter, Liza Minnelli; Lucie Arnaz; Sigourney Weaver; Princess Yasmin Khan; and others. But I don't think Kay needed to look outside herself. The willful, shameless, impetuous Eloise was all her. This was something she reminded people of with increasing outrage and indignation as the world fell in love with the character and that love manifested itself by rapid identification. Every girl and woman who felt she had an inner rabble-rouser claimed that she was Eloise.

I should say right here that I'm probably the only female in the English-speaking world who did not think she was Eloise. I was an only child on good terms with my parents. When we took our occasional road trips around the West, we stayed only in motels—not hotels with big swimming pools. Even as a child, Eloise struck me as a little unhinged. The cool factor is nil, but I have to confess: I was always a Madeline girl.

Don't tell the ghost of Kay Thompson.

Kay created her own licensing company with partner Bob Bernstein to merchandise the hell out of Eloise—not something routinely done back then. There were Eloise dolls, of course. Eloise clothes, Eloise wigs, Eloise luggage, Eloise bath towel-and-washcloth sets, Eloise postcards, and an Eloise emergency kit (complete with Bazooka bubble gum, turtle food, crayons, sunglasses, and Do Not Disturb doorknob signs from the Plaza). The hotel introduced a children's menu, a Tricycle Garage, and an Eloise display room down the hall from Kay. An oil portrait of Eloise enjoyed a place of pride on the wall in the hotel's Palm Court, where it still hangs today.

As time went on, the nation's possessive embrace of Eloise began to irk. Kay did not like it when Knight was given credit for his sweet illustrations. After a while, she did not like it when fans would claim to "be" Eloise. *She* was Eloise, goddammit. Things got even weirder when she grew jealous and resentful of the child cast to play Eloise in CBS's *Playhouse 90* adaptation.

At first, Kay adored Evelyn Rudie. But when people started calling Evelyn "Eloise" Rudie, her affections cooled. One night at the Plaza, Kay and Evelyn ran into Eartha Kitt, who was performing at the Persian Room that week. Eartha said, "This is the new Eloise!" and Kay decided shortly thereafter that she would voice the character. Her completely unworkable method: Every time Evelyn was to speak, she would either need to have her back to the camera, her hand over her mouth, or a book in front of her face. Kay, crouching behind the nearest large piece of furniture closest to the mic, would then squeak out the line.

Of course it didn't work, but people were afraid to tell Kay until the very last minute—because by this time, a lot of people were afraid to tell Kay things she didn't want to hear. Which had become most things. At the 11th hour little Evelyn "Eloise" Rudie wound up delivering her own dialogue, but the show was panned anyway.

No matter. Eloise was an official cultural phenomenon, and three more books were published: *Eloise in Paris* (1957); *Eloise at Christmastime* (1958); and *Eloise in Moscow* (1959).

Kay accepted an advance for *Eloise Takes a Bawth* in 1962. By then her collaboration with Hilary Knight was on the rocks. She still despised that he got any credit for his work, and was loath to share any of the royalties. When he submitted his illustrations, she refused to approve them, and the project languished until her editor at Simon & Schuster simply gave up. Two generations later the project was revitalized, and *Eloise Takes a Bawth* was published in 2002, using Knight's illustrations.

Nevertheless, Kay's possessiveness of the character knew no bounds, and even as the years passed, she continued to be mama-bear fierce. In celebration of the 40th anniversary of Eloise, a bookstore in New York staged a huge window display. Kay called up to complain that the display advertised Eloise and not *Kay Thompson's* Eloise. It was 1995, and Kay was 86 years old.

IN 1957, KAY COSTARRED IN *Funny Face* with Fred Astaire and Audrey Hepburn, where she stole the show with the aforementioned "Think Pink!" number. Her role as Maggie Prescott was inspired by Diana Vreeland, editor-in-chief of *Harper's Bazaar* (see Chapter 23). It would be her only notable* Hollywood role. Let us pause for a minute to appreciate the irony. It took the success of a children's book, which has absolutely nothing to do with her staggering gifts as an arranger, singer, or dancer, to finally land Kay an A-list movie role.

Funny Face was a hit, and every newspaper in New York (seven, at the time) heralded Kay Thompson as a blazing new star in the Hollywood firmament. She was 48 years old, and had been at it for almost 30 years. Kay had made it—both on her own terms and in every sense of the word. One of life's mysteries is why getting exactly what you want doesn't make you happier, or any easier to live with.

Movie offers rolled in like the waves at Malibu during a Pacific storm. Theater offers, too. Noël Coward pressed her to star in a play he had opening on Broadway, but Kay trotted out her by-now ancient and threadbare excuse that she was still wounded by being fired from *Hooray for What!* a quarter of a century earlier.

It was all nonsense. In the end, her ego got in the way of everything. If she couldn't be completely in control, she didn't want any part of it. She entertained roles in movies that would become pop classics—*Auntie Mame, Thoroughly Modern Millie, The Pink Panther*—then passed on all of them.

In 1962, on a whim, Kay moved to Rome, where she sped around the city on her Vespa and fell in love for a minute or two with an American executive at the company that made Playtex bras. She rented a fancy, three-story apartment, painted the walls Mediterranean Sea blue, and varnished her coffee table with nail polish. Often, she sat on her rooftop terrace watching the gaudy Roman sunsets and thinking—just for a moment—that this is the life. She had a favorite hangout, the Blue Bar, where she liked to play the piano and sing. A favorite was "My Funny Valentine."

The great Italian director Federico Fellini took an interest in Kay and invited her to his office to see if they might work together. She knew he

---

* Later she would play a bit role in the 1970 flop *Tell Me That You Love Me, Junie Moon*, with her beloved goddaughter, Liza Minnelli—but the less said about that, the better.

was only interested in seeing whether he might use her to play one of his grotesque characters. She would have been perfect, of course. But she passed.

Kay was a kook—the kind they don't really make anymore. Throughout her curious career, she always behaved like a diva, like a woman who was entitled to more. Arrogance isn't usually something people accept in women, unless they are extraordinarily beautiful. Kay was merely extraordinarily gifted—and believed that alone earned her the right to be herself.

CHAPTER 25

LAVERNE COX

Undaunted

LAVERNE COX TELLS A STORY ABOUT being a kid in Mobile, Alabama. I don't know when this is, because Laverne does not give her age. (Life is challenging enough as an African-American trans woman; throwing some good old-fashioned ageism on top of the heap of bigotry, phobia, and well-meaning misunderstanding is not something she's up for just now.)

Every day Laverne took the bus home after school, and every day when she got off, kids would chase her. She would start to run the moment her foot hit the ground. Sometimes they caught her and beat her up. On this day, her tormenters were members of the school band. When they wrestled her to the ground, they beat her with their drumsticks. A parent saw what happened and called the principal, who called Laverne's mother. Laverne didn't want her mother to know, because her mother felt the problem could be solved if Laverne fought back. But Laverne was afraid and didn't want to fight back. Thus, every time she got beat up, she was treated as if it were her own damn fault.

Laverne Cox is best known for her role as the credit card scammer and hairdresser Sophia Burset in the Netflix hit women's prison drama *Orange Is the New Black*. She was born Roderick Laverne Cox in Mobile, Alabama, where she and her identical twin brother, M. Lamar, were raised by their mom. As early as third grade, she identified as female. In conversation with *Time* magazine about her landmark June 2014 cover she said, ". . . I just thought that I was a girl and that there was no difference between girls and boys. I think in my imagination I thought that I would hit puberty and I would start turning into a girl."

When she did hit puberty, the only thing she turned into was someone who liked boys, which compounded her growing confusion and shame. A teacher had already told her mother that unless she took Laverne in hand, "your son is going to end up in New Orleans wearing a dress." Whatever that meant, exactly, Laverne knew it was shameful; she imagined her grandmother sitting in heaven, looking down on her with great disappointment. So she swallowed a bottle of pills she found in the medicine cabinet. She went to sleep expecting to join her grandmother, but instead woke up with a stomachache to end all stomachaches. She never told a soul, even her mother.

In the end, Laverne was saved by her creative drive: her strong desire to be an artist and to make a living as a performer. She studied dance and acting at Indiana University Bloomington, and then Marymount Manhattan College. Before landing the role of Sophia in *Orange Is the New Black,* she'd only portrayed sex workers. Seven hookers preceded the role that would change her life. *Orange Is the New Black* premiered in 2013, and then came all the firsts: first openly trans woman to be nominated for a prime-time Emmy, first trans woman on the cover of a major magazine *(Time),* first trans woman wax figure at Madame Tussauds! She attended the 2015 White House Correspondents Dinner and collected a hug from First Lady Michelle Obama. In 2017, she became the first transgender person to play a transgender person on a scripted network show (*Doubt,* on CBS, which got yanked after two episodes for unknown reasons).

Laverne Cox has clearly arrived. She's become the star she always dreamed of being, and could be forgiven for kicking back a little and enjoying the fruits of her success. She could focus on her acting career, attend A-list parties, present awards (as she did at the 2017 Grammys), show up for magazine cover shoots, or score some awesome couture from designers eager to dress her stunning, statuesque bod—all while politely deflecting questions about being transgender (most of which tend to be awkward, offensive, and pretty clueless). She could have saved herself a lot of effort, frustration, and the need to summon every last ounce of patience she possesses. She could have just gone on and lived her life. She could have refused to deal with it. But she's committed to the simple human cause of showing the world that trans people are also human, and has no intention of keeping quiet or going away. She is undaunted.

In 2014, Katie Couric interviewed Laverne and transgender model Carmen Carrera on her talk show, *Katie*. In an effort, I imagine, to do the hard-hitting journalist thing, Couric asked questions like "Was the whole process painful, physically, for you?" and "Your private parts are different now, aren't they?"

It's impossible to find a correlation to such questions for a cisgender person. The best I can do is to recall the time I was on the *Today* show to talk about a funny essay I'd written for some magazine about being in a relationship with a guy 16 years my junior. Ann Curry and I yukked it up in the predictable "You go, girl!" fashion, discussing how much Bon Jovi I was expected to endure and whether I worried that he would one day leave me for a woman his own age.* But what if instead she had focused on the state of my middle-aged vagina? What if she asked, "Is sex painful for you? How much lube do you have to use?"

In the wake of Couric's interview with Laverne, the Internet was swift and unforgiving, condemning her interview tactics mercilessly.

But Laverne, however miffed she may have been privately, welcomed Couric's awkward, invasive let's-talk-genitals question, because it gave her a chance to push the conversation in a meaningful direction. If the conversation had been all platitudes and analysis of TV roles, Laverne would never have found the opening to say: "The preoccupation with

---

* Answers: More than you might expect; I should hope he would leave me for a younger woman. If he left me for someone my age, I'd kill him.

surgery objectifies trans people. We then don't get to deal with the real lived experiences, with the reality of trans people's lives. So often we're targets of violence. Our unemployed rate is twice the national average. If you're a trans person of color, it's four times the national average. The homicide rate in the LGBT community is highest among trans women. If we focus on transition, we don't get to talk about those things."

This was a daytime women's talk show. Mothers trying to get their babies to go down for a nap were watching, women home with the flu, or folding laundry, or figuring out what to cook for dinner. Laverne could easily have done a typically feminine thing and played it off. She can be very funny. She could have said, "Oh, Katie, I'll just leave it to your imagination," and then changed the subject. But now that she is in the public eye, visibility and education have become part of her job; she is using her celebrity to bring awareness to what she calls "the lived life" of a trans person, day by day. The blog posts she writes for *HuffPost* are well-considered essays with titles like "Voter Suppression and the Transgender Community" and "Everybody's Trans: Gender Oppression Hurts All of Us."

In 2015, Laverne posed nude for *Allure*. She had previously declined their offer, twice. I'm sure she wondered whether, aside from the risk of career suicide, she was setting herself up for some serious backlash—on a par with getting beaten up by the band kids, or worse. "But I'm a black transgender woman," she observed. "Black women are not often told that we're beautiful unless we align with certain standards. Trans women certainly are not told we're beautiful. Seeing a black transgender woman embracing and loving everything about herself might be inspiring to some other folks. There's beauty in the things we think are imperfect."

True enough, but she looks pretty dang perfect in the stunning black-and-white portrait that eventually ran in the magazine. The camera loves her, it turns out. In summer 2017 Beyoncé tapped Laverne to be one of the faces of her Ivy Park fitness line. Laverne is so breathtaking it's just plain ridiculous.

It's not overstating things to say that just walking down the street as a transgender person in America is to risk your life. Hate crimes against transgender people tripled between 2014 and 2015; the rate was highest against African-American trans women. In August 2013, a woman named Islan Nettles was walking down a New York street when a guy started flirting with her, realized she was trans, and beat her to death.

That Laverne is fully aware of these dangers, and nevertheless chooses to put herself out there, challenging assumptions and making people think, takes a lot of guts. It makes her a brave woman, which in my book makes her difficult: bold, unafraid to kick ass, and unwilling to minimize herself—an action women have often taken to avoid conflict and unpleasantness. With grace and a hell of a lot of dignity, Laverne welcomes her detractors. It's a lesson we could all stand to learn.

CHAPTER 26

HILLARY RODHAM CLINTON

Ambitious

I HAVE A WHITE HOUSE STORY that involves First Lady Hillary Clinton—or more accurately, her office in the West Wing. I was parked there for a spell on the morning of January 24, 2000—the same day the president unveiled a $27 million equal pay initiative for American women. I was there for a magazine story. President Clinton's announcement was set for 11 a.m., and I was very early.

The tiny, swingy-haired page couldn't figure out what to do with me in the meantime, so she invited me to hang out in the first lady's office. Hillary wasn't there, but I remember being struck by how friendly her office seemed, filled with presents from her travels and an energetic staff. A young aide wearing pearls offered me a glass of water. To pass the time, I asked her whether she enjoyed working for the first lady, and she said she loved it. I then asked what the best part of working for her was, and her face opened in a grin. "She makes me feel smart!" Then I asked what the first lady did for fun, and she said, "the StairMaster."

During the 2016 presidential campaign, when people hated Hillary with the sort of loathing reserved for the world's evil despots, I remembered this day. I don't think the young assisant wearing pearls had any idea what I was doing there. I don't think she told me that she loved her job because her boss made her feel smart for any nefarious reason. She could have said the job was just okay, and that the great thing about working for Hillary was the benefits. I felt as if this gave me a secret glimpse of Hillary, who took the time to make a young staff member feel her intelligence was appreciated.

I carried this memory throughout the campaign—even when I felt she was making mistakes, counting her chickens, and failing to show us the woman I thought, based on this tiny experience, I knew her to be.

Hillary Diane Rodham was born on October 26, 1947. From what I can tell, she was difficult straight out of the gate—by which I mean she was a brilliant overachiever. She was a straight-A student, and both a Brownie and a Girl Scout. (I have no evidence of this, but I feel as if I can safely say she was one of those Girl Scouts who earned more badges than anyone else in the troop.) In high school, she was elected vice president of the student council her junior year. In 1964, her senior year, she ran for president—and in a bit of foreshadowing that would never be permitted in a cheesy novel, lost to a boy who allegedly told her she was stupid if she thought a girl could ever be elected. It was one thing to collect merit badges and excellent grades—those are plentiful. But whenever there's a single position up for grabs—an important one that confers both power and prestige—only a very confident, ambitious girl will go for it.

After she graduated from Wellesley in 1969 (honors, commencement speech that drew a standing ovation, and so on), she entered Yale Law. "I was taking a law school admissions test in a big classroom at Harvard," Clinton told the Humans of New York blog in 2016. "My friend and I were some of the only women in the room. I was feeling nervous. I was a senior in college. I wasn't sure how well I'd do. And while we're waiting for the exam to start, a group of men began to yell things like: 'You don't need to be here.' And 'There's plenty else you can do.' It turned into a real 'pile on.' One of them even said: 'If you take my spot, I'll get drafted, and I'll go to Vietnam, and I'll die.' And they weren't kidding around. It was intense."

Hillary was rattled but controlled herself—something she would be criticized for later—did well, and was admitted. She continued her focused, disciplined, high-achieving work while also being pursued by fellow student Bill Clinton. There's a picture of the two of them in 1971 or so. He's got a lot of hair and an unfortunate beard. She is rocking an excellent Gloria Steinem look, with straight center-parted hair and wire-rimmed aviator glasses. Their coats are ill-fitting and their pant legs too short. They shine with smarts and optimism. As everyone who watched the 2016 Democratic Convention by now knows, he asked her to marry him. She said no.

After they graduated in 1973, Bill Clinton flunked the District of Columbia bar exam but passed the test in his home state of Arkansas. Hillary, who could have stayed in the Northeast and launched a stellar career, then betrayed her difficult-woman heritage and followed him there. She, who was so independent—who already aspired to be a senator, or even the president—*followed her man*. And it wasn't as if she was following him to an elite place like New York City, where she might more easily satisfy her ambition to become the Darth Vader of American politics. With respect to her boyfriend's home state (Arkansas brought us the first Wal-Mart), the opportunities for an outspoken Yankee woman to make her mark were less certain. And still she followed her heart.

I remain mystified as to why Hillary never gets points for that decision from the folks who wish she were a more traditional woman. Hillary haters are happy to reach back decades to collect evidence that she's an evil, radical feminist but fail to acknowledge that changing your own plans to support your man is as traditional as it gets. Still, when Bill and Hillary did get married on October 11, 1975, she kept her own name. That created a stir, even though it was an era when women all over the country were doing it.*

Bill was elected governor of Arkansas in 1978. While she was first lady, Hillary worked as a patent and intellectual property attorney. She co-founded a children's advocacy group, and served as the chair for the Rural Health Advisory Committee.

If you squint, you can see the seeds of Hillary's problem sprouting right here. She improved health care for the poorest rural Arkansans, but the committee appointment that allowed her to do so was made by her husband. She did a good thing, but it was a good thing done by the *wife* of the governor, a female who had not been elected. I can easily imagine some unemployed

---

* I've been married twice and have never changed my name. Lucky I don't intend to run for president.

man's man from Huntsville scoring free checkups and vaccines for the entire family, cussing out the uppity first lady as he rolls down his sleeve.

On February 27, 1980, Chelsea was born; in November, Bill Clinton lost his bid for reelection. Suddenly, Hillary was both a new mom and the breadwinner. She continued to work. She took care of her baby (and probably a mopey husband). When Bill Clinton ran for governor again in 1982, she quit her job to devote herself to the campaign full time, and started calling herself Mrs. Bill Clinton. In 1983, she was named Arkansas Woman of the Year, and in 1984 she was even named Arkansas Mother of the Year. Now we're talking. This is all good, all wifely. All first lady–conforming.

And yet, again, no points given. Instead, she would earn the moniker "the Lady Macbeth of Little Rock." Shakespeare's iconic antiheroine, as you may recall, was famous for suppressing her femininity in favor of ambition and the pursuit of power. Dozens of media outlets adopted the name and ran with it. Hillary Clinton had given up a lot for her marriage and family. But she didn't give up everything, and that fact made her suspect. In other words, difficult.

When Bill Clinton was elected president in 1992, Hillary, who was now 45, had not yet figured out that anything she said could and would be held against her until the zombie apocalypse. Nevertheless, feeling a little spicy during an interview that same year on *60 Minutes,* she said this: "I could have stayed home and baked cookies and had teas, but what I decided to do was to fulfill my profession, which I entered before my husband was in public life."[*]

I remember watching the coverage on TV. Hillary was so confident, so frank and sassy. She wasn't smiling when she said it. She was serious. I cannot believe that after 12 years of first ladying in a southern state, she still didn't realize that she must smile at all times. (She may have been forgiven for reasoning that because the only men who smile when they talk are serial killers about to start in on the ritual torture, there was no reason for her to do so. Or maybe she was already figuring out that she would never be forgiven for anything, so what the hell.) Anyway, over time Hillary trained herself

---

[*] You know, like millions of other college-educated women of that time.

not to be frank and sassy, but to be measured, careful, and tapped down. Which would lead to accusations of being phony and untrustworthy.

WHAT PEOPLE CAME TO DESPISE so thoroughly about Hillary Clinton is that she simply would not quit. Her ambition couldn't be knocked out of her by Bill's affairs. It couldn't be knocked out of her by the public humiliation of the Monica Lewinsky scandal; by her husband's circus of an impeachment; by the never-ending Whitewater investigation; or by that thing involving cattle futures. She just kept going. And yet when it appeared as if she'd been felled by traditional "woman matters"—her man cheated, her man lied—her approval ratings rose like the sun. Analyze that!

Hillary was elected senator of New York State in 2000, was reelected in 2006, and ran for president against Barack Obama in 2008, losing in a vicious and heavily covered primary campaign. In 2016 she was the first woman to run for president on a major party ticket. She lost the electoral college (232 to 306) but won the popular vote by a count of almost three million.** This brings us to a distressing moment in American history, where the least experienced person to ever run for president prevailed over the most experienced person to ever run for president.

Hillary's many enemies aren't all the misogynists who during the election sported T-shirts and pins saying "Life's a bitch: don't vote for one." Many are intelligent and worldly. Some actually followed the cattle futures thing and know why it was shady. Still, their hatred for her was and is off the charts. Seriously, it was a presidential election, folks, not an arranged marriage. Citizens of the Republic were merely being encouraged to vote for her, not accept one of her kidneys for transplant.

In October 2016, a month before the election, the *Atlantic* ran a feature headlined "Fear of a Female President." It cited the power of the "precarious

---

** She won a total of 65,844,610 votes—48.2 percent–compared with Trump's 62,979,636 votes–46.1 percent–according to David Wasserman of the nonpartisan *Cook Political Report*. Other candidates took about 5.7 percent of the popular vote.

manhood" theory, which "posits that while womanhood is typically viewed as natural and permanent, manhood must be 'earned and maintained.' " Because manhood is won, it can also be lost. Scholars at the University of South Florida and the University of Illinois at Urbana-Champaign reported that when asked how someone might lose his manhood, college students rattled off social failures like "losing a job." When asked how someone might lose her womanhood, by contrast, they mostly came up with physical examples like "a sex-change operation" or "having a hysterectomy."

Among the emasculations men fear most is subordination to women. This fear isn't entirely irrational. A 2011 study in the *Journal of Experimental Social Psychology* found that men who have female supervisors enjoy less prestige than men whose bosses are male. Given this, it's cause for celebration that there are *any* woman bosses anywhere. As a wise friend says, "Yes, things can be better, but they can always be worse."

Hillary was a woman who did the natural woman things (have a baby), and also wanted to do the earned and maintained man things (run a country). She wanted the most powerful job in the world, which stirred up something terrifying in the lizard brains of a large part of the population.

Which brings us to the lunacy over her private email server—possibly the most boring scandal in the history of mankind, yet one that would not go away. Briefly, when Hillary was secretary of state, rather than using her state.gov email address, she used a private server and a personal account. When her unusual setup was discovered—the *New York Times* broke the story—she turned over roughly 30,000 emails to the State Department, and destroyed another 30,000 more, deemed to be personal. She didn't violate the letter of the law, but it does seem either sloppy or underhanded, depending on your point of view. Naturally, the point of view of her detractors was that she should be stoned in the public square.

During the campaign I conducted a little impromptu experiment in my neighborhood Starbucks. I went table to table and asked people if they knew what a server was, as in private email server. I live in Portland, Oregon, one of the nation's most tech-savvy cities. Out of the dozen or so people I queried,

half of them thought it was, like, an extra computer under your desk. One woman laughed and said for a long time she thought the server was a person, as in "I'm Todd, I'll be your email server."

One guy turned out to be a network engineer and gave me a mini TED talk on the matter. In his opinion, if Hillary was using a private email system, it would have been set up by a professional IT firm. Any modern email "server" (actually a service) on a privately hosted server is years ahead of government-managed systems in its security. He was pro–private email server.

I LIKE HILLARY, have always liked Hillary. She was the *first* first lady with a postgraduate degree, and I liked that about her. Because I hail from the solid middle class and made my way in the world under my own steam, I feel solidarity with her. I think she made some missteps during her campaign. (Did she really have to come out with "basket of deplorables," the ready-made Internet meme and campaign slogan for the opposition?) It's a natural impulse to try to parse what went wrong—but the bottom line is that Hillary Clinton is the most difficult kind of difficult woman: one who loudly and proudly possesses the ambition of a man. During the third debate she looked radiant in a white pantsuit, a slash of red lipstick. She looked energized and fully alive. She whipped out stats like a rap star on speed. She talked back, sassed a little. She was in her element, being difficult. She didn't win, but survived being this difficult. She thrived being this difficult. She showed all of us that difficulty is a power that doesn't desert us when we suffer—even the defeat of a lifetime. Which inspires millions of the rest of us to step up.

CHAPTER 27

JANIS JOPLIN

Defiant

WHEN I WAS IN GRADE SCHOOL in the late 1960s, a gang of older teenage girls in the neighborhood adopted me as their mascot. They were 16 years old and smoked pot and longed to flee our Southern Californian suburb for San Francisco, where it was all happening. They could not possibly be more cool. One day, hanging out at the mall, we spied a rack of albums for sale at, of all places, the Singer Sewing store (in a bid to lure young people into the store, they'd started selling records). The ringleader sent me in to pinch a copy of *Cheap Thrills,* the new album by Big Brother and the Holding Company. Inside the store, the salesperson was nowhere to be seen, so I grabbed two. As a reward, they let me keep one. I played it over and over again on my record player in my bedroom, screeching and moaning "Piece of My Heart" into my salt-shaker microphone, pinching my eyebrows together and throwing my hair around. Janis Joplin was a revelation.

My mom worked tirelessly to impress upon me that girls should be polite and soft-spoken. They should be good listeners. They should be careful not to be too expressive, or risk startling the rest of the human race and sending it into a panic. Complaining was very unattractive, and should be indulged in only with my best friend. Crying in particular tended to upset people, and should be done in private, if at all; no one looked good doing it. And the other thing girls should be was as pretty as possible at all times.

Then came Janis, who not only refused to hide her feelings; she refused to even dial them down a notch. She flaunted them. She owned them with every cell in her body. She moaned and crooned and groaned and panted and screeched and shrieked. I just loved her.

JANIS JOPLIN WAS THE FIRST CERTIFIED female rock star. She was the lead singer of Big Brother and the Holding Company, one of a handful of bands making up the psychedelic music scene in San Francisco during the late 1960s. For a few early months in 1965, they *were* the psychedelic music scene.* When Big Brother played the 1967 Monterey Pop Festival, they left everyone in the dust. Or rather, Janis did. Her yowling, howling, crooning, broken-hearted rendition of the classic blues song "Ball and Chain" was raw, aggressive, and sexy. It was unlike anything anyone had ever heard from the lungs and heart of a middle-class white female. The most popular girl singers of the age were safely feminine. Joan Baez and Judy Collins come to mind, with their silky hair and dulcet tones.** They were graceful fawns in the forest, dipping a dainty hoof in a clear pond of sweet water, while Janis was a monster truck with a broken muffler hauling ass down a rutted, pot-holed southern road.

Janis Lyn Joplin was born in Port Arthur, Texas, in 1943, two years before the end of World War II and the official beginning of the baby boom. She was an agreeable child and excellent student, but in her senior year of high school discovered booze, the Beats, the blues, teenage rebellion, and the joy of shooting her mouth off. In 1962, after a halfhearted attempt at college, she drifted between Austin,

---

* The Grateful Dead, Jefferson Airplane, and Quicksilver Messenger Service were also practicing in old Victorians that were on the verge of being condemned, making the neighbors' ears bleed as they figured out their sound.

** What about Grace Slick, you may wonder. I don't know what to tell you. She wasn't Janis.

Los Angeles, New York, and San Francisco before finally settling in Haight-Ashbury, where she joined Big Brother, already a well-established Bay Area band. Her performance at the 1967 Monterey Pop Festival caught the eye of the music industry brass in attendance that day; within a year, she would be a star. Big Brother's first major recording was the psychedelic masterpiece *Cheap Thrills,* certified gold on release in August 1968, selling more than a million copies (and shoplifted by many enterprising preteens).

With hot pink and purple feather boas pinned in her hair, long beaded necklaces, bracelets stacked up to her elbows, skimpy tops, satin bell-bottoms, macramé vests, and a bottle of Southern Comfort at her side, Janis was for a brief time the undisputed queen of rock-and-roll. Still, she was often troubled, and didn't care who knew it. She yearned for love, took up with people who couldn't love her, and turned away people who would. She fretted that the world would discover she was a fraud. She was heartbroken when people didn't recognize her on the street. She worried that she was ugly. She drank a staggering amount and struggled with a moderate heroin habit until her accidental overdose on October 4, 1970, at the age of 27.

PORT ARTHUR IS AN OIL REFINERY TOWN on the Gulf Coast, 91 miles east of Houston and a stone's throw from Louisiana. It's a town of billowing smokestacks, tall gas flares topped by ever-burning flames, oil jacks that pump ceaselessly as a heart, and row upon row of squat white petroleum storage tanks. It's one of the most humid places in the country, where the air smells of rotten eggs, fireworks, and scalded plastic. (I'm told people who live there don't notice after a while.) There are tidy, well-heeled neighborhoods too, with shady streets, manicured front lawns, and churchgoing neighbors. The Joplins lived on one such street.

Janis's father, Seth, was an engineer at Texaco. Her mother, Dorothy, was a housewife, focused on raising Janis and her two younger siblings, Laura and Michael. They were a Texas-style *Leave It to Beaver* family. Janis, older than Laura by six years, was sent to Sunday school and joined the Bluebirds. She showed some singing ability, but no one made much of it. Aside from her intelligence (which was viewed as a liability in a girl), she seemed poised for an expected future: attending Lamar State College of Technology in neighboring Beaumont for training as either a teacher or a nurse before marrying a local boy and settling down. That was pretty much the lone option for a young woman in Port Arthur, Texas, in the late 1950s.

Then as now, the biggest natural advantage a woman has is beauty. It may be skin-deep, but when has that bothered the teachers, employers, suitors—even parents—in charge of doling out the time, attention, favors, promotions, and marriage proposals? When Janis turned 14, it became apparent that she would be just this side of homely, a reality she struggled with her entire life.

Puberty is more transformational for some of us than others. Janis's blond curls darkened to dust-bunny brown, and she gained weight. Worst of all, she was smacked with a catastrophic case of acne that no amount of pancake makeup could disguise. Her mother took her to the dermatologist, who blamed the victim; Janis was told to keep her hands off her face and avoid fried foods. She did, but nothing helped. In school, she was desperate to fit in, at first. She joined the Future Teachers of America and was part of a group that decorated the gym for dances and made posters for student elections. But at some point, being relegated to the invisible army of female do-gooders and behind-the-scenes helpers was too dispiriting.

Junior year she took up with a group of senior boys who were artistic and outlaw-ish: Jim Langdon, a jazz musician; David Moriaty, who remained a friend after she left Texas; and Grant Lyons, who turned her on to the music of Leadbelly and Bessie Smith, Janis's primary musical influences and inspiration. The older boys also turned her on to the Beat poetry of Lawrence Ferlinghetti, Allen Ginsberg, and Gary Snyder. Already an avid reader, she devoured Jack Kerouac, and took his thoughts about racism to heart. Port Arthur was segregated in 1958, and the large African-American population—40 percent of the town—lived on the wrong side of the tracks. One day in Janis's social studies class, the topic of the rights of Negroes came up. Everyone solemnly affirmed the wisdom of segregation, except Janis, who stood up and said, "Society's treatment of the black person is wrong. They are people like you and me."

After that, the bullying began in earnest. Janis was called a weirdo, a nigger lover, a pig—and, of course, a whore, that all-purpose insult for women who refuse to obey. Boys with whom she'd never exchanged a single word spread rumors about banging her in the backseat of their cars. (This was not an era when parents marched down to the high school and demanded justice.) Janis's reaction was not to lie low, as another girl might have. Instead, she doubled down. If someone passed her in the hallway and made oinking sounds, she spun on her heel and yelled at them to fuck off. Janis was rebellious and mouthy to a degree the good people of Port Arthur had rarely seen. And you know what? It made her feel good and alive.

It was a 40-minute drive from Port Arthur across the border into Louisiana, where you could hear live music at the bars in Vinton and get seriously shit-faced. The bars were whites-only, but there were a few where you could sneak in and hear black musicians playing what Janis and her crowd considered to be real music. However, it was well known among the high school rebels that the best music was in New Orleans, a daring four-hour drive across the state. Few people had the chops to try to get away with it.

One night during her senior year, Janis talked some of the boys in her gang into making the trip.* They got smashed, barhopped until

---

* In time-honored fashion, Janis lied to her mother, telling her she was spending the night at a girlfriend's house.

the wee hours, then suffered a minor wreck on the way home. Cops arrived, parents were called, and by Monday the gossip had spread throughout the high school. The reputation of the boys had soared— what cool cats, living on the edge!—while Janis was branded the class slut. No one believed they'd gone all that way merely to hear some good bands.

Given Janis's complete failure before this time to woo the boys in her class, this might initially have seemed like an improvement in her social status—at least someone wanted to have sex with her! But Port Arthurians were a judgmental lot, and she was now fully ostracized. The irony is that the boys in her crowd were completely uninterested in her. They lusted after other girls—the pretty ones—and she always went home alone.

JANIS GRADUATED FROM high school in 1960. In 1962, she enrolled in the fine arts program at the University of Texas, Austin, ostensibly to become a painter. She moved into The Ghetto, an apartment house near campus where the political activists, artists, and folk singers lived. She and her Autoharp joined a bluegrass band called the Waller Creek Boys. They had a regular Wednesday night gig at a converted gas station called Threadgill's Bar & Grill. It was owned by country singer and yodeler Kenneth Threadgill, who supported Janis and believed in her talent—a kindness she would never forget. For two bucks you could drink beer until the wee hours, listening to Janis sing Leadbelly's and Bessie Smith's greatest hits in her mournful alto.

In 1962, Texas college coeds still wore beehive hairdos, straight skirts, white shirts with Peter Pan collars, and flats. Boys had short hair and dressed like their fathers. Shelley Fabares was the top-selling white female singer of the year with "Johnny Angel," which topped out at number six on the Billboard charts.

Janis could not have been more different. She wore raggedy-hemmed jeans, denim work shirts, and no bra. She was freakish enough to be newsworthy for a *Daily Texan* story headlined "She Dares to Be Different." (Oh, they had no idea.)

Janis might have stayed in Austin indefinitely. She loved performing at Threadgill's, where she was developing a following. People were starting to think that however weird she might be, she could really sing.

The Greek system was big at UT, and every year Alpha Phi Omega held the Ugliest Man on Campus contest as a fundraiser for charity. For five dollars, frat boys nominated each other, sorority girls secretly nominated boys who'd spurned them, and it was all good, clean early-1960s fun. Someone entered Janis into the contest. She didn't win, as legend holds. But given how self-conscious she was about her looks, she didn't need to.

A week later, ugly, manly Janis was gone.

She hitchhiked to the Bay Area with Chet Helms, a long-haired friend who'd been there before. Janis wowed the crowds at popular coffeehouses in North Beach, Santa Cruz, and Palo Alto, who were used to agreeable-sounding guitar strummers, rather than an angst-ridden, acne-scarred Texas woman who sang her guts out. Around this time, during her first foray to San Francisco, she started using both speed and heroin. She was never one for acid; her mind was active enough, she didn't need hallucinations on top of everything else. But anything that could be shot into a vein to distract her for a while from her ever-aching, ever-wounded heart? She was all over that.

Oh, she made some bad decisions. She shot her mouth off to a Hells Angels gang and got herself beat up. She was bisexual, and took up with an assortment of men and women who loved her either too much or not enough. Still, she had friends who cared about her, and when they saw how strung out she was, how skinny and dirty and arm scratching and crazy-eyed, they pooled their money and bought her a bus ticket back to Port Arthur.

Back she went to her parents' house. She enrolled as a sociology major at Lamar State College. She bought modest gathered skirts and long-sleeved blouses to cover the track marks. She saw a psychiatric social worker, briefly. She told him that if she could just be a good Port Arthur girl, she would be able to bury her ambition, her passion to sing, her need for the needle. For all of Janis's intelligence, she seemed happy to be a mystery to herself. Another theory: The only thing that made her singing come alive was her tsunami of unarticulated feelings—and perhaps intuitively, she realized that sorting them all out would compromise her gift.

There was also something else: While in San Francisco she'd fallen in love with Peter de Blanc,* whom she knew through speed user circles. A few weeks after Janis had returned to Port Arthur, Peter dropped in and asked Seth Joplin for his daughter's hand. He was on his way to New York to do something or other. The family was apparently not overly impressed with Peter, but it hardly mattered. Janis was engaged! She embarked upon the traditional bride-to-be activities of the time: selecting a china pattern, assembling a hope chest, shopping for a wedding gown, and stitching together, with her mother and sister, a Texas Lone Star quilt for the marital bed.

Then, suddenly, Janis stopped hearing from him. Peter de Blanc had disappeared.

Back she went to singing, to plotting another escape. Back she went to Austin, to singing at Threadgill's. For a short time, Jekyll and Hyde merged: She hurled herself back into the blues in her modest skirt and poufy bun. Guys who'd known her when she was at UT, and were still hanging around town, didn't notice her square ensemble as much as how good she'd gotten. Her feelings poured out of her. Her voice was raw and unadorned. Her charisma was weird and affecting.

I'm making it sound so simple and freewheeling. Janis was tortured. She felt Texas was safer, better, and "good" for her, while also boring, closed-minded, and an artistic dead end. She couldn't make peace with

---

* This may not have been his real name, not surprising given all that would transpire.

this fact. She might have dithered in Austin indefinitely, but in 1966, her old pal Chet Helms, now a self-styled music promoter who would go on to become the so-called father of 1967's "Summer of Love," talked her into coming back—again!—to San Francisco to audition for Big Brother and the Holding Company.

Years later, Janis would recall it like this: "How I happened to join Big Brother? Well, Chet Helms sent Travis Rivers to get me. What I usually say is that I wanted to leave Texas, but that's not what really happened. I didn't want to leave. But he was such a good fuck! How could I not go?"

The less-groovy truth—completely at odds with the spirit of the laid-back times—is that Janis was driven, ambitious, competitive, and itching for success.

AT THAT TIME, BIG BROTHER was the house band at the Avalon Ballroom, managed by Bill Graham, the granddaddy of the modern rock concert, who also ran the Fillmore Auditorium. The band consisted of psychedelic rock specialist "Weird" Jim Gurley; self-taught bassist Peter Albin; San Francisco State student Sam Andrew; and artist and Spaghetti Factory waitperson Dave Getz on drums. Like many bands of the time, they spent perhaps as much time coming up with the band name as they did practicing. (Second runner up: Tom Swift and His Electric Grandmother.) They called their sound "freak jazz"—and from all reports, it was sort of progressive/hard rock/raga riffs/fuzz tone/feedback distortion/blues.** Their stated mission was "to speak to all the children of the earth," which may have led to their desire to bring in a "chick singer," given that 51 percent of the aforementioned children are female. More likely, they hoped it would distinguish them from the other rock bands popping up daily like head shops on Haight Street.

** I cannot begin to imagine what this sounds like; please use your imagination.

When Janis auditioned, at the age of 23, she wasn't particularly impressed, and the feeling was mutual. Part of the issue was a difference in musical style—a diplomatic way of saying that Janis was pretty much a stone-cold genius, while BBHC excelled at being very loud. But Helms had persuaded both parties to give it a chance. So when they asked her to join them, Janis said hell yes.

In July 1966 the band moved to a big house in Lagunitas, a tiny rural community in Marin County. Frank Zappa once said (possibly around the same time), "The older you get, the more you realize life is like high school." I wonder if Janis realized this as she settled in with her male bandmates and their wives and girlfriends. There she was again, one of the guys, but still essentially alone. At the end of the night, they all crawled into bed with their old ladies, and she was left to ponder the injustice of it all. When Big Brother wasn't rehearsing, she hung out at a local roadhouse where she drank herself into a stupor and played pool with the Grateful Dead, who lived down the road.

The Lagunitas idyll lasted only a few months—long enough for Janis to make the all-important transition from Texas beatnik in drab work shirts and jeans to would-be sparkly hippie princess. Her inspiration was Jim Gurley's wife, Nancy, a small-boned creature with a master's degree in English, whose interpretation of counterculture couture ran toward high priestess/gypsy queen. Oh, the velvet gowns! The satin, lace, and endless swags of glittery necklaces! Janis decided that would be the look she would adopt, once she had a little money. To demonstrate her adoration and devotion to Nancy, she rather ostentatiously slept with Jim. You know, as one did in those days. Nancy was apparently a little miffed, but nothing a joint couldn't fix.

Bead making was Nancy's thing. (So was dropping acid, with a speed chaser.) The proper way to bead involved using a slender needle to ease a small glass bead onto a piece of waxed leather thread, followed by tying a tiny knot, then slipping on the next bead. Janis, determined to stay clean, used beading to keep her hands busy and away from dope. But one day it simply got away from her and she shot up with the others. In a single afternoon, she, Nancy, and another girl, Rita, pinwheel-eyed on speed, whipped out a 15-foot beaded curtain.

This is as good a place as any to say that in those years, everyone sat around doing a lot of drugs. I don't think I have it in me to carefully reconstruct the scenes, which are numerous and all essentially identical: People do the drug. They say things they believe to be profound or funny but are generally neither. Someone puts on a record. People bob their heads to the music. If the drug is of the upper persuasion, they may dance around like maniacs until they collapse in a heap. Whether on uppers or downers, some guy plays an air guitar. People start making out, then either forget they're doing it or disappear into another room for a proper balling.* Time passes. A lot of time passes. Someone orders a pizza.

In those pre-Internet days acronyms weren't really a thing. No SMH, BTW, LOL, YOLO, or all the rest. It's unfortunate, because if there's one place we could really use a universally accepted acronym, it would be as a placeholder for what happened during the many hours, days, and weeks in the 1960s and '70s when people did drugs. If there is one thing more boring than sitting around while other people do drugs, it's listening to them tell stories about sitting around doing drugs—and I'm afraid that's what a true accounting of Janis's life during these years would entail. A popular acronym affirmed by the Oxford English Dictionary would be really handy here. Something like SADD, Sat Around Doing Drugs.

SADD, SADD, SADD.

THE MONTEREY POP FESTIVAL, held June 16 to 18, 1967, became the template for all the outdoor music festivals to follow. The lineup included

---

* I seem to have a lot of friends who miss certain things about the 1960s and '70s: the music, the flowing attire, the fact that no one had answering machines, much less more advanced technology. No one misses the word "ball."

pretty much everyone still in heavy rotation on your local classic rock station: Canned Heat, Steve Miller Band, The Who, Jimi Hendrix, Grateful Dead, The Mamas & the Papas, Otis Redding, Ravi Shankar, Jefferson Airplane, and Big Brother and the Holding Company. This is the concert at which Jimi Hendrix set his guitar on fire with lighter fluid, bashed it onto the stage a good half dozen times, then tossed the shredded bits into the audience. Still, I would argue that Janis's performance was more memorable. Documentarian D. A. Pennebaker captured brilliant, unexpected moments in his film *Monterey Pop:* the way Janis's feet lift out of her kitten heel sandals when she really belts it out; the expression on the face of Mama Cass, sitting in the front row and mouthing "Wow!"; Janis's sweet, awkward bow at the end, and her girlish skip offstage.

In a matter of weeks, she was being celebrated as the bright, off-the-rails young thing helping to usher in the new age of sex, drugs, and rock-and-roll. She was applauded for operating with no filter, beloved for doing all the dope, screwing all the guys, and shrieking and cussing about her repressed middle-class childhood.

JANIS'S SIBLINGS, LINDA AND MICHAEL, saw a different side of their sister. In 1992 Linda, who has a master's in psychology and a Ph.D. in education, would publish her own memoir—*Love, Janis*—in an effort to rehabilitate her sister's image. They insisted she wasn't just a "ballsy mama" but a kind, normal girl who'd been influenced by a bad crowd. And, you know, they weren't crazy or in denial.

Until her death, Janis faithfully wrote long, very sweet letters home. The world's most cheerful, detailed-oriented summer camper has nothing on Janis when it came to writing letters. She wrote about her gigs, how much money she was making, her apartment, her neighborhood, her new clothes, her dog, George. She included magazine articles from *LOOK* and *Newsweek* on the Haight-Ashbury scene, then reassured her family these were mere distortions. The golly gee willikers tone is unmistakable. In a letter dated April 1967 she wrote, ". . . guess who was in town last week—Paul McCartney!!!! (he's a Beatle)."

In the same missive, she cagily breaks the news about her infamous black-and-white topless portrait, taken by photographer Bob Seidemann. In it, her chest is festooned with many beaded necklaces, styled so that one nipple pokes out coyly between the strands. "Also, they're bringing out a poster of me!" she writes chattily. "Maybe you've read in *Time* magazine about the personality posters. They're big, very big photographs, Jean Harlow, Einstein, Belmondo, Dylan, & Joplin. Yes, folks, it's me wearing a sequined cape, thousands of strings of beads & topless. But it barely shows because of the beads. Very dramatic photograph & I look really beautiful!! If it wouldn't embarrass you, I'll send you one. I'm thrilled!! I can be Haight-Ashbury's first pin-up."

Bob Seidemann, weighing in on the experience of being on the other side of the camera, saw it a bit differently. He found Janis to be aggressive and kind of a pain in the ass. During the shoot, she was naked from the waist up, mostly covered by the sequined cape. Throughout, she kept yowling, "Oh motherfucker! I want to take my fuckin' clothes off." She stripped, even though Seidemann told her to keep her clothes on. Later, she laid into him because she wasn't seeing any money from the sale of the poster. "You motherfucker, you're taking all the money I'm making for you."

Which one was the "real" Janis? Why can't it be both? Or many things, for that matter. Why couldn't she be a sweet daughter; kind sister; witty, compassionate friend; vulnerable lover; defiant genius; complicated, difficult woman? Why can't we all be that?

IN THE SUMMER AND FALL OF 1967, Big Brother played a number of gigs, including the Summer Solstice festival in Golden Gate Park (a benefit for the Free Clinic, and also for the Zen Mountain Center). Groovy peace and love vibes notwithstanding, the band was not getting along. By "not getting along," I mean the guys were put out because since Monterey, word on the street was that the band was holding Janis back.

In February 1968, they made their East Coast debut at Anderson Theater on the Lower East Side. Janis was a basket case, intimidated by the thought of playing New York. She fretted that they would just be written off as a gang of "street freaks" from the Haight.*

In her satin, beads, feathers, and bracelets, Janis brought it. Her scorching, vocal cord–shredding rendition of "Piece of My Heart" had people on their feet. They rushed the stage, which she encouraged and flat-out adored. She gave four encores that night. The *New York Times* gave the show a rave, writing, "The lines can start forming now, for Miss Joplin is as remarkable a new pop music talent as has surfaced in years." Two weeks later, after successful gigs in Boston, Providence, and Detroit, they returned to New York to play the Fillmore East. Lines *had* formed, snaking down the street for many blocks—a crush of people there to see Janis. Not long after that, the group was booked and billed as Janis Joplin and Big Brother and the Holding Company. (You can imagine how well that went over.)

Also in 1968, Janis spent some of her newly acquired rock star moola on a 1965 Porsche. She paid $3,500 for it, and commissioned Big Brother roadie Dave Richards, who obviously possessed some serious art chops in addition to his music equipment–hauling skills, to do a custom psychedelic paint job. Richards covered the Porsche with turquoise, orange, and pink flowers, butterflies, astrological signs, mushrooms, skulls, and even a portrait of the band. The car instantly became as famous as its driver; in 2014, it sold at auction for $1.76 million.

---

* She wasn't being oversensitive. Frank Zappa and the Mothers of Invention refused to play at Monterey Pop because Zappa thought the Bay Area bands were subpar.

IN THE FALL OF 1968 —despite the fact that *Cheap Thrills* was a massive hit—Janis's manager, Albert Grossman, announced her plan to leave the band. Hastily, a new band was tossed together. It was called the Kozmic Blues Band, but there was nothing "kozmic" about it. Not their fault, really. Janis was 25, and didn't have a managerial bone in her body— something no one really thought about before handing her four musicians for whom backing her was merely a gig. Also, the whole of her musical education consisted of getting up in front of a crowd half-crocked and singing her guts out. What was she supposed to do with a bunch of musicians she hardly knew? And what were they supposed to do with her?

In February 1969, all four performances at the Fillmore East were sold out. The mainstream press was there, as well as Mike Wallace and a *60 Minutes* camera crew. The band wasn't terrible, but Janis was. *Rolling Stone,* in a cover story, called her the "Judy Garland of Rock" and declared her performance "stiff and preordained." In March, she appeared on *The Ed Sullivan Show,* and played Fillmore West to a hometown crowd. *San Francisco Chronicle* writer Ralph Gleason said she should "go back to Big Brother, if they'll have her." The Rolling Stones and Tina Turner played Madison Square Garden on Thanksgiving 1969. Janis was pressed into doing a duet with Tina, which she managed to botch, being too drunk to stand up.

Only a year earlier, Janis had been fresh and original: the glorious, anarchistic embodiment of the age. Sexual and rebellious, her energy untamed, she was like nothing anyone had ever seen. In retrospect, it was probably time for her style to evolve. But she was afraid to change for fear of losing the love of her audience. Instead, she lost her way for a bit. Whenever she felt insecure or overwhelmed, she acted out, swaggering and cussing and stomping around. Really, she could be obnoxious. Once, while interviewing a roadie, she made a big production of squeezing his bicep, then cackling that he didn't seem strong enough to carry the equipment, much less have sex with her.

In the meantime, now she was famous. Like most people who imagine the arrival of fame will bring joy, Janis was confused, and sometimes flat-out pissed off, that celebrity brought more problems than it solved.* Whenever her entourage went out to eat and drink, Janis felt obligated to pick up the bill, then would complain bitterly that people were taking advantage of her. She bought a house in Larkspur, in Marin County, and installed a wet bar made of redwood burl, a sunken tub, and a dog door for her beloved George. Junkies and hangers-on came and stayed. She would fly into a rage and kick them all out, then weep with loneliness. She expected everyone to know who she was, and when they didn't, she panicked that her career was on the skids. Once, she called Bob Dylan just because she could. "Hey Bob, it's Janis!" she roared. "Janis, who?" he said. She wept. Whether alone or in the middle of one of her raucous parties, she knocked back a quart of tequila; because it wasn't her signature Southern Comfort, now largely a publicity prop, she believed she was doing better.

During lucid moments Janis admitted to friends that she was in deep trouble. She knew she needed help, that her drinking—there was never any mention of drug use; everyone who knew her believed she'd kicked the needle long ago—was affecting her voice and ability to perform. This sort of clarity never lasted. There would always be someone crashing through the door, sliding into the booth beside her, or skipping backstage with a bottle of something, and she would never say no. On tour she developed a routine: Arise at a respectable hour, drink until passing out in the afternoon, "rest" until showtime, sober up enough to perform, rest afterward by getting drunk.

In January 1970, Janis's circumstances improved. It's something you learn as you get older: If you can just hang on, things will eventually get

---

* A question for another time is why everyone wants to be famous when it so rarely ends well.

better. The Kozmic Blues Band disbanded, replaced by the Full Tilt Boogie Band. She was better with this setup; her voice was maturing. It was richer, more nuanced. Unfortunately, her shows were less electrifying than they'd been in the past, and also less well attended.

This had more to do with changing times than with Janis, but she took it as implicit criticism anyway. For being an emblem of the 1960s, Janis wasn't especially political—by which I mean not at all. The moment she stood up in her 11th-grade social studies class and spoke out on behalf of civil rights was her first and last overtly political act. She paid almost no attention to what was going on in the world: quite a feat in an era when presidential candidates and famous civil rights leaders were being assassinated right and left, and pregnant actresses were being slaughtered in their fancy homes by hippie lunatics.

Closer to home, if you were a rock star, was Altamont. On December 6, 1969, at the Altamont Speedway Free Festival, four people died. One drowned in an irrigation ditch, two were killed in a hit-and-run, and audience member Meredith Hunter was stabbed by a Hells Angel as he tried to climb onstage. The fallout was a souring of the concert scene. Concert promoters became strict about crowd behavior, forbidding singers to urge the frenzied audience to stomp and dance in the aisles or rush the stage. At outdoor venues, barriers appeared between the front row and the stage, in an effort to maintain order. But Janis loved nothing more than getting people stirred up to the brink of rioting. Managers, publicists, and minders would beg her to tone it down. "I'm not gonna tell 'em to get out there and dance, but if they do it, man, I won't say a word! If they break those barriers, I *ain't* tellin' 'em to sit down. I won't! I won't!"

The genuine, generous side of Janis could still be glimpsed now and then. In July she canceled a $15,000 gig to travel to Austin for Ken Threadgill's 61st birthday party. Threadgill, you remember, supported her and believed in her when she was a weirdo and would-be ugliest man on campus. She had come straight from Honolulu, where she and the

Boogie Band had delivered a solid, seasoned performance. She serenaded Ken Threadgill with an acoustic version of "Me and Bobby McGee" and presented him with a gift from Hawaii. " . . . I brought him one thing I knew he'd like," she said. "A good lei." She dropped the flowers around his neck and laughed girlishly.

IN THE FIRST DAYS OF OCTOBER 1970, Janis was relatively happy. Things were going well, in fact. She and the band had been in the Sunset Sound recording studio in Los Angeles, finishing up the new album, *Pearl*. On October 1, she laid down a sly, a cappella version of a new song, "Mercedes Benz." She was in good spirits. She had a new boyfriend, Seth Morgan, with whom she was talking marriage.

On the last night of her life, she listened to an instrumental track for a song called "Buried Alive in the Blues." She was invigorated at the thought of laying down the vocal track the next day. At the end of the session she tooled her famous psychedelic Porsche down Sunset to have a drink with a few pals at Barney's Beanery. She drank two screwdrivers and expressed her joy that the band was coming together and that the new album would most surely be a hit. A little after midnight she returned to her room at the Landmark Hotel, alone.

There are various thoughts about why this particular hit of heroin was fatal. Some say she had not been using at the time, and thus had failed to build up the proper tolerance. Some say this particular smack was especially pure, and thus potent.

During the early morning hours of October 4, she died.

Janis was a pioneer of difficult womanhood for a generation who'd been taught that above all a woman must be nice, polite, and well behaved. She put the music world on notice that a female singer didn't have to be angelic, but could be nasty, powerful, and ballsy. Her life was not easy, and she was often her own worst enemy. But she demonstrated that women don't need to constantly be policing their feelings, that being alive means being on speaking terms with every dark corner of our hearts. That we should not be afraid to let it all out. Some might call that difficult. I call it being human.

CHAPTER 28

LENA DUNHAM

Imperfect

I WAS IN A HOTEL ROOM, on a layover on my way to Paris, when I watched the premiere of *Girls* in the spring of 2012. This is the only remotely cool personal detail about me in relation to the hyper-cool Lena Dunham and her Emmy Award–winning HBO comedy series about four millennials who live in Brooklyn and stagger through the early years of independence. Lena's cool quotient may fluctuate in relation to how people are feeling about her latest tweet; Instagram post; ill-considered political statement; tattoo acquisition; questionable red carpet outfit; degree of nudity; weight loss or gain, or recent magazine cover photograph. But there is one unhip horror of which she will never be accused: She is not a middle-aged woman.

I am old enough to be Lena Dunham's mother. I even have a daughter who is currently the same age Hannah, Marnie, Jessa, and Shoshanna were in that first season when the nation was losing its mind over the hilariously self-involved, clueless eponymous girls—especially the perfectly terrible sex Hannah and Adam had on a broken-down couch that could have used its own condom. Weirdly, this makes me a much better appreciator of *Girls* than the girls for whom the show was created.*

Because I came of age in the 1970s, and went to film school in the '80s, I feasted on a cinematic diet of poorly lit European art films that

---

* Somewhat icky factoid: Twenty-two percent of viewers during that first season were men over 50. I'll leave you to make of that what you will.

revealed the occasional dense bush or flaccid penis (not to mention Bertolucci's *Last Tango in Paris,* with the butter scene). I also sat through any number of student films starring the filmmakers' normal-looking friends doing drugs and having bad sex—and thus my jaw didn't drop when I watched Hannah, in that first episode, struggle to take off her tights on Adam's couch. I thought she got it just right, and I laughed my head off, remembering. During that first short half-hour premiere, viewers were put on notice: Lena is a normal-looking person who's going to show 20-something life in all its cringe-worthy glory.

MUCH HAS BEEN MADE ABOUT Lena Dunham's privilege, as if the fact she was born to two celebrated, well-connected New York artists accounted for her drive and talent, or the ability to get a pilot green-lighted at HBO. For the daughter of photographer Laurie Simmons and painter Carroll Dunham, the main signifier of how Life Has Been Unfairly Good to Lena is the Tribeca loft in which she and her younger sister Grace grew up.* That loft, with its chic white walls and white floor, was one of the stars of *Tiny Furniture,* the $25,000 film Lena shot over the course of three weeks in 2009, which led eventually to her HBO deal for *Girls.* Success begetting success, she soon landed a three-plus-million-dollar book deal to write a collection of personal essays, published in 2014 as *Not That Kind of Girl: A Young Woman Tells You What She's Learned.* Lena claimed to be inspired by Helen Gurley Brown's 1982 best-selling self-help guide *Having It All,* but I didn't see it. Really, it's just an uneven collection of personal essays that might have been written by Hannah, had her Season 3 e-book deal panned out. Still, Lena took the money and wrote—and good for her.

Lena's real advantages lay in having a close relationship with her mom

---

* That her mother bought the place, housed inside a former textile warehouse, back in the '70s when Tribeca was still sketchy, before the invasion of J.Crew, is overlooked.

and dad, and witnessing from a young age what it means to live a life in the arts. She was spared the learning curve that most of us go through, first being seduced by the romance of the creative life, which features much drinking, pot smoking, talking, and suffering before figuring out that it's just like anything else: a beastly amount of hard work, long hours, late nights, boredom, and revision, revision, revision. "My parents taught me that you can have a creative approach to thinking that is almost scientific," Lena observed. "You don't have to be at the mercy of the muse. You need your own internalized thinking process that you can perform again and again."

On screen, as Hannah Horvath, Lena Dunham is not so savvy. Actually, she's whatever's the opposite of savvy, with her endless chattering, self-absorption, lack of self-awareness, and—cardinal sin—being unlikable. Because viewers apparently have trouble distinguishing between Hannah the character and Lena the creator, Lena has been branded as unlikable as well. The main thing viewers struggled with was that Hannah had a normal, slightly chubby body, and still insisted on being naked. She dared to be, week after week, season after season, a young woman okay in her less-than-perfect body.

It's ridiculous that this was the primary act that made Lena Dunham difficult—that what was seen as either appalling or "brave" was being naked while not being a supermodel. On Instagram she wrote: "Let's get something straight: I didn't hate what I looked like—I hated the culture that was telling me to hate it. When my career started, some people celebrated my look but always through the lens of 'isn't she brave? Isn't it such a bold move to show THAT body on TV?' "

Maybe people simply confused courage with confidence. As a creator, Lena was confident that her imperfect body would hold your attention—so confident that even if she, as a director, shot herself at unflattering angles doing unflattering things, you'd be unable to look away. Once, when asked when she felt the most sexy, she answered without hesitation: "When I'm directing." That's a difficult woman talking right there. She claims her power in her actions, not in the perceptions of others.

For my middle-aged white woman money, Lena Dunham's genuine act of bravery rested in the compassionate portrayal of Hannah's parents. Loreen (Becky Ann Baker) and Tad (Peter Scolari) are academics in their late 50s who teach, presumably, at Michigan State in East Lansing. They are also actual humans with their own struggles, desires, and secrets. Even though the show is not about them, they serve as more than props, punch lines, or cautionary tales of what will happen to the main character if she doesn't follow her dream/embrace her passion/take the teaching job in France/say no to the boring, yet safe, boyfriend/dare to age.

This isn't to say there's a dearth of well-rounded, compelling middle-aged characters on TV. But they always find themselves in what I think of as Eileen Fisher television—shows that are well made and stylish, with no expectation that anyone under 45 will tune in.*

In Season 1, Episode 6 of *Girls,* Hannah goes home to East Lansing for a weekend with her parents. While she goes off to a sad party with Eric, the cute pharmacist she'd met earlier in the day when she'd picked up Loreen's prescription (which we assume is hormone replacement-related), Loreen and Tad celebrate their anniversary with a nice dinner out and shower sex.

"Wet and wild!" exclaims Tad. Loreen moans as her boobs slap about. But the evening proves to be too much crazy for Tad. Between the heavy meal out, the booze, the frisky sex, the hot water, he passes out, slips, and falls. Hannah walks in the door after her own awful one-night stand with Eric the pharmacist only to hear her mom yelling in distress. She bursts into the bathroom to see her dad passed out. He's naked, and her mom is naked. It's the first time we see Hannah assess the situation quickly and take charge, helping to cover her dad and move him to the bedroom. There's more to the story of Loreen and Tad—no spoilers here. But kudos to Lena for making them complex characters—and for

---

* *Grace and Frankie,* starring Lily Tomlin and Jane Fonda, comes readily to mind, as well as any other show featuring women over 50 who fail to still look fetching in a sleeveless sheath, à la Julia Louis-Dreyfus in *Veep.* (I'm not upper arm–shaming Lily and Jane, I promise.)

also giving them the full cringe-worthy *Girls* treatment, including awkward nudity.

In 2015, while *Girls* was heading into the final stretch of its run (the final season aired in 2017), Lena and her friend Jennifer Konner started *Lenny,* a weekly newsletter for young (and not so young) feminists. When I signed up I thought, *Leave it to Lena Dunham to make* newsletters *cool again.* Her provocative Tweet storm–inducing pieces include "Supporting Reproductive Rights When You're a Person of Faith"; "One of a Kind: On the Healing Power of Sexual Fantasy"; and "The All-American Menstrual Hut." She's also been vocal about her fight for birth control rights, which includes the care she receives for her own complicated and ongoing personal battle with endometriosis (she posted a picture of herself in the hospital getting treatment after a horrific episode following the Met Gala).

This determined outspokenness has made Lena one of those women about whom people say "Why won't she just go away?" And it's to her credit that she has no intention of shutting up in order to make people like her. Full disclosure: I also find her annoying at times. She's a difficult woman, and sometimes difficult women grate on our last nerve. But here's a radical notion: *That's okay.*

The cries of outrage over her remark that she wished she'd had an abortion to better empathize with women who'd undergone the procedure could be heard in outer space. Should she have said it? No. Has any man on the planet ever said something stupid and been forgiven within the time it has taken me to write this sentence? You know the answer.

Recently, I watched Lena on *73 Questions,* the vogue.com video series where a guy with a camera follows you around while shooting off intimate queries. Lena wore a striped tank top, hip-slung jeans, and high heels. She appeared cute, smart—not perfect but perfectly acceptable. It's a measure of how difficult she is that I didn't worry, seeing her this way, that her unruly self was going to be sucked into the celebrity machine, where she would be turned into a likable size 2 star who wears the right message T-shirts but otherwise doesn't rock the boat. Lena is far too difficult for that.

CHAPTER 29

CARRIE FISHER

Proll

I CRIED WHEN I HEARD Carrie Fisher died, a couple of days after Christmas in 2016. People all across the galaxy did: *Star Wars* nerds, avid readers of her novels and memoirs, mental health advocates, self-proclaimed killjoy feminists. The coroner's report, released six months later, reported that traces of heroin and cocaine had been found in her system. Some fans left the club, outraged that it wasn't a simple, noncontroversial heart attack caused by too much fish and chips (she was on her way home from London) that ended her life. But Carrie was never easy, never well behaved, never secretive about her demons. She was never not controversial in life, so why should her death be any different?

I've always claimed Carrie as a very distant cousin, if the definition includes going to the same film school as George Lucas, who gave us Princess Leia. I entered USC School of Cinematic Arts not long after *Star Wars* had become a Hollywood blockbuster and was on its way to becoming a cultural phenomenon on a par with . . . well, nothing. There had never been anything like *Star Wars* before in the history of cinema. We studied it as if it were a holy text. We collected arcane trivia about the production long before anyone else. (I still have an early draft of the screenplay, where R2-D2 *talks* instead of beeps.) I had seen the movie many times in class, but only twice at Grauman's Chinese Theatre: once, with a boy I'd met in Switzerland (a real Swiss shepherd), who wept at the wonder of it; and once with my dad, an engineer and industrial designer, who seemed to enjoy it but whose only comment was, "You know, there's no sound in space."

There weren't any (or many) women in film school in those days, either. I recall production classes in which I was the only girl among the nerds. No one had much to say about Princess Leia. (*Return of the Jedi* was still a year or so in the future, and guys had not yet beheld her perched beside Jabba the Hutt in her metal bikini.) Instead they obsessed over camera angles and the sound effects. I, on the other hand, was completely taken with Leia: a fearless, principled, snarky tomboy in eyeliner. She could not be intimidated by authority, and seemed impervious to torture. She lied when it suited her, shot first without bothering to ask questions, and failed to get all dewy-eyed with gratitude when she was rescued. She was fierce, but caring. I didn't think Carrie Fisher was a great actress, but I smelled a whiff of smirk in her line readings. A kindred spirit.

BORN OCTOBER 21, 1956, to movie star Debbie Reynolds and star crooner Eddie Fisher—the most famous couple in Hollywood—Carrie never wanted to be in show business. From the day she could sit up, she had a front-row seat at the slow-motion catastrophe that is megacelebrity. Still, entertainment was the family business, and it was easier to fall into that than, say, law school. In 1975, she scored a bit part in *Shampoo,* with Warren Beatty. In 1977, *Star Wars* was released, and whatever hope she may have had for living under the radar was destroyed, along with Leia's home planet of Alderaan. She would appear in other movies—some good ones. But to filmgoers, she would always be spunky Leia, in her drapey white gown and cinnamon bun hairstyle.

In 1987, Carrie published a damn good autobiographical first novel: *Postcards From the Edge*. It became a pretty good movie starring Meryl Streep as a recovering addict living in the shadow of her fabulous, self-involved mother, played by Shirley MacLaine, for whom every day offers another chance for a star turn. The book became a *New York Times* best seller, as did her three subsequent novels and three memoirs. Her one-woman show, *Wishful Drinking*, was a hit on Broadway; in 2015, she reprised her role as Leia in *The Force Awakens** to great acclaim. In 2016, she and her mother co-starred in the touching documentary *Bright Lights: Starring Carrie Fisher and Debbie Reynolds*. Whatever rifts existed from the *Postcards From the Edge* era seemed to have largely healed.

Layered between these accomplishments was a lot of suffering and struggle, all played out in the public eye. At the age of 28, after a drug overdose and a stretch in rehab, Carrie was diagnosed with bipolar disorder. Rather than try to play off her erratic behavior as mere addiction—always a more glam option than straight-up mental illness—she came out as bipolar, advocated for it, and wore her disease with grace and her trademark searing humor. "I'm actually in the Abnormal Psychology textbook," she once said. "Obviously my family is so proud. Keep in mind though, I'm a PEZ dispenser *and* I'm in the Abnormal Psychology textbook. Who says you can't have it all?"

CARRIE WAS A MERE BABE OF 19 when she was cast as Princess Leia—the same age as her mother when *she* was cast as Kathy Selden in *Singin' in the Rain*. By the time Carrie was born in 1956, Debbie was America's Sweetheart, a stone-cold A-list movie star. She had further burnished

---

* On deciding to take the role: "I've been Princess Leia for 40 years, so what, I'm suddenly going to stop now?"

her star by marrying teen idol Eddie Fisher, who ruled the charts in the early 1950s (between 1950 and 1956, he had 35 songs in the top 40). Their courtship consisted essentially of Eddie saying in an interview that if he could date anyone, it would be Debbie Reynolds, and so their managers arranged it. Debbie was blond and sunny. Eddie was dark and boyishly handsome. As a couple, they were white hot. One struggles to make a contemporary comparison: Britney and Justin? Kim and Kanye? Brangelina? None of these couples are surrounded by the aura of sweet, Internet-less innocence that enveloped Debbie and Eddie. Sixteen months after ~~having~~ Carrie, her brother, Todd, was born—and the perfect family was now complete.

Oh, those home movies. In both *Wishful Drinking* and *Bright Lights*, you can see golden Debbie with her sweet babies in the bright California sun. Pool parties, Easter egg hunts, Carrie and Todd going round and round on their tricycles. Only because of what we now know does Carrie seem more expressive and animated than her little brother. She grimaces, grins, scowls, and howls. Her dark eyes snap with intelligence. In a few shots, Carrie drags Todd around by his ankles. Debbie smiles at it all, because that's what stars did.

In 1958, when Carrie was two, her father left her mother for Elizabeth Taylor (see Chapter 2). Debbie would go on to marry Harry Karl, whom she did not love but who was the opposite of Eddie. Karl was a shoe store magnate, a "millionaire businessman" who lost his money on bad investments and gambling debts, then plowed through Debbie's fortune. They wound up divorced when Carrie was 17.

To my knowledge there are no studies that quantify how much a child suffers when her parents are involved in Hollywood's scandal of the century—probably because the only children who would have been qualified to participate in the study would be Carrie and Todd. How isolating it must have been, and how bizarre. Old copies of *Photoplay* feature Debbie, toddler Carrie, and baby Todd on the cover, with headlines ranging from "The Night My Children Kept

Me From Dying" to "What Debbie Tells Her Children About Liz and Eddie."

One of Carrie's first memories was sitting on the lawn watching a cameraman fall through the shrubbery, trying to snap a picture. After she could walk but was still a small child, she remembered fans would lunge over her and shove her aside, trying to shake hands or touch her mother. She believed her mother belonged to everyone but her. She believed her father left—or so Carrie would confess to him in 2010, three months before he died—because she wasn't funny enough. Even as a toddler she tried to be amusing, to keep him from leaving.

THERE'S A CLIP IN *BRIGHT LIGHTS* of Debbie doing a nightclub act in 1971 or so. She's wearing a black jacket, hot pants, and stockings—and weirdly, a white boater straight out of *The Music Man*. Carrie is in the audience, and Debbie coaxes her up to sing a song "for your old mother." (Debbie was 39.) Carrie is wearing a velvet dress, as you would for a special occasion. Her hair is long and shiny, and she looks younger than 15. When she opens her mouth and belts out "Bridge Over Troubled Waters," in a theatrical contralto to rival Judy Garland's, you can see the stirrings of her adult default attitude: "facerious," a perfect word I made up just now to describe her singular mingling of the serious and the facetious. Look, Mom, she seems to be saying, I'm singing my heart out like some over-the-hill nightclub diva in a beaded ensemble, even though I'm barely old enough to babysit.

Carrie's wasn't a trained voice—nor would it ever be, since dismissing her vocal gifts was one way of rebelling against her parents. The child of two of the most beloved and celebrated singers of the age would refuse to sing! I should clarify: She would refuse to use her voice in a professional capacity. Setting aside her 1982 guest appearance on *Laverne and Shirley* (where, dressed in a green satin bunny costume, she sang "My Guy" to guest star Hugh Hefner), she generally used her voice as a secret weapon, like a knife tucked into a boot.

In 1973, at 17, Carrie enrolled in the Central School of Speech and Drama in London. Her goal of avoiding show business at all costs wasn't going so well. At her mother's urging, she had quit high school to act in the ensemble of *Irene,* Debbie's Broadway musical. In the racy *Shampoo,* she went on to play the braless and bandanna-clad "sexually liberated" teenage daughter of one of hairdresser Warren Beatty's clients, who seduces him with the immortal words, "Wanna fuck?"* She struck upon drama school in London because it was a way of getting as far as possible out of the house—while still pleasing her mother, who was also footing the bill.

She read for *Star Wars* over Christmas vacation in 1975, because why not? A goofy low-budget sci-fi flick? What harm could there be in that? When she received the pages for the audition and saw that Princess Leia said things like, "A battle station with enough firepower to destroy an entire system!" she thought, oh yeah. For Lucas's part, he cast her because even at 18 she was formidable but also warm and shrewd, as a warrior princess would be.

Is there anything that remains unknown about the making of *Star Wars?* A quick scroll through Amazon reveals dozens of encyclopedias, atlases, compendia, and definitive stories behind the making ofs. Despite my inside track at USC, I'm not sure I can add anything new.

Oh wait, yes I can.

In *The Princess Diarist,* published a month before she died, Carrie confessed to an affair with Harrison Ford during filming. "I've spent so many years not telling the story of Harrison and me having an affair on the first *Star Wars* movie that it's difficult to know exactly how to tell it now," she wrote.

---

* Debbie lobbied without success to change the line to "Wanna screw?"

It happened thus: After a surprise 32nd birthday party for George Lucas, they started smooching in the car, which led to them smooching in her flat, which led to "a one-night stand that lasted three months." He was 34, married, already movie star–like. She was 19, had had exactly one serious boyfriend (from drama school)—and, although she pretended to be an experienced woman of the world, she was freaking out. She wondered, in teen girl parlance, whether he "liked" her in the same way she "liked" him. During the week they practiced their true acting skills by pretending to be two people not having an affair; on the weekend, they got it on in her flat.

He didn't talk much. He was an absolute mystery to her, one of those strong silent types in whom we always presume there are cavernous depths of heart and soul that only we can plumb.** She wrote in her diary about spending a lot of time trying to make him smile (". . . obviously I have not heard of child labor laws"). Once, in a pub, she pulled off an imitation of his gruff swagger that had him shuddering with soundless laughter, and she counted that moment among the greatest in her love life. When the film wrapped, and so did the affair, she claims he tried to buoy her spirits by saying, "You have the eyes of a doe and the balls of a samurai." I'm sorry, but I call bullshit. That line is classic Carrie Fisher.

IN 1983, CARRIE MARRIED PAUL SIMON, the genius lyricist half of Simon and Garfunkel. (Their union would crash and burn after only 11 months.) They had met when Simon visited the set of *Star Wars*. He was, as she noted, a short Jewish singer, just like her father, Eddie. It was tempestuous from the start, based on a shared sensibility, a passion for words and each other and, apparently, a lot of cocaine. In fairness to everyone involved, I can assure you that pretty much

---

** Most of the time these guys are just boring; we all learn the hard way.

everything in the entertainment world involved a lot of cocaine in the early 1980s. I was, at the time, just out of film school, and it wasn't unusual to be offered a Perrier and a line during a pitch meeting.

Carrie/Leia started snorting coke on the ice planet of Hoth—that is, on the set—during the filming of *The Empire Strikes Back*.* Allegedly, even John Belushi, who would die of an overdose in 1982, advised her to dial it back a little. She didn't love cocaine, but it was what was around, and she would ingest anything that offered a respite from the intensity of being Carrie. Every morning when her eyes clicked open—that is, if she'd managed to sleep at all—a tsunami of thoughts and feelings surged into her mind, a literal brainstorm every waking moment. She'd found that LSD made her feel more normal. The spinning inner monologue was transformed into visual hallucinations. A change is as good as a rest! Plus, if she dropped acid with friends, everyone was out of their gourds, and she didn't feel so alone. Among prescription drugs she favored Percocet, and once confessed to having taken upwards of 30 a day, just to quiet her mind.

In 1980, when she was 24, a doctor diagnosed her as bipolar. She thought he was just telling her that because who in his right mind would want to tell Princess Leia she was a garden-variety drug addict? When she was shooting the unbelievably awful *Under the Rainbow,* she weighed 90 pounds—I'm sure everyone thought she looked hot and fabulous—and was so sleep-deprived that she had a seizure on the set.

In 1985, after filming wrapped on Woody Allen's *Hannah and Her Sisters,* she accidentally overdosed on the aforementioned Percocet and sleeping pills.

Afterward, she was ready to listen to her doctor. She suffered from bipolar II—characterized by more and deeper depressive episodes— and hypo-, rather than full-blown, mania. Her lows were lower and longer, her highs less manic. When coupled with all the freewheeling

---

* Also known as The Best Star Wars.

self-medication, they laid waste to relationships, self-regard, and good career management.**

Turns out she *wasn't* just a celebrity with fairly standard addiction issues, but a woman with mental illness. A far less glamorous state of affairs.

In 1987, Carrie wrote her first book, *Postcards From the Edge.* It begins: "Maybe I shouldn't have given the guy who pumped my stomach my phone number, but who cares?" Then we come to: "Instant gratification takes too long." Then, reading farther along: "You know how I always seem to be struggling, even when the situation doesn't call for it?"

Oh, I was jealous of Carrie when *Postcards* was published. First *Star Wars,* now a hilarious first novel that got a ton of attention, plopped onto the best-seller list, and was turned into a movie starring Meryl Streep? My generous response to her success: Why does she get everything?

In the 1990s, Carrie wrote several more novels and fattened her bank account with good money made doctoring scripts. *Outbreak, The Wedding Singer,* and *Lethal Weapon 3* all benefited from her kick and sparkle. She also fell in love with a new guy, Hollywood "power" agent Bryan Lourd, who after three years famously left her to marry a man. ("He told me later that I had turned him gay by taking codeine again. And I said, 'You know, I never read that warning on the label.'")

Before their split, Carrie and Bryan had Billie, born in 1992, whom Carrie raised as a single parent. This broke her heart in a way she never was able to alchemize into uproarious material, reminding her of being raised alone by her mother after Eddie left.

Carrie sought treatment, and her disease was largely under control. But bipolar disorder isn't a tidy disorder. Your meds work until they

---

** Example of poor role selection: *Under the Rainbow,* a devastatingly unfunny spoof costarring Chevy Chase and involving a Nazi spy, Japanese assassin, and gang of actors cast as the citizens of Munchkinville, all staying in the same hotel while filming *The Wizard of Oz.* Carrie wasn't the only one doing a lot of drugs in the 1980s.

don't. Often, a manic state is like a flood busting through a levy. In 1998, after a particularly bad manic patch, Carrie was institutionalized. I know all this because Carrie talked about it in writerly detail on *Primetime With Diane Sawyer* in December 2000. I vividly remember the interview.

Carrie was 44, prettier and more charismatic than she'd been as a younger woman. She wore her hair, still brown but strategically lightened, in a cheeky bob. Her voice had become raspier with age.

She described the exhausting, frenzied thoughts that led to compulsive monologuing, which in turn exhausted everyone around her. The sleepless nights, often many in a row, and the impulse to act on every bad idea that involved shopping, traveling, and sex ("Wow! Who are *you*, strange man who I suddenly want to bone?"). She described the two sides of herself: Rollicking Roy, the life of the party, and Sediment Pam, "who stands on the shore and sobs." When people said they "loved" Carrie, who they really loved was Roy. She would call friends and whisper, "Roy's in town." And the party would begin.

"When we were shooting *Harry Met Sally*, I stayed up all night snorting heroin. You can imagine how proud my parents must be," she said.

She talked about the time on the psych ward. Every day, her goal was just to feel less. In the hospital she went six days without sleep. She hallucinated, she jabbered at the television. She felt as if she could reach out and touch her mood with the palms of her hands (it felt cool to the touch), and out her window saw gleaming, futuristic cities. Bryan visited her in the psych ward, and she begged him to take their daughter, because she never knew whether she was coming back. But she did come back, of course.

"So, happily ever after?" asked Sawyer.

"There's no such animal. It's everything ever after."

A woman less difficult might have stayed mum about the whole thing. Carrie's life may have been public, but medical records are not. She could easily have confessed to her fondness for prescription painkillers and no one would have been the wiser. There's a certain glamour associated with excess that doesn't quite spill over to being perceived as batshit crazy.

But Carrie was on the front lines of oversharing. She was TMI-ing in advance of the abbreviation. She had no interest in protecting her image as a sexy space princess, or even the princess of so-called Hollywood royalty. She talked about it all, including electroconvulsive therapy (ECT). This had to have taxed even her candid nature. Carrie came of age during a time when admitting to ECT was career-ending. (To wit: After admitting he'd suffered from depression and had undergone ECT, Senator Thomas Eagleton, on the ticket with George McGovern for a hot second in 1972, was booted off faster than you could say *One Flew Over the Cuckoo's Nest.*)

Not everyone celebrated Carrie's openness. Some people found her confessions to be just too much. The *Washington Post,* reviewing *The Princess Diarist,* predicted her honesty would make readers cringe. I conducted an unscientific survey of maybe two dozen men, and found that the more hard-core their *Star Wars* fandom, the less interested they were in seeing Carrie Fisher in any other role aside from Princess Leia. Most were unaware that she'd become a powerful, outspoken advocate for mental illness as just another human flaw, no better or worse than any other. "I am mentally ill. I can say that," she'd been known to say. "I am not ashamed of that. I survived that, I'm still surviving it, but bring it on. Better me than you."

PEOPLE HAVE ALWAYS ASSUMED that since the *Star Wars* trilogy had been such a massive hit, the Brink's truck must roar up once a week and toss bags of money on Carrie's front porch. But the only person who got stupidly rich was George Lucas. Carrie, just old enough to vote when she signed her contract to play Princess Leia, signed away her "likeness"

and all merchandising rights. She was paid scale, and had no profit participation.

In her 2008 one-woman show *Wishful Drinking*, she discussed this inequity, and she was not sanguine about having her likeness superimposed on a shampoo bottle (when you unscrewed her head, shampoo poured out of her neck). Or a PEZ dispenser, or a lunch pail, or all the other Leia *objets* that have haunted her existence, while not making her a sou richer. She joked in her facerious way about how, because she never owned her likeness, she had to pay George every time she looked in the mirror.

Still, for a 20-year-old she was rolling in dough. She blithely hired a business manager someone recommended and forgot all about it. When she needed money, she got some—until sometime in her 40s, when she discovered she was more or less broke.

She thus began a lucrative side gig as a lap dancer. For Carrie, "lap dance" was code for signing autographs at Comic-Cons, of which there are hundreds all over the world. Truly, she could have made an entire career out of signing autographs for $70 a pop. She once referred to *Star Wars* fame as "an under-populated, empathy-free zone." Being female, the zone was even more sparsely populated, with Carrie/Leia its queen and only citizen.

She would dutifully show up at some god-awful convention center, where the light makes even a dewy 20-year-old look sallow and blotchy, armed with her middle-aged woman's body, thinning hair, failing eyesight, perimenopausal irritability. She would get writer's cramp signing pictures of her ravishing, dewy self for hours on end, weekend after weekend. Can you imagine? In this culture that values appearance above every other female trait, there she was valiantly staring at herself in that damn metal bikini, aware that not only would she never wear a metal or any other bikini ever again, but that she might not even have the courage to squeeze into a Lands' End one-piece. This is setting aside all the men—not looking so hot themselves, let's face it—eager to tell her how she was their very first crush.

Once, a mother brought her little daughter, dressed as Leia in a tiny robe, with tiny buns capping her tiny ears, and the daughter took one look at Carrie and started wailing, "I don't want the old one!"

Carrie felt as if she were both Leia and the custodian of Leia; given that she was also Roy and Pam, you can see how exhausting her life could be.

IN 2008, CARRIE WENT ON THE ROAD with *Wishful Drinking*. Developed in L.A. at the beginning of the year, it also enjoyed runs in Berkeley, Seattle, and Washington, D.C., before a limited run on Broadway at Studio 54.* It closed in January 2010, and the reason I'm being so precise about the dates is so you understand how it was that tiny five-foot-one-and-a-half-inch Carrie Fisher came to weigh 180 pounds, thus committing the most unpardonable female sin in our hallowed land. For two years she was on the road. During those two years she didn't exercise and ate large meals very late at night (room service, please). Also, for an addict living one day at a time, a pint of ice cream now and then, mostly now, seemed utterly harmless.

She was not unaware. She knew the jeans and skinny tees had been pushed to the back of her closet and she was living in leggings and tunics. But it wasn't until she Googled herself and found someone had written, "WTF happened to Carrie Fisher? She used to be so hot. Now she looks like Elton John," that she realized it was time to take herself in hand.

There was nothing for it but to lose the weight. And she did: Fifty pounds in nine months, at the age of 54. Anyone, male or female, able to maintain the focus and discipline to drop 50 pounds—especially staring down the

---

* Yes, *that* Studio 54.

barrel of 60*—is a badass of near-superhero proportions. "I thought I was getting old," she quipped. "It turns out I was mostly getting fat."

But she was also getting old.**

When Carrie reprised her role as Leia in *Star Wars: The Force Awakens,* released in 2015, Twitter erupted with the usual nasty, pointless insults. In fairness, Carrie did disappoint every male fan of the original trilogy by refusing to spend her life maintaining the illusion that she was still that lithe, slim-waisted girl in a metal bikini. She could have, you know. Rather than write books, doctor scripts, speak out on behalf of those with mental illness, parent to the best of her ability, and care for Eddie and Debbie in their dotage—for she always adored her parents, despite the crap they put her through as a child—she could have obsessively tended her figure. She could have spent her life working out multiple times a day and lived on air and cigarettes, in the manner of a working supermodel. Instead, she had a full, messy, imperfect life.

When the ageist body-shaming schmucks came after her on Twitter, she was not silent. To her "fans" who blasted not Carrie's performance, but her body, face, voice, posture—what am I missing?—she had the following retort:

@carrieffisher: "Please stop debating about whether OR not [I've] aged well. Unfortunately it hurts all 3 of my feelings. My BODY hasnt aged as well as I have. Blow us."

CARRIE FISHER WAS NOT THE FIRST Princess Leia. In 1975, during casting, there was another, much younger girl named Terri Nunn whom George Lucas had tapped for the role. Nunn was 15, fine-boned and

---

* There is always doing it for your health, but at a certain point people tend to say fuck that too. I'm eating that piece of cake.

** Because who isn't?

cool in demeanor. A somewhat textbook princess. She would have been fine. In fact, she looked much more like Mark Hamill's actual twin than did Carrie Fisher. George Lucas is famously not great with actors. For all his visionary genius, he's much better with starships, droids, and explosions. But he immediately saw something in Carrie: that she could be warm, tough, funny, and fierce, all at the same time. She was a princess with a blaster, but also a girl capable of becoming a woman who could lead people.

I hope she realized before she left us that it was her huge heart, her humor, and her complex personality that made Princess Leia difficult, and thus immortal.

ACKNOWLEDGMENTS

ENGLISH NEEDS A BETTER WORD than gratitude to express my deep appreciation for my editor Hilary Black. There are editors; then there is Hilary, who had my back while I wrote and thought and rewrote and ate too many artisanal donut holes (I live in Portland) and developed an eye twitch and emailed like a lunatic. She is *sui generis*. Allyson Johnson, project editor, also deserves a big raise and a week off. Make that two. Thank you to everyone else at National Geographic: Melissa Farris, Nicole Miller, Ann Day, Kelly Forsythe, Daneen Goodwin, and Jessie Chirico. Judith Klein, thank you for the herculean task of manuscript wrangling. Kimberly Glyder, your glorious illustrations make my heart sing.

I am indebted to David Forrer for his endless faith in me. Also at Inkwell: Kim Witherspoon, Richard Pine, Michael Carlisle, Nathaniel Jacks, and Corinne Sullivan.

Writers of Renown, thank you for listening to me talk about "my women" over the years: Allison Frost, Angie Muresan, Deb Stone, Colleen Strohm, Dan Berne, Peter Wallace, Laura Wood, Debbie Guyol (thank you, too, for your razor-sharp copyediting eye). Danna Schaeffer, I owe you a year's worth of kir royales for your sage advice and sharp observations. Deb Nies and Melea Seward, #thankyou, #whatwouldIdowithoutyou?

To the Collioure crew, *merci bien* to James Allen, Candace King, Jen Obermeyer, Wayne Obermeyer, Scott Hornyak, Jorge Argonz, Dan Berne, Aliza Bethlahmy, Kathy Budas, and Randy Rollison, for your company and good cheer during crunch time. Time for an aperitif.

To Kim Dower, dear friend, your love, encouragement have buoyed me since our lemon bread days. Words can't convey my appreciation.

Finally, to Jerrod Allen, the Man of the House, and Fiona, my little tomato: Thank you for being my people.

SOURCES

I BUILT A SIZABLE LIBRARY OF indispensable sources during the writing of this book. The following is a list of the books and articles whose pages became dog-eared, whose sentences I underlined and highlighted, as I strove to understand my subjects. I'm deeply indebted to the authors, who generously shared their ideas, passion, wisdom, and authority with the wider world.

This is far from a complete list of works about—and in some cases by—the difficult women whose lives I've explored. A complete bibliography can be found on my website: www.karenkarbo.com.

J. K. ROWLING

J. K. Rowling (@jk_rowling) | Twitter

J. K. Rowling: A Bibliography 1997–2013, Philip W. Errington (Bloomsbury Academic, 2015)

"Mugglemarch: J. K. Rowling Writes a Realist Novel for Adults," Ian Parker (*New Yorker,* October 1, 2012)

Very Good Lives: The Fringe Benefits of Failure and the Importance of Imagination, J. K. Rowling (Little, Brown and Company, 2015)

ELIZABETH TAYLOR

The Accidental Feminist: How Elizabeth Taylor Raised Our Consciousness and We Were Too Distracted By Her Beauty to Notice, M. G. Lord (Walker Books, 2012)

Elizabeth Taylor: A Private Life for Public Consumption, Ellis Cashmore (Bloomsbury Academic, 2016)

Elizabeth Takes Off: On Weight Gain, Weight Loss, Self-Image, and Self-Esteem, Elizabeth Taylor (G. P. Putnam's Sons, 1988)

How to Be a Movie Star: Elizabeth Taylor in Hollywood, William Mann (Houghton Mifflin Harcourt, 2009)

GLORIA STEINEM

"Here's the Full Transcript of Gloria Steinem's Historic Women's March Speech," Diana Bruk (*ELLE,* January 21, 2017)

My Life on the Road, Gloria Steinem (Random House, 2015)

Outrageous Acts and Everyday Rebellions, Gloria Steinem (Random House, 1987)

"Road Warrior," Jane Kramer (*New Yorker,* October 19, 2015)

"Showgirls, Pastrami and Candor: Gloria Steinem's New York," John Leland (*New York Times,* October 7, 2016)

AMY POEHLER

"Amy Poehler and Tina Fey: When Leaning In, Laughing Matters," Melena Ryzik (*New York Times,* December 3, 2015)

"Amy Poehler: Sweet Queen of Comedy with a Wicked Streak," Hephzibah Anderson (*The Guardian,* October 18, 2014)

Yes Please, Amy Poehler (Dey Street Books, 2014)

RUTH BADER GINSBURG

"Heavyweight: How Ruth Bader Ginsburg Has Moved the Supreme Court," Jeffrey Toobin (*New Yorker,* March 11, 2013)

My Own Words, Ruth Bader Ginsburg (Simon and Schuster, 2016)

Notorious RBG: The Life and Times of Ruth Bader Ginsburg, Irin Carmon and Shana Knizhnik (Dey Street Books, 2015)

Sisters in Law: How Sandra Day O'Connor and Ruth Bader Ginsburg Went to the Supreme Court and Changed the World, Linda Hirshman (Harper Perennial, 2015)

"What Ruth Bader Ginsburg Taught Me About Being a Stay-at-Home Dad," Ryan Park (*The Atlantic,* January 8, 2015)

JOSEPHINE BAKER

Jazz Cleopatra: Josephine Baker in Her Time, Phyllis Rose (Doubleday, 1989)

Josephine, Josephine Baker and Jo Bouillon (Harper & Row, 1977)

Josephine Baker in Art and Life: The Icon and the Image, Bennetta Jules-Rosette (University of Illinois Press, 2007)

Josephine Baker and the Rainbow Tribe, Matthew Pratt Guterl (Belknap Press, 2014)

The Many Faces of Josephine Baker: Dancer, Singer, Activist, Spy, Peggy Caravantes (Chicago Review Press, 2015)

RACHEL MADDOW

Drift: The Unmooring of American Military Power, Rachel Maddow (Crown, 2012)

"Rachel Maddow, the Lovable Wonk," John Powers (*The American Prospect,* March 26, 2012)

"Rachel Maddow: The Rolling Stone Interview," Janet Reitman (*Rolling Stone,* June 14, 2017)

COCO CHANEL

Coco Chanel: A Biography, Axel Madsen (Bloomsbury, 1990)

Chanel and Her World: Friends, Fashion, and Fame, Edmonde Charles-Roux (Vendome Press, 2005)

Coco Chanel: An Intimate Life, Lisa Chaney (Viking, 2011)

The Secret of Chanel No. 5: The Intimate History of the World's Most Famous Perfume, Tilar Mazzeo (Harper, 2010)

MARTHA GELLHORN

Gellhorn: A Twentieth-Century Life, Caroline Moorehead (Henry Holt & Co, 2003)

Hemingway & Gellhorn, directed by Philip Kaufman (HBO, 2012)

Selected Letters of Martha Gellhorn, Caroline Moorehead (Henry Holt & Co, 2006)

Travels With Myself and Another: A Memoir, Martha Gellhorn (Viking, 1978)

SHONDA RHIMES

"Shonda Rhimes Opens Up About 'Angry Black Woman' Flap, Messy *Grey's Anatomy* Chapter and the 'Scandal' Impact," Lacey Rose (*The Hollywood Reporter,* October 17, 2014)

"Shonda Rhimes on Power, Feminism, and Police Brutality," Robbie Myers (*ELLE,* September 23, 2015)

Year of Yes: How to Dance It Out, Stand in the Sun and Be Your Own Person, Shonda Rhimes (Simon & Schuster, 2015)

EVA PERÓN

Evita, First Lady: A Biography of Evita Perón, John Barnes (Grove Press, 1978)

Evita: In My Own Words, Eva Perón (Mainstream Publishing, 1997)

Evita: The Real Life of Eva Perón, Nicholas Fraser and Marysa Navarro (W. W. Norton & Company, 1996)

Perón and the Enigmas of Argentina, Robert Crassweller (W. W. Norton & Company, 1987)

HELEN GURLEY BROWN

Bad Girls Go Everywhere: The Life of Helen Gurley Brown, the Woman Behind Cosmopolitan *Magazine,* Jennifer Scanlon (Oxford University Press, 2009)

Enter Helen: The Invention of Helen Gurley Brown and the Rise of the Modern Single Woman, Brooke Hauser (Harper, 2016)

I'm Wild Again: Snippets From My Life and a Few Brazen Thoughts, Helen Gurley Brown (St. Martin's Press, 2000)

Not Pretty Enough: The Unlikely Triumph of Helen Gurley Brown, Gerri Hirshey (Farrar, Straus and Giroux, 2016)

Sex and the Single Girl: The Unmarried Woman's Guide to Men, Careers, the Apartment, Diet, Fashion, Money, and Men, Helen Gurley Brown (Bernard Geis Associates, 1962; reprinted Barricade Books, 2003)

EDIE SEDGWICK

Edie: An American Biography, Jean Stein with George Plimpton (Knopf, 1982)

Edie: Girl on Fire, David Weisman and Melissa Painter (Chronicle Books, 2006)

"Happy Birthday, Edie Sedgwick," Lynn Yaeger (*Vogue,* April 20, 2015)

ANGELA MERKEL

Angela Merkel: The Authorized Biography, Stefan Kornelius (Alma Books, 2013)

Angela Merkel: A Chancellorship Forged in Crisis, Alan Crawford and Tony Czuczka (Bloomberg Press, 2013)

Angela Merkel: Europe's Most Influential Leader, Matthew Qvortrup (The Overlook Press, 2016)

"The Quiet German," George Packer (*New Yorker,* 2014)

BILLIE JEAN KING

Billie Jean, Billie Jean King with Frank Deford (Viking, 1982)

Game, Set, Match: Billie Jean King and the Revolution in Women's Sports, Susan Ware (The University of North Carolina Press, 2011)

A Necessary Spectacle: Billie Jean King, Bobby Riggs, and the Tennis Match That Leveled the Game, Selena Roberts (Crown, 2005)

Pressure Is a Privilege: Lessons I've Learned From Life and the Battle of the Sexes, Billie Jean King and Christine Brennan (LifeTime Media, 2008)

JANE GOODALL

Beyond Innocence: An Autobiography in Letters, the Later Years, Jane Goodall, edited by Dale Peterson (Houghton Mifflin Harcourt, 2001)

In the Shadow of Man, Jane Goodall (Houghton Mifflin, 1971)

Jane Goodall: The Woman Who Redefined Man, Dale Peterson (Houghton Mifflin Harcourt, 2006)

My Friends, the Wild Chimpanzees, Jane Goodall (National Geographic Society, 1969)

VITA SACKVILLE-WEST

Behind the Mask: The Life of Vita Sackville-West, Matthew Dennison (St. Martin's Press, 2015)

Portrait of a Marriage: Vita Sackville-West and Harold Nicolson, Nigel Nicolson (Weidenfeld & Nicolson, 1973)

Sissinghurst: Vita Sackville-West and the Creation of a Garden, Vita Sackville-West and Sarah Raven (St. Martin's Press, 2014)

Violet to Vita: The Letters of Violet Trefusis to Vita Sackville-West, 1910–1921, edited by Mitchell A. Leaska (Viking, 1990)

Vita: The Life of V. Sackville West, Victoria Glendinning (Alfred A. Knopf, 1983)

ELIZABETH WARREN

Elizabeth Warren (@SenWarren) | Twitter

A Fighting Chance, Elizabeth Warren (Metropolitan Books, 2014)

This Fight Is Our Fight: The Battle to Save America's Middle Class, Elizabeth Warren (Metropolitan Books, 2017)

"The Outsider," Glenn Thrush and Manu Raju (*Politico Magazine*, March/April 2015)

MARGARET CHO

I Have Chosen to Stay and Fight, Margaret Cho (Riverhead, 2005)

I'm the One That I Want, Margaret Cho (Ballentine Books, reprint 2002)

"Shaved and Savage: Has Comedian Margaret Cho Finally Gone Too Far?" Ann Friedman (*The Guardian*, November 3, 2015)

AMELIA EARHART

20 Hrs., 40 Min.: Our Flight in the Friendship, Amelia Earhart (G. P. Putnam's Sons, 1928; reprinted National Geographic Adventure Classics, 2003)

East to the Dawn: The Life of Amelia Earhart, Susan Butler (Da Capo Press, 1997)

The Fun of It: Random Records of My Own Flying and of Women in Aviation,

Amelia Earhart (G. P. Putnam's Sons, 1932; reprint edition Academy Chicago Publishers, 1977)

The Quotable Amelia Earhart, edited by Michele Wehrwein Albion (University of New Mexico Press, 2015)

FRIDA KAHLO

The Diary of Frida Kahlo: An Intimate Self-Portrait, Carlos Fuentes (Abrams, 2005)

Devouring Frida: The Art History and Popular Celebrity of Frida Kahlo, Margaret A. Lindauer (Wesleyan University Press, 1999)

Frida: A Biography of Frida Kahlo, Hayden Herrera (HarperCollins, 1983)

Frida Kahlo: Face to Face, Judy Chicago (Prestel, 2010)

Frida Kahlo: The Paintings, Hayden Herrera (HarperCollins, 1991)

Kahlo, Andrea Kettenmann (Taschen, 2015)

NORA EPHRON

Crazy Salad and Scribble Scribble: Some Things About Women and Notes on the Media, Nora Ephron (Vintage, 2012)

I Feel Bad About My Neck: And Other Thoughts on Being a Woman, Nora Ephron (Knopf, 2006)

I Remember Nothing: And Other Reflections, Nora Ephron (Knopf, 2010)

Nora Ephron: The Last Interview and Other Conversations, Nora Ephron (Melville House, 2015)

"Seeing Nora Everywhere," Lena Dunham (*New Yorker,* June 28, 2012)

She Made Me Laugh: My Friend Nora Ephron, Richard Cohen (Simon & Schuster, 2016)

DIANA VREELAND

"The Cult of Diana," Amy Fine Collins (*Vanity Fair,* November 1993)

Diana Vreeland, Eleanor Dwight (William Morrow, 2002)

Diana Vreeland: The Eye Has to Travel, directed by Lisa Immordino Vreeland and Bent-Jorgen Perlmutt (Glass Studio, 2011)

Diana Vreeland: The Modern Woman: The Bazaar Years, 1936–1962, edited by Alexander Vreeland (Rizzoli, 2015)

DV, Diana Vreeland (Knopf, 1984)

Empress of Fashion: A Life of Diana Vreeland, Amanda Mackenzie Stuart (Harper, 2012)

Diana Vreeland Memos: The Vogue Years, edited by Alexander Vreeland (Rizzoli, 2013)

KAY THOMPSON

Eloise: A Book for Precocious Grown-Ups, Kay Thompson and Hilary Knight (Simon & Schuster Books for Young Readers, reissue edition, 1969)

"Eloise at 55: The Legacy of Kay Thompson," NPR staff (Weekend Edition, NPR, December 4, 2010)

It's Me, Eloise: The Voice of Kay Thompson and the Art of Hilary Knight, Jane Bayard Curley and Kay Thompson (The Eric Carle Museum of Picture Book Art, 2017)

Kay Thompson: From Funny Face to Eloise, Sam Irvin (Simon & Schuster, 2010)

"Oh Kay! Rex Reed Recalls Kay Thompson," Rex Reed and *New York Observer* staff (*New York Observer*, July 20, 1998)

LAVERNE COX

"Laverne Cox: The G2 Interview," Rebecca Nicholson (*The Guardian*, June 14, 2015)

"Laverne Cox's Most Revealing Interview Yet," Melissa Maerz (*Entertainment Weekly*, June 10, 2015)

"The Transgender Tipping Point: Laverne Cox Talks to *TIME* About the Transgender Movement," Katy Steinmetz (*TIME*, May 29, 2014)

HILLARY RODHAM CLINTON

The Destruction of Hillary Clinton, Susan Bordo (Melville House, 2017)

Hard Choices: A Memoir, Hillary Rodham Clinton (Simon & Schuster, 2014)

Living History, Hillary Rodham Clinton (Simon & Schuster, 2003)

A Woman in Charge: The Life of Hillary Clinton, Carl Bernstein (Knopf, 2007)

Hillary's America: The Secret History of the Democratic Party, Dinesh D'Souza (Regnery Publishing, 2016)

JANIS JOPLIN

Buried Alive: The Biography of Janis Joplin, Myra Friedman (William Morrow & Company, 1973)

Love, Janis: A Revealing New Biography of Janis Joplin with Never-Before-Published Letters, Laura Joplin (Villard, 1992)

Pearl: The Obsessions and Passions of Janis Joplin, Ellis Amburn (Warner Books, 1992)

Scars of Sweet Paradise: The Life and Times of Janis Joplin, Alice Echols (Metropolitan Books, 1999)

LENA DUNHAM

"Downtown's Daughter," Rebecca Mead (*The New Yorker,* November 15, 2010)

"Is It Evil Not to Be Sure?: An Excerpt from Lena Dunham's College Diary," Lena Dunham (Lenny, May 17, 2016)

"Lena Dunham Is Not Done Confessing," Meghan Daum (*The New York Times Magazine,* September 10, 2014)

Not that Kind of Girl: A Young Woman Tells You What She's "Learned," Lena Dunham (Random House, 2014)

CARRIE FISHER

Carrie Fisher (@carrieffisher) | Twitter

"Carrie Fisher Opened Up About Her Demons—And Knew She Wouldn't Have a Hollywood Ending," Joe Mozingo, Soumya Karlamangla, and Richard Winton (*Los Angeles Times,* June 20, 2017)

Postcards From the Edge, Carrie Fisher (Simon & Schuster, 1987)

Shockaholic, Carrie Fisher (Simon & Schuster, 2011)
The Princess Diarist, Carrie Fisher (Blue Rider Press, 2016)
Wishful Drinking, Carrie Fisher (Simon & Schuster, 2008)

ABOUT THE AUTHOR

KAREN KARBO is the author of multiple novels, works of creative non-fiction, and a memoir. Her genre-bending Kick-Ass Women series includes *Julia Child Rules: Lessons on Savoring Life; How Georgia Became O'Keeffe: Lessons on the Art of Living; How to Hepburn: Lessons on Living from Kate the Great;* and the international best seller, *The Gospel According to Coco Chanel: Life Lessons from the World's Most Elegant Woman.* Her novels, *Trespassers Welcome Here, The Diamond Lane,* and *Motherhood Made a Man Out of Me,* were named *New York Times* Notable Books, as was her memoir, *The Stuff of Life.* Her work has also appeared in *Elle, Vogue, Outside,* the *New York Times,* the *Los Angeles Review of Books, Condé Nast Traveler, Salon, Slate,* and other magazines. Recently she was selected as one of 24 authors for the inaugural Amtrak Residency. She is the recipient of a National Endowment for the Arts Fellowship in Fiction, an Oregon Book Award for Creative Nonfiction, and a winner of the General Electric Younger Writer Award. Karen and The Man of the House (her partner of 16 years) live with their three dogs in Portland, Oregon.

READING GUIDE

What are Karen Karbo's criteria for being termed a "difficult woman." Do you agree? If not, why not? (Don't be afraid to be difficult!)

How would *you* define a "difficult woman"?

Have you ever had to choose between being true to yourself or being accepted and loved?

Do you live your life on your own terms or give in, change your opinion, oblige others both in your career and in your personal life?

Did you ever dare to break the rules? If so, which rule(s) did you break? If not, which rule or rules do you wish you had broken?

What is your definition of a heroine?

What do you think it means to be female?

Have you ever held yourself back from giving a "smart" answer, or being "overly" competitive?

Does the word *ambitious* mean different things when applied to a man or a woman? What about the words *passionate, outspoken, opinionated,* and *persistent?*

If you could choose three women profiled in this book (alive or dead) with whom you could have dinner, who would you choose?

Were any of the women in this book role models for you when you were growing up? Why?

Are there any women in the book you do not admire? Why?

Of the 29 iconic women included, with whom do you identify the most? Which one do you wish you could be? Why?